INDIA AND THE PATENT WARS

A volume in the series
THE CULTURE AND POLITICS OF HEALTH CARE WORK

edited by Suzanne Gordon and Sioban Nelson

A list of titles in this series is available at cornellpress.cornell.edu.

INDIA AND THE PATENT WARS

Pharmaceuticals in the New Intellectual Property Regime

MURPHY HALLIBURTON

ILR PRESS

AN IMPRINT OF

CORNELL UNIVERSITY PRESS

ITHACA AND LONDON

First published 2017 by Cornell University Press
First printed in paperback, 2017

Printed in the United States of America

Library of Congress Cataloging-in-Publication Data

Names: Halliburton, Murphy, 1964– author.
Title: India and the patent wars : pharmaceuticals in the new
    intellectual property regime / Murphy Halliburton.
Description: Ithaca : ILR Press, an imprint of Cornell University Press,
    2017. | Includes bibliographical references and index.
Identifiers: LCCN 2017016268 (print) | LCCN 2017022708 (ebook) | ISBN
    9781501713972 (pdf) | ISBN 9781501713989 (ret) | ISBN 9781501713460
    (cloth : alk. paper) | ISBN 9781501713477 (pbk. : alk. paper)
Subjects: LCSH: Drugs—India—Patents. | Patent laws and legislation—
    India. | Pharmaceutical industry—India. | Medicine, Ayurvedic—
    Economic aspects—India. | Intellectual property—India. | Patents
    (International law)
Classification: LCC KNS1150.M44 (ebook) | LCC KNS1150.M44 H35
    2017 (print) | DDC 346.5404/86—dc23
LC record available at https://lccn.loc.gov/2017016268

Cornell University Press strives to use environmentally responsible suppliers and materials to the fullest extent possible in the publishing of its books. Such materials include vegetable-based, low-VOC inks and acid-free papers that are recycled, totally chlorine-free, or partly composed of nonwood fibers. For further information, visit our website at cornellpress.cornell.edu.

This book is dedicated to Amy, Luca, and Sophie.

Contents

Acknowledgments   ix

Note on Names of Medications   xi

Introduction   1

1. The Invention and Expansion of Intellectual Property   21

2. The New Patent Regime: The Activists and Their Allies   36

3. Ayurvedic Dilemmas: Innovation, Ownership, and Resistance   55

4. The Gilead Model and the Perspective of Big Pharma   91

5. The View from Hyderabad: The "Indian" Pharmaceutical
Industry and the New Patent Regime   116

Conclusion   140

Notes   151

References   163

Index   179

ACKNOWLEDGMENTS

I would like to thank the many individuals and organizations whose assistance enabled this long-term research project to become a book. This work is the product of bits and pieces of investigation and writing that started around 2003 and continued through 2015. I am especially grateful to representatives from India- and United States–based biomedical pharmaceutical companies who took the time to meet with me and discuss their perspectives on patent controversies and drug access issues and to the practitioners of ayurvedic medicine and representatives of ayurvedic pharmaceutical companies who offered their views on the same topics and shared their concerns about biopiracy. The many conversations I have had with Krishna Ravi Srinivas and my meeting with his colleague T. C. James, both of Research and Information System for Developing Countries, New Delhi, were important to shaping my ideas, and I am grateful to my long-term friend and colleague Dr. K. Gireesh for introducing me to informants in Kerala and for his insight and camaraderie during my stays in Thiruvananthapuram.

This book benefited from several opportunities I had to present my research on patent controversies, starting in 2004 with a colloquium talk at the City University of New York Graduate Center at the invitation of my colleagues in the Department of Anthropology. My analysis of these issues developed further through subsequent presentations, including a colloquium at the Department of Sociology and Anthropology at Lehigh University in 2011, arranged by Bruce Whitehouse, and a South Asia Studies Seminar talk at the University of Iowa in 2012, at the invitation of Fred Smith. I also benefited greatly from speaking about these issues with Dr. Mala Ramanathan and her graduate students at the Achutha Menon Centre for Health Science Studies in Thiruvananthapuram, India, in 2014.

Research for this book was supported in part by a Professional Staff Congress–CUNY Research Award to support travel to India in 2004 and 2005. The book also draws on fieldwork conducted in Kerala, India, in the 1990s that was supported by grants from the Wenner Gren Foundation and the National Science Foundation.

I am grateful to the editors and staff at Cornell University Press for their interest, support, and work on this project. Frances Benson and Sioban Nelson's editorial insight and support was invaluable, and I am especially indebted to Suzanne Gordon, who carefully read and edited several versions of this manuscript, challenging me to move outside my comfort zone of academic discourse and develop a voice that can speak to a popular audience as well as to specialists. I believe I have taken at least some steps toward this goal because of her efforts.

Portions of this work appeared in earlier articles I wrote on the new global patent regime. Some of the discussion of ayurvedic practitioners' resistance to the new patent regime in chapter 3 appeared in my article "Resistance or Inaction? Protecting Ayurvedic Medical Knowledge and Problems of Agency," *American Ethnologist* 38(1): 85–100, 2011. Examples in chapter 2 of activist efforts to mitigate the effects of the patent regime appeared in "Drug Resistance, Patent Resistance: Indian Pharmaceuticals and the Impact of a New Patent Regime," *Global Public Health* 4(6): 515–527, 2009, and part of the discussion of the emergence of the concept of intellectual property in chapter 1 appeared in my "Introduction" (Special Issue—Intangible Property at the Periphery: Expanding Enclosure in the 21st Century), *International Journal of Cultural Property* 19(3): 233–249, 2012.

NOTE ON NAMES OF MEDICATIONS

Throughout this book, the brand names of medicines are written with an initial capital (for example, Viread) and generic names are written in lower case (for example, tenofovir). The registered trademark symbol "®" is not used next to brand names in this text, but all brand names mentioned are registered trademarks.

INDIA AND THE PATENT WARS

INTRODUCTION

We live in a world where more and more ideas and experiences are becoming forms of property. Intellectual property laws have expanded throughout the globe, and a broad range of creations and realms of human experience have been cordoned off, with legal fences being put around the sharing of innovations and cultural practices. Yoga routines, genetically engineered mice, French gastronomy, and the cultural practices of Afro-Brazilians have all been subject to ownership claims under a new global regime of intellectual property protections. We are also seeing extensions of laws that protect more familiar forms of intellectual property. Copyright laws now keep vast collections of film and literature out of the public realm, while new patent laws make it harder both to share medical knowledge and to produce generic versions of medicines. United States court decisions, multinational corporations, and the World Trade Organization (WTO) are major contributors to this new regime in which knowledge that was once considered part of the public domain has become the property of individuals, corporations, and communities.[1] At the same time, counterefforts such as the Access to Knowledge movement, Creative Commons licensing, and Doctors Without Borders' Access to Essential Medicines program struggle to keep artistic creations, medications, and scientific knowledge in the public realm.[2]

In this new property regime that spans the globe from Indonesia to Brazil to the United States, India has been the site of some of the most fraught battles over the ownership of pharmaceutical knowledge. A center of medical knowledge for centuries, India is home to several non-Western medical systems that are taught in colleges and practiced in hospitals, and the country provides many of the world's Western, biomedical drugs through its growing pharmaceutical sector.

Over the last ten years, as I spoke to people in the United States about the research I had been doing on controversies over patents in India, some would make comments about Indian companies "stealing" products from US companies or "violating" patents by producing "copies" of medications that were patented elsewhere. What most people who knew a little about this controversy did not know was that nothing illegal was going on. Before the WTO implemented its global patent rules, each country created its own patent laws tailored to its own priorities and concerns. India's pre-WTO patent law had a provision stating that, for medications, *only the process for making the medication, but not the medical product itself, could be patented.* Thus, different companies could make the same medicine if they could find a different way to manufacture the drug, and, until recently, Indian companies were free to create their own versions of drugs that were patented elsewhere, whether antidepressants, treatments for AIDS, medications for erectile dysfunction, or the various statins, such as Pfizer's Lipitor, that have been making huge profits for multinational drug companies.

The Indian government included this special product patent exception back in 1970 because it wanted to avoid monopoly control of medicines. Medications, because they could save a life or cure a disease, were not like other kinds of inventions in the minds of Indian lawmakers. In the United States, on the other hand, medicines have long been protected by product patents, and laws have conformed more closely to the interests of pharmaceutical corporations, allowing what some critics today consider to be frivolous patents on slight modifications of drugs, known as "me-too" drugs, that offer no increase in efficacy. Over the course of the 1990s and

2000s, the WTO required member nations to change their laws and conform to a single, United States–style intellectual property regime. In other words, India had to make its patent laws more like those of the United States because of the WTO's mandate. The deadline India and other developing countries were given was 2005, and India met this requirement when it passed its 2005 Patents (Amendment) Act.

One employee of a multinational pharmaceutical corporation whom I spoke to about this topic displayed the usual disdain for Indian companies "stealing" other companies' ideas. National autonomy did not matter. India's earlier law with its product patent exception was simply wrong in the view of this employee. If an Indian company made the same drug this person's company patented, it should be illegal, and the 2005 law made it so. It was only later that I learned that the company this person worked for was one of several that produced products based on knowledge from India's ayurvedic medical system for which no royalties or other compensation were ever paid. While corporations have become more vigilant about safeguarding what they feel to be their intellectual property, the Indian government has been shoring up protections for what it considers to be Indian proprietary knowledge, such as the pharmacopoeia of ayurvedic medicine. This book examines the new world of increased restrictions on the use of medical knowledge, and on the production of the drug products that derive from this knowledge, and asks what is gained and lost in this new system of control.

While the WTO mandate, known as the Trade Related Aspects of Intellectual Property Agreement, or TRIPS, limited the sharing of Western pharmaceutical knowledge and production by expanding patents, some were concerned that it would also enable what is known as "biopiracy," which is the plundering of local or indigenous knowledge to create commercial products for multinational companies. Indigenous peoples and practitioners of non-Western systems of medicine in India, Brazil, and elsewhere became concerned that multinational companies would come prospecting for their knowledge about medicinal plants. They would learn of, say, a tropical shrub that treats stomach disorders used by the Ka'apor people in the Amazon or a tuber that has anti-inflammatory properties well known to practitioners of ayurvedic medicine in India, and they would then isolate the active ingredient in the plant to create a new product for which they would acquire patent rights. These concerns were not far-fetched, as the first effective antipsychotic in Western psychiatry was derived, and patented, by isolating the active ingredient in *Rauwolfia serpentina,* a plant used in Ayurveda to treat mental disorders. And an important early anesthetic was derived from an extract, curare, used by indigenous people in South America and made into a medication by a US company. These innovations were developed by pharmaceutical laboratories that eventually became, respectively, part of Novartis and Bristol-Myers Squibb, and both of these companies have been recently involved in patent disputes in India, asserting property rights for their own innovations. More recently, US and European patents have been issued based on knowledge from India of the properties of turmeric and the neem tree.[3] There are numerous other examples of treatments derived from local or indigenous knowledge around the world, from birth control pills to cancer treatments. In fact, the legal scholar Ikechi Mgbeoji, in his study of biopiracy, estimates that "over one-quarter of modern drugs prescribed all over the world are directly derived from plant life forms, and most of them are products of . . . traditional knowledge of the uses of plants."[4] If Mgbeoji's assessment is correct, the struggle between corporate and indigenous knowledge of the medicinal effects of plants could be quite extensive.

It was unclear, however, how the WTO's new provision on intellectual property would affect non-Western medical systems, since it was oriented toward protecting corporate products and individual inventors and did not seem to change any rules that pertain to indigenous knowledge.[5] Still, many in India, Brazil, and elsewhere were wary of the potential exploitation of local knowledge, and in light of these concerns, India implemented laws based on the Convention on Biological Diversity, which was signed at the 1992 Rio Earth Summit, to provide protection for and benefit-sharing of indigenous knowledge. The Indian government also established the Traditional Knowledge Digital Library (TKDL) to codify knowledge and practices it considers national property, from yoga to the arts to treatments from Indian medical systems.

The most prized aspect of India's local knowledge that the government is trying to protect is Ayurveda, a contemporary, institutionalized medical system that has ancient roots. Ayurvedic medicine has grown in popularity in the West, but it is not quite the "holistic," "natural," or "spiritual" healing system that many people in the West believe it to be. Those outside of South Asia tend to imagine Ayurveda as akin to other "alternative" healing systems. These views are often shaped by a New Age outlook that sees all non-Western medicines as having something in common and as being holistic, natural, or spiritual, whereas in fact these healing systems vary greatly and are often as material and pragmatic as they are holistic or spiritual.

Ayurveda actually has a lot in common with Western biomedicine; both systems intervene in the physiology of the body through the use of pharmaceuticals and other therapeutic modalities. One could argue that Ayurveda is more holistic than Western biomedicine in the sense that it takes into account diet, the season, and other environmental factors more often than biomedicine does. But a typical ayurvedic medical consultation will focus on symptoms and physiology as understood in ayurvedic terms. The patient will describe symptoms, and the doctor—or *vaidyan,* as ayurvedic practitioners are often known—will palpate the patient's body, perhaps listen with a stethoscope (since Ayurveda has adopted some tools of Western biomedicine), and ask the patient questions. Then the vaidyan will make a diagnosis, using one of the Sanskritic terms for diseases in Ayurveda, such as *asmari* or *kapha unmada,* and assess the effect on the three *dosas,* or bodily characteristics, *vata, pitta,* and *kapha,* and other factors. Sometimes the diagnoses have clear correspondences to Western medical diagnoses, such as *asmari,* which is kidney stones, and sometimes they are harder to translate, such as *kapha unmada,* which resembles depression but has different characteristics.[6]

Though its earliest texts date back about two thousand years, Ayurveda is a contemporary, thriving practice. It is taught in ayurvedic medical schools throughout India, and it features schema for understanding health and illness, such as the dosas, bodily substances known as *dhatus,* and myriad other factors. These schema help practitioners understand the effects of food and environmental factors on health and illness and are the basis of an extensive pharmacopoeia of ayurvedic plant-based medicines that some fear will be copied and patented. Research journals present new clinical studies in Ayurveda, but the issue of whether Ayurveda offers new inventions or is based on past truths of medical insight is unclear and, as we shall see, a problem for how ayurvedic knowledge relates to patent law. Ayurvedic medications are produced in factories that process and refine raw plant materials, but ayurvedic pharmaceutical producers do not isolate active chemical entities as is done in Western biomedicine.

Thus Ayurveda is arguably more "natural" than biomedicine, even though plant ingredients are pulverized, evaporated, cooked, and otherwise processed by machines in factories to make ayurvedic drugs. Some ayurvedic doctors prefer not to prescribe factory-produced medicines and instead mix medicines, which they tailor to specific patients' problems, in their own offices. Thus minor innovations are constantly created in the practice of ayurvedic medicine. Sometimes individual doctors' formulations have been kept secret, but no legal ownership rights have been claimed for these creations—that is, until the WTO upped the ante in the world of intellectual property by creating an environment that led practitioners to be more protective about their innovations.

India is also a major producer of pharmaceuticals of Western medicine, or what is referred to as "biomedicine" in this book. Medical anthropologists prefer the term "biomedicine" partly because this medical system is no longer, and rarely has been, exclusively "Western." Also, there are other medical systems that derive from the same Western—specifically Greek—origins of biomedicine, such as India's *Unani* medical system. In India, "biomedicine" is known as "English medicine," "modern medicine," and "allopathy." The term "alternative" medicine is not used because several medical systems, including biomedicine, Ayurveda, and homeopathy, are considered mainstream, but biomedicine is the dominant system in terms of government and private financial and institutional support.

The Indian biomedical pharmaceutical sector is huge, and India-based companies, many of which operate in countries all over the world, have been a source of inexpensive medications for individual consumers and public health programs, supplying low-cost antiretrovirals for AIDS treatment programs in sub-Saharan Africa, which has 70 percent of the global burden of HIV/AIDS, and cost-saving generic drugs to US consumers. While the role of Indian pharmaceutical companies in supplying affordable medications for the international AIDS crisis has received media attention, the degree of consumption of Indian pharmaceuticals in the United States and other high-income countries is less well known. Eighty percent of the active ingredients in all drugs consumed in the United States are produced in India and China.[7] In addition to active ingredients, many of the final drug products are produced by Indian companies. US consumers may not be aware that 40 percent of the prescription medicines they pick up from their pharmacies come from India, even though a company name such as Aurobindo, Ranbaxy, or Sun Pharmaceuticals appears on the label.[8]

Indian pharmaceutical companies, however, have had to rework their business practices after the World Trade Organization enacted TRIPS, and India had to change its Patents Act to allow product patents for medications. Now drug products can be patented in India and can only be produced with permission, usually in the form of a license from the patent holder, and an accompanying payment of royalties.

This seemingly slight change from process patents to product patents in 2005 confers exclusive market control of medications to single companies and could have major international public health effects if this causes prices of essential medicines to rise. Already, controversy has stirred over the effects of the new patent regime, with court cases mounted in opposition to new patents and applications for licenses to override patent rights in the name of public health submitted in India, Brazil, and other places. Meanwhile, some multinational drug companies have voluntarily licensed the right to produce some of their medications to Indian companies, keeping the prices of certain treatments for HIV/AIDS relatively low for now. These trends need careful monitoring, since thirty-seven million people in the world are living with HIV, and only 46 percent of them have access to these lifesaving medications.[9]

Practitioners of Ayurveda have been concerned by the new patent regime but uncertain about how it would affect them, since Ayurveda relates ambiguously to the provisions of patent law. Patents protect innovations that are useful, novel, and non-obvious and that are individually created rather than the product of collective, shared knowledge. Innovation in Ayurveda is both individual and collective, novel yet always in dialogue with classic principles. It is based on knowledge about the physiological effects of plants but does not involve isolating active ingredients, which would make their therapies patentable since one cannot patent plants (unless they have been genetically modified). In some ways, biopiracy does not seem to threaten the practice of Ayurveda directly, since biomedical products, which use chemically isolated ingredients rather than plant materials, would not be used by ayurvedic practitioners, and ayurvedic pharmaceutical producers should be able to continue to use medicinal plant materials even if active chemical ingredients extracted from them were patented by others. But this patent system seems unjust to Ayurveda's defenders, since it protects rights for biomedical products but does not defend ayurvedic innovation in the same way—confirming that science and the law, like any other social practices, are culturally inflected.[10] For example, reserpine, the antipsychotic drug developed from ayurvedic insights, which is now used as an antihypertensive, continues to make over $200 million a year in sales for the biomedical drug companies that produce it, but no ayurvedic practitioners have seen a share of these profits.[11] In response, ayurvedic activists are digitizing ayurvedic knowledge through the TKDL as a resource to use in opposing patents while some ayurvedic practitioners are developing products that they think are patentable, possibly changing the practice of Ayurveda in the process.

In exploring controversies over the ownership and control of medical knowledge in a post-WTO world, this book highlights the vicissitudes and dangers of this new environment while revealing moments of opportunity for a more equitable future in this regime of ownership that may affect access to medicine for a large portion of the world's population. To do so, the book takes into account actors that have much at stake in the new patent environment, including activists concerned with the price of essential medicines, United States– and India-based pharmaceutical companies, and ayurvedic practitioners and producers.

Overextending Intellectual Property

The idea of intellectual property and its application in the new patent regime are not wholly nefarious, oppressive, and without productive consequences. Like the legal scholar and critic of the current IP regime, James Boyle (2008), I do not object to intellectual property in principle. The idea of giving an innovator a temporary monopoly over an innovation conditional on the public disclosure of how the innovation works balances individual and public interests and was an improvement on an earlier system where innovators simply kept the formulations behind their creations secret. This secret often died with the innovator rather than becoming part of the public domain as innovations now do after twenty years under patent law. What is problematic is the overextension of intellectual property law and the use of obfuscating myths of individual invention that justify it. Scholars have examined myths that support principles of intellectual property showing that claims of individual invention obscure the collective and incremental nature of innovation in medicine, science, and the arts.[12] Patents, for example, protect the collective invention of employees of a corporation only because a corporation is legally, though not actually, an individual, while the collective knowledge of a community or an indigenous medical system is not patentable.

Before the WTO, when nations crafted their intellectual property laws with greater autonomy, people around the world were freer to borrow, share, or appropriate each others' knowledge and creations. Today, because patent cordons are being reinforced mostly at the behest of powerful commercial interests, less privileged forms of knowledge are also being cordoned off, leading to a loss of creativity, a reluctance to share knowledge, and a shrinking of the public domain. This reinforces observations by critics who lament the loss of an intellectual commons that comes from both sides of intellectual property struggles, the powerful interests that advocate for expansive IP law and the groups that resist these expansions by establishing defensive claims.[13]

In Indonesia, the government's defenses of indigenous knowledge and arts—from contemporary theater to textiles to classical dance—through new intellectual property laws limit the borrowing of ideas from Indonesian cultures by outside artists. This restricts the possibility of cultural exchange and works against the interests of the artists the Indonesian government claims to be defending, who want their products to be used and circulated by outsiders.[14] Likewise, people in India and the Indian state often celebrate how their cultures, medicines, and sciences have been adopted around the world—from yoga to Gandhian nonviolence to the concept of zero in mathematics and even ayurvedic medicine—but such contributions to global patrimony, and even the discovery of new treatments for diseases, may be threatened by the Traditional Knowledge Digital Library and other attempts to encode and protect knowledge systems.

Even before the rise of modern globalization, cultural hybridity was commonplace, and the adoption and sharing of different cultural and scientific ideas—borrowing that today might be considered forms of piracy—was the norm. We take for granted that, until recently, we had been living in a world where an open public domain was maintained, often simply because there were fewer laws limiting the circulation of innovations. Europeans did not have to pay royalties to China every time they made pasta, brewed tea, or set off fireworks because of the Chinese origins of these innovations. Mathematicians and engineers did not have to figure out which numerical concepts came from Indian, Greek, or Arab sources and get the necessary permissions to continue their work.[15] While restrictions on the sharing of knowledge and innovation, whether artistic or scientific, represent a loss to human creativity and scientific discovery, researchers who examine recent IP controversies argue that we need to be wary of the ideal of an open public domain, which, like many rational-actor or level-playing-field ideals, ignores social inequalities that give more powerful interests a greater ability to extract and benefit from communal resources.[16] It is also not appropriate to suggest that both sides—the corporate interests and the defenders of local knowledge—share equal blame for the current partitioning of the world's knowledge. The defenses of Ayurveda, yoga, and the arts in India, Indonesia, and elsewhere are best seen as a reaction to the corporate actors who initiated this standoff.

Reacting to Globalization: Power, Complexity, and Vulnerability

In analyzing the struggles between activist, corporate, and government actors, this book provides an example of how people react to and resist forces of globalization. Global initiatives and agreements constantly reshape the socioeconomic world we live in today, and understanding and reacting to these forces—or what I call "constellations" of power to refer to their multilayered nature and their complexity—can be daunting. WTO mandates, such as TRIPS, free trade agreements, such as NAFTA and the proposed Trans-Pacific Partnership (which contains new IP protections), and the constant movement of industrial production in pursuit of low-cost labor regularly remake our world, but it can be difficult to discern what will be their effects.

Thus, this examination of the current struggle over intellectual property claims considers the legibility of power, which refers to how difficult it is to understand a system of power, such as the new patent regime, for people whose lives it affects and even for the journalists, researchers, and activists who assess such systems and decide what to do about them. For a long time, analyses of power and resistance considered power relations that were relatively easy to read or where the threat, and who was behind it, was clearer. For example, labor exploitation of peasants and indigenous people and the seizure of land by Hispanic elites led to the Mexican Revolution and similar uprisings in the twentieth century.[17] The threat of fascist and authoritarian leaders like Mussolini and Suharto was also relatively easy to perceive.[18] The political scientist James Scott famously argued that often resistance does not result in open revolt but takes place through what he called "everyday forms of resistance" such as foot dragging, work slowdowns, pilfering, and other methods, but the conditions people were reacting to were relatively clear to those who were affected: landlords were raising the rent, mechanization was putting people out of work.[19]

Today, amorphous "forces of globalization" are harder to decipher. They are mysterious, daunting, and difficult to figure out how to resist. These networks of power are also like rhizomes, to use a popular metaphor proposed by social scientists and philosophers for analyzing science, technology, and social networks.[20] A tree is hierarchical and centralized, with a trunk from which branches break off and divide into smaller branches, ending up at the smallest level like capillaries in the human body, and all dependent on the center. The rhizome, on the other hand, is a mostly subterranean structure of roots that goes out in every direction, constantly forming new junctions and networks from which plant shoots pop up at various intervals. Unlike the tree, there is no center in the rhizome. The structure continuously reproduces itself as it moves out through space in multiple directions. There is no trunk, stem, or root structure that, if severed, affects the whole organism. If one were to cut the roots of the rhizome, it would continue to send out new branches and shoots in different directions as long as there were space and nutrients. The new global intellectual property regime is in some ways like the tree, since the WTO was central in its implementation, but it has taken on the structure of a rhizome, sending shoots up in different countries as laws are changed and new supporters or adherents are added to the network. Some supporters at new nodes in the network appear at first to be resistors, as in the case of those in India who are working to protect Ayurveda through the TKDL. Although this effort is aimed at protecting knowledge from misappropriation, it at the same time affirms the principles of intellectual property of the new regime by preparing to mount oppositions to patents using provisions of patent law—specifically by proving that biomedical pharmaceuticals derived from Ayurveda are based on prior knowledge and therefore not patentable. This amounts to an agreement to the principles of patent law that are central to the new IP regime.

In trying to understand what she calls "the state of globalization" today, the social anthropologist Shalini Randeria speaks of the unwieldy and complex nature of contemporary forces that involve webs of corporate and government actors and multiple legal regimes.[21] In earlier studies of power and resistance mentioned above, people objected to policies of their landlords, bosses, or government leaders. Today, the government and local officials are as likely to be allies as adversaries, since the "law today transcends state boundaries in complex and significant ways due to a proliferation of actors, arenas, methods and forms of rulemaking and dispute resolution located at different sites around the world."[22] Randeria considers the multiple legal regimes that India must negotiate, including TRIPS and the Convention on Biological Diversity, and concludes that "in the new architecture of global governance, power is diffuse and elusive."[23]

Francis Gurry of the United Nations World Intellectual Property Organization (WIPO) similarly points to the growing complexity that international policies and agreements have taken on in the wake of TRIPS, where organizations, such as the Convention on Biological Diversity, the Food and Agriculture Organization, and UNESCO, have suddenly had to work intellectual property positions into their agendas, when they did not have to do this in the past. The dynamics of power and resistance have been a major focus of social science research for several decades now, but this diffuse character of power—which renders it illegible and makes strategies of resistance difficult to devise—has not been central to that research.[24]

Thus global constellations of power, like the new intellectual property regime, are multilayered and constantly changing, and attempts to resist them can lead to unanticipated results. A rhizomatic structure is difficult to dismantle or resist. In the case of the effect of the new IP regime on ayurvedic medicine, the threat is hard to decipher, and ayurvedic practitioners and activists have engaged in a variety of reactions, which include deliberate inaction, hoping that by "lying low" and not engaging with the new regime there will be no threat. Defenders of Ayurveda must deal with an extra layer of complexity, since they are trying to understand how their system of medicine relates to patent law and whether and how their knowledge needs to be defended, but few people have the legal, political, and ayurvedic expertise to assess these issues. For biomedical pharmaceutical production, there is a little more clarity.

If one severs the roots of a rhizome, there will be little effect on the plant network. Similarly, creatures of mythology, such as the hydra or the cyclops, seemed daunting, but they always had some vulnerability that the hero could find to subdue the creature. This is somewhat like what activist groups and government representatives in India have managed to do through legal maneuvering within the new patent regime, notably by adding an obscure-sounding provision to the country's new patent law, Section 3d. While they have not actually "subdued" the new regime, we might say these efforts have "domesticated" it by limiting its negative effects in India and for places that depend on India's low-cost drug supply. This story of heroism is not well known, most likely because it involves legal technicalities that seem complicated and obscure, but basically, small activist groups in India, such as an organization of HIV-positive people assisted by a handful of activist lawyers, have been able to defeat patent applications by multinational companies in the India Patent Office, and their efforts are aided by Section 3d's rigorous standard for patents to be awarded in India.

Section 3d creates a more balanced patent law that resembles the original principle of intellectual property as a temporary and limited social contract that protects real innovation, rather than what IP has become today, a tool for expanding the reach of private property. The oppositions based on Section 3d prevent what some have seen as frivolous patents that have been awarded in other places, such as the United States, for me-too drugs. Section 3d requires that new versions of drugs show greater effectiveness than the older versions to obtain a patent. While this does not sound like an unreasonable requirement, it has brought the ire of the pharmaceutical industry. This provision prevents Indian patents of several medications that were profitable for pharmaceutical companies elsewhere, and it was added, at the behest of leftist parties, to India's new intellectual property laws. Corporations got what they wanted in the WTO with TRIPS, but they did not anticipate India adding this section that would limit its effects. Needless to say, "big pharma" did not see the creation of Section 3d as heroic, but rather as an unfair restriction on their property rights. Swiss-based multinational giant Novartis challenged Section 3d in India's Supreme Court, but in a decision handed down in 2013, the court ruled this provision was legal and allowable under TRIPS.

The metaphor offered earlier of trying to defeat a mythical beast is appropriate because it calls attention to the fact that global constellations of power such as the new patent regime are complex and intimidating. The metaphor's weakness is that it depicts a uniformly dangerous and malign threat whereas the new patent regime is not so simple, and, unlike a mythical beast, it has its allies. Enthusiasts of the "free market" model believe that increasing corporate profitability through strict property controls will float all boats and spur economic growth in many sectors, and strong IP protections will create incentives for corporate innovation in all WTO member states. There are many problems with such "free market" ideals—and one of them is that TRIPS is more about WTO and government intervention in favor of corporate interests than freeing markets— yet the new patent environment is not wholly nefarious, and it has led to unexpected opportunities that have some benefits, such as development of new products by Indian pharmaceutical companies. These products do not merely add more drugs to the overly medicated privileged strata of society in India and high-income countries; they also show promise in addressing neglected diseases of low-income areas that large, multinational pharmaceutical companies ignore.

Finally, this book takes pharmaceutical companies seriously as important, and unavoidable, actors with legitimate concerns. Without a doubt these corporations have an unfair share of power to conform economic policy to their interests, but we will see how the caricature of an all-powerful "big pharma," often found in social science and public health research, ignores the complexities and varied agendas of pharmaceutical producers.

Studying Pharmaceutical Producers

This book builds on other work that has explored the expansion of intellectual property rights in the last few decades.[25] Most of those studies focus on Europe or North America and explore these issues from legal and textual sources. Less attention has been paid to the most significant sites of current patent struggles, such as India, one of the world's largest pharmaceutical producers with a history of sharing medical knowledge with the West, and we have not learned much about how actual people in pharmaceutical production respond to the new legal regime.[26] I chose to follow these issues over an extended period of time, tracking the maneuvers of the WTO, pharmaceutical corporations, and Indian government protections of indigenous medical knowledge in the media from the period before 2005, when India implemented the new intellectual property rules, and for several years after. Like other work on the new patent regime, this book depends on documentary and legal sources, but I supplemented these observations with insights from pharmaceutical producers involved in the struggles and opportunities created by the new patent environment by speaking with individuals involved in the protection of ayurvedic knowledge and employees of ayurvedic and biomedical pharmaceutical companies in India and the United States.

The issues considered in this book are constantly emerging and evolving, making it challenging to offer definitive pronouncements on them. As I was including genes in the list of objects that are now subject to IP claims in this introduction, the United States Supreme Court ruled that naturally occurring, unaltered genes could not be patented, striking down Myriad Genetics' claim to own the BRCA breast cancer genes but affirming that synthetic genes could be patented.[27] Meanwhile, legal precedents continue to emerge from India, such as the 2013 Indian Supreme Court decision upholding Section 3d of the 2005 Patents Act. While the terrain is always shifting, it is valuable to try to make an accounting of where we are and where we are heading.

My own assessment of the effects of the patent regime has changed over the course of my research on this issue. In an earlier analysis of the emerging patent environment, I raised the concern that the new regime will have a dire impact on global public health because it will most likely raise the price of medications that have been developed since the new regime came into effect, such as treatments for new forms of HIV/AIDS that are becoming resistant to the first line of antiretroviral drugs (ARVs). This could have a devastating effect on ARV programs in low-income countries.[28] Yet in the case of tenofovir, one of the most important first- and second-line AIDS treatments that has come out under the new patent regime, the price in low-income countries has come down dramatically, from $200 per person per year to $26 per person per year, because of voluntary licensing agreements that the patent owner, Gilead Sciences, issued to multiple Indian generic pharmaceutical manufacturers, allowing them to produce the medications. Thus one of the earliest and most well documented examples of pricing under the new patent regime was not what I, and others, anticipated. This raises the possibility that the effects of the new patent laws may not be as dramatic as expected. As we will see later, such voluntary licensing practices have their limitations, and we will have to monitor whether the tenofovir scenario is repeated with other essential medicines as drug production under the new regime continues.

Also, some were concerned that the new patent environment would result in Indian pharmaceutical companies being acquired by multinational producers and becoming a source of cheap scientific labor for making medications. This has not happened—or not happened yet—and this concern assumes a simplistic opposition between multinational "big pharma" and a vulnerable Indian generic sector. Many India-based companies are large and multinational. Meanwhile, some foreign-based companies are generic producers, and some India-based companies have developed and marketed their own branded products. The first pharmaceutical developed and patented under India's new law by an India-based company is Ranbaxy's Synriam (arterolane maleate and piperaquine phosphate),[29] an antimalarial that will help treat a disease that has been neglected by other multinational companies.

Despite my training in anthropology, this book is not heavily ethnographic, although it uses ethnographic methods and presents ethnographic perspectives not typically offered in other assessments of the new intellectual property regime. I based some of my claims on following institutions, the implementation of laws, and efforts by activists over the last twelve years through information I gathered from the media and other public records such as press releases and documents available on interest-group websites. The analysis of the emergence of a new legal regime and its impacts on public health, practitioners, and corporations does not easily lend itself to the fly-on-the-wall orientation of participant observation, the signature method of anthropology, which in this case would ideally involve observing people in the workplace. Still, I gained important insights from doing field research. Discussions with ayurvedic practitioners and producers who were not directly working on projects such as the TKDL but who were concerned about patent issues were the easiest to initiate and provide an important perspective. Fieldwork around ayurvedic practitioners working on the TKDL or inside pharmaceutical companies was not as feasible, although it was attempted with limited success. I did also manage to meet with, and interview, other important stakeholders and activists in India and the United States. This blend of methods is an effective way—but not the only way—to study the emergence of a new legal regime. It enabled me to take account of slowly evolving processes along with the views of local actors, and it is appropriate when one is "studying up" powerful institutions as I did in examining pharmaceutical company policies and practices.

In the 1970s, the anthropologist Laura Nader urged researchers to "study up," which refers to doing ethnographic work on powerful institutions, not just marginalized people, everyday practices, or exotic others.[30] Efforts to study up have become increasingly popular, but as Hugh Gusterson points out, based on his ethnographic studies of nuclear weapons scientists, people in powerful institutions or elite positions usually do not welcome scrutiny and they often have the means to avoid it. This difficulty in studying up Gusterson labeled the "Roger and Me syndrome," a reference to the Michael Moore documentary where Moore tries to interview the CEO of General Motors, only to be turned away repeatedly by security personnel. Gusterson thus advocated "polymorphous engagement" with powerful subjects, which involves a variety of methods, including interviewing where possible, conducting ethnographic observations in peripheral spaces, such as workplace cafeterias and waiting areas, and doing research based on news and other textual sources.[31]

The research in India was conducted during brief fieldwork in Kerala in 2004 and 2005 that focused on meetings with ayurvedic practitioners and producers and legal and public health experts. In a subsequent visit in 2012, I conducted interviews with ayurvedic practitioners, legal analysts, and pharmaceutical company representatives in Hyderabad, Delhi, and Kerala. Hyderabad, a historical, multicultural city that was once the center of a large kingdom ruled by a succession of Nizams, is now the pharmaceutical hub and a high-tech boomtown of southern India. Delhi is one of the nation's megacities, home to several pharmaceutical companies as well as government workers who analyze national policy, including intellectual property provisions. Kerala is a state in southern India where I have conducted ethnographic research on a range of issues related to medical anthropology and public health. The state is, in essence, the ayurvedic pharmaceutical hub of India, the lesser-known counterpart to Hyderabad, and Kerala is renowned for its concentration of ayurvedic physicians and institutions, including clinics, hospitals, and even psychiatric facilities. Many have come to Kerala seeking the region's local knowledge about medicinal plants, starting with Hendrik Adriaan van Rheede, a Dutch official stationed in Cochin, who, in the seventeenth century, compiled the famous *Hortus Malabaricus*, an encyclopedia of botanical knowledge from this part of India that aided the development of biological science in Europe.

Observations about ayurvedic medical practices are based on these visits as well as fieldwork conducted since the early 1990s on ayurvedic treatments for psychopathology, and I continued to monitor developments related to the new IP regime in the Indian media during an eight-month stay in India in 2013–2014 that was focused on a different research topic.[32]

The process of trying to speak to representatives of pharmaceutical companies that were key players in the new patent regime was fraught with challenges characteristic of the "Roger and Me" syndrome. I believe that pharmaceutical companies in the United States and India want to avoid direct interaction with researchers. They prefer to control what is said to the public through press releases and presentations on their websites, but those pharmaceutical employees I was able to speak with were forthcoming and helpful in discussing how they respond to the new patent environment, although they were, no doubt, a self-selected group. Thus in addition to analyzing pharmaceutical company perspectives on patent controversies and presenting an encouraging example of price reductions through partnerships between United States–based Gilead Sciences and several India-based companies, I will examine corporate obfuscation showing how companies' preference for one-way communication contributes to the difficulty in deciphering systems of power today.

The History of Intellectual Property and the Current Regime

The next two chapters examine the development of intellectual property law in Europe and the recent expansion of this type of property relation around the world while also highlighting features of India's changing patent laws and activists' attempts to use these laws to oppose patents. The book then moves on to examine the perspective of pharmaceutical producers, showing how ayurvedic practitioners and producers, United States–based pharmaceutical companies, and Indian pharmaceutical companies navigate the new terrain of intellectual property.

Chapter 1 sketches the history of the concept of intellectual property from its emergence in fifteenth-century Europe through its expansion in the late twentieth century with the World Trade Organization TRIPS agreement. Chapter 2 considers the public health effects of the change from a process to a product patent regime in India, the primary supplier of essential medicines for low-income countries, and examines how activists in India, such as the Lawyers Collective and the Indian Network for People Living with HIV/AIDS, have defeated recent patent applications.

Chapter 3 highlights the history of the sharing of medical knowledge between India and the West and analyzes the divergent reactions of practitioners and producers of ayurvedic medicine to the new patent regime, some of whom oppose the regime and some of whom try to create proprietary ayurvedic medicines. Chapter 4 presents the perspective of multinational pharmaceutical companies, with a special focus on Gilead's voluntary licensing program that has allowed Indian companies to make several of Gilead's antiretroviral products, bringing down the price of important medicines for AIDS in low-income countries. We will learn that for these companies, the main priority under the new patent regime is to protect their markets in wealthy and middle-income countries, and the main problem of drug access may turn out to be for the poor who live in middle-income countries such as Brazil and China. Chapter 5 critiques the distinction between "multinational" pharmaceutical companies, or "big pharma," and "Indian" pharmaceutical companies used in many analyses, and presents discussions with representatives from two Indian pharmaceutical companies, which address patent licenses, economies of scale—the special capacity of the Indian pharmaceutical sector—and prospects for research and development in India, which has recently produced new drugs for cancer and malaria.

Before further examining the role of these actors involved in pharmaceutical creation and production, it will be necessary to understand where the concept of intellectual property came from. Intellectual property does not really exist until innovators create this concept starting in fifteenth-century Venice. This is a particular European view about property relations built largely on romantic ideals of individual innovation, and it is remarkable that these culturally specific ideas about ownership have spread to the point where most of the globe is conforming to a single intellectual property regime.

1

THE INVENTION AND EXPANSION OF INTELLECTUAL PROPERTY

In a compelling study of our shrinking creative and cultural commons, *The Public Domain* (2008), the legal scholar James Boyle alerts us:

> We are in the middle of a second enclosure movement. While it sounds grandiloquent to call it "the enclosure of the intangible commons of the mind," in a very real sense that's just what it is. . . . Once again things that were formerly thought of as common property, or as "uncommodifiable," or outside the market altogether, are being covered with new, or newly extended, property rights. (45)

The first enclosure movement, which developed over the course of the fifteenth to nineteenth centuries in England, involved the privatization of what were once common lands, while this second enclosure movement involves the privatization of creative and intellectual realms through intellectual property laws. Despite sounding the alarm about the new enclosure movement, Boyle's book opens with a defense of the basic principles of intellectual property law.

In the case of patent law, Boyle explains that this kind of protection is preferable to the previous method of gaining a commercial advantage through the maintenance of secrecy that was used, for example, by medieval guilds. The problem with secrecy is that the invention does not get broadly produced so that the greater society can enjoy its benefits, and its usefulness to society may die with the death of the innovator. Some ayurvedic doctors use this method of keeping their formulas to themselves to control the use of their innovations. Most ayurvedic practitioners I spoke to were not, however, enthusiastic about this method. They explained that they preferred that knowledge be shared, and they complained that formulations that were kept secret died with their "owners." A patent, which is a time-limited contract between the innovator and society, and not a guarantee of enduring ownership, ensures that innovations remain as public resources after the expiration of a patent and after the death of an inventor. Boyle explains that through this contract, society is assuring innovators that if they publically disclose their invention—in enough detail so that others will be able to recreate it—the state will give them a temporary monopoly to produce the invention or transfer the rights to benefit from its production. After the term of the patent expires, the invention will become part of the public domain, available for anyone to produce. Should the inventor not wish to divulge how the invention works after the expiration of the patent or if the inventor dies, society will have an explanation of how the invention works "on file," even though the form of the record of the patented invention has changed over time.[1]

Boyle goes on to explain the other key forms of intellectual property, copyrights and trademarks that protect artistic works and symbols of trade, and then asks:

> But does intellectual property work this way now, promoting the ideal of progress, a transparent marketplace, easy and cheap access to information, decentralized and iconoclastic cultural production, self-correcting innovation policy? Often it does, but distressingly often it does the reverse. The rights that were supposed to be limited in time and scope to the minimum monopoly necessary to ensure production become instead a kind of perpetual corporate welfare—restraining the next generation of creators instead of encouraging them. (8–9)

Boyle adds that through extensions of the life of copyrights to, in many cases, over a century, at least in the United States, "most of twentieth century culture is under copyright—copyrighted but unavailable. Much of this, in other words, is lost culture" (9). This is because books, films, and music are often not made available to the public because of fear of infringement.

Although the life of a copyright has been extended to over a hundred years, in most cases the life of a patent remains at twenty years. It is the enforcement of patents that has been extended, along with the application of United States–style patent law through the WTO, which includes product patents for medications and overrides much local variability in patent provisions. A key rationale of patent law, the assurance that after investing in research and bringing a new drug to market others cannot come along immediately and copy it, is now used as "a kind of black-mail" where "industry leaders and lobbyists routinely warn that lower prices will reduce funds for R&D and result in suffering and death that future medicines could reduce."[2] Such appeals to the importance of re-covering investments, however, obscure the significant amount of public money that goes into innovations for which corporations claim exclusive rights. Nonetheless, pharmaceutical companies have effectively mobilized the ideology of intellectual property and the threat of diminishing future drug development to advocate for the expansion of their property claims.

The Invention of Intangible Property

Anthropologists have tried to determine whether intellectual property or similar protection for intangible forms of property exists outside of European societies or before capitalism and its sanctification of private property became the global norm. Their findings have, however, been ambiguous. In 1928, Robert Lowie claimed something like intellectual property, or "incorporeal property," to use his term, existed in precapitalist societies in the form of rights to songs and secrecy of certain kinds of knowledge. He cites, for example, research on the Eskimo, among whom "a commu-nistic trend as to economic necessaries is coupled with strict individualism as to the magical means of securing food," and describes the process by which ritual knowledge and songs may be "purchased" among Blackfoot

Native Americans.[3] A. Irving Hallowell retorted that this indicates something like mere possession, which is not equivalent to formal property rights, since such claims do not have the "commercial flavor" seen in contemporary property claims.[4] Countering those who argue that non-Western peoples do not have principles that resemble intellectual property and believe only in communal ownership, Michael Brown offers examples of Kiowa and other Native American practices of individual ownership of songs, designs, and other forms of intangible property. He adds that "the rules controlling the flow of ideas and information are often hard to reconcile with Western practices and, perhaps more significantly, with the replicative technologies spawned by the Industrial Revolution."[5]

It is difficult to determine whether practices such as secrecy about knowledge and "owning" songs constitute predecessors to what we know as intellectual property. If Michael Brown is right, it may be the "replicative technologies," such as mass printing and mass manufacturing, that spur the creation of actual legal protections for intellectual property. Doctors of ayurvedic medicine speak about the maintenance of secrecy of some doctors' formulations as if it is similar to intellectual property law. This practice may predate the commodification of medical products that developed with colonialism and capitalism, or it may be a more recent response to commodification, a defense against the practice of making and selling medical products for a profit.

The emergence of modern intellectual property law can be more distinctly defined. The granting of patents as privileges to market inventions—but not as ownership of the concept behind the invention—dates back to fifteenth-century Venice. The elements of modern patent law—which protects the information that is the basis of an invention—can be traced to transformations in claims of ownership and ideas about mental and physical labor in eighteenth-century Europe and the United States.[6]

The science historian Mario Biagioli highlights a shift that occurred around 1790, when the state stopped conceiving of patents as privileges and began protecting patents as rights. New specification requirements for patents replaced the principle that the invention was a material thing the inventor presented before representatives of the state to claim ownership. Patent laws adopted in France and the United States in the late 1700s required a precise description of the invention on paper and resulted in the protection of the idea behind the invention as property: "Allowing for the emergence of the idea as a distinct entity, specifications made possible for that idea to become the immaterial 'essence' of the invention."[7] This is the basis of the social contract behind patent law that we have today, where the state gives the innovator a temporary monopoly on his innovation in exchange for the innovator's public disclosure of the invention in enough detail so that others can reproduce it after the patent expires or the inventor dies.

Similar principles emerged in the development of copyright law after the passage of the Statute of Anne in England in 1710. The statute claimed that "printers, booksellers, and other persons have of late frequently taken the liberty of printing, reprinting, and publishing, or causing to be printed, reprinted, and published, books and other writings, without the consent of the authors or proprietors of such books and writings, to their very great detriment, and too often to the ruin of them and their families." "For the encouragement of learned men to compose and write useful books," it awarded exclusive rights to print books to their authors and to those booksellers and printers to whom the authors assigned their rights.[8] Thus the book trade's "claims of proprietorship extended not only to the particular books they published, but to the content of those books."[9]

Starting in the late 1700s, Wordsworth and other Romantic authors promoted the ideas that creative works came from an individual wellspring of creativity and that writers could be said to own these works. Before then:

> Writers, like other artisans, considered their task to lie in the reworking of traditional materials according to principles and techniques preserved and handed down to them in rhetoric and poetics—the collective wisdom of their craft. In the event that they chanced to go beyond the state of the art, their innovation was ascribed to God, or later to Providence. Similarly, in the sphere of science, invention and discovery were viewed as essentially incremental—the inevitable outcome of a (collective) effort.[10]

References to the romantic myth of the individual inventor in this book thus invoke two meanings of "romantic": it is "romantic" in the sense that it is an ideal and not a reflection of the actual practice of innovation, and it is "Romantic" in that it evokes a literary movement that inspired the idea of individual creativity in literature which is, in turn, linked to the notion of individual creativity in science.[11]

Another important distinction emerged in copyright debates in eighteenth-century England: when "the law not only came to differentiate between mental and manual labour, it also came to *privilege* the labour of the mind over that of the body."[12] The argument used by publishers was that the mental faculty is what separates man from beasts. A further hierarchy that was essential to modern intellectual property law emerged in the mid-nineteenth century, privileging mental creativity over "mere" mental labor. From the late eighteenth to early nineteenth centuries in Germany, the Republic of Letters similarly distinguished between the creative work of the intellectual and the craftwork of artisans. Artisans were denied the status of scientific authors because "they merely manipulated preexisting materials rather than creating something truly novel."[13] While the principles of patent law value "true innovation" over "mere manipulation," much "innovation" in pharmacology today is achieved by "merely manipulating" preexisting innovations and concepts. Currently, the element of creativity remains enshrined in the legal requirement that an invention be original and non-obvious to obtain a patent. The US Patent Act of 1952, which in its amended form is the reigning patent law in the United States, requires that inventions be novel, non-obvious, and useful, and the patent applicant must disclose the invention in enough detail that "any person skilled in the art to which it pertains" can make it.[14] Despite this seeming adherence to the standards of intellectual property law, US patent law appears very liberal in awarding patents compared to India's 2005 Patents Act.

Intellectual property law received several boosts in the expansion of its realms of coverage and the extension of its protections in the last thirty years, especially in the United States. US intellectual property law is important for understanding the new global patent regime, since the WTO TRIPS agreement is essentially an expansion of US IP law to the rest of the world, and US interests are behind other expansions of IP law contained in bilateral agreements between nations and the proposed Trans-Pacific Partnership. In *Diamond v. Chakrabarty,* a landmark 1980 United States Supreme Court case that allowed the patenting of certain life forms, the microbiologist Anand Chakrabarty, working for General Electric, created a genetically modified bacterium that can be used to break up oil spills. The US Patent Commissioner challenged Chakrabarty's attempt to patent this bacterium on the supposition that life forms cannot be patented.

The case went to the Supreme Court, which decided that while existing life forms cannot be patented, this engineered organism could be because it was sufficiently altered by human intervention and was sufficiently novel.[15]

Also in 1980, Congress passed the Patent and Trademark Law Amendment Act—better known as the Bayh-Dole Act—which facilitated the commercialization of innovations developed at universities and nonprofit institutions. While this did not greatly increase the orientation of university research toward the production of commercial products, it continued a trend of privatizing scientific knowledge and not just the knowledge pertaining to specific inventions. In a study of patenting of university research, David Mowery and colleagues warn:

> "Privatization" of knowledge inputs that formerly were part of the "scientific commons" through patenting may impede the progress of research. Increased academic patenting may also enhance incentives for faculty or universities to delay publication, restrict sharing of research materials, and/or limit the sharing by faculty of their research results with the scientific community.[16]

Such limitations on the sharing of knowledge are already occurring, according to Mowery and coauthors, and it is due not only to the Bayh-Dole Act but also to US patent law's overly broad definition of the "usefulness" of inventions.

Ten years after Bayh-Dole, the California Supreme Court ruled in *Moore v. The Regents of the University of California* that the plaintiff John Moore did not have property rights over a cell line derived from his spleen. This cell line was used to create patented products by his physicians after he went for cancer treatment at UCLA Medical Center. The court ruled that Moore's doctors should have informed him of the potential commercial use of his cells but decided that Moore did not have property rights over his cells, which were eventually developed into products by Sandoz Pharmaceuticals and Genetics Institute, Inc.[17] Moore was not entitled to property rights because he did not do any work on his cell line. But his doctors did. That is, the doctors mixed in their labor with his cells, to invoke the classic rationale for property rights from the seventeenth-century English philosopher John Locke, which is still at the root of property claims.

Aided by the Bayh-Dole Act, the Regents of the University of California agreed to split the profits from products derived from Moore's cell line with Moore's doctors, and an agreement was made with Sandoz and Genetics Institute, Inc., to commercially produce products from the cell line, such as treatments for AIDS and cancer. Moore was not included in this profit-sharing agreement.

Another landmark decision regarding the patentability of biological material was handed down in 2013 when the United States Supreme Court overturned Myriad Genetics' patent claim for the BRCA gene that is linked to an increased likelihood for developing breast cancer. Because this gene was naturally occurring and was not created or significantly modified by Myriad, Myriad did not have property rights. While striking down Myriad's claim, the court affirmed the patentability of modified genes, paving the way for increasing investment in such products.[18]

In 1992, copyright protection received a major boost when the Sonny Bono Copyright Term Extension Act extended copyrights to seventy and, in some cases, one hundred years, including extensions that were retroactive. With the advent of the Internet, additional provisions were passed, including the Digital Millennium Copyright Act, which limits the use, distribution, and sharing of digital materials.[19] The full story of copyright is beyond the scope of this book, but it is important to note that there is an affinity between the idea of the creative genius of the writer and that of the scientific innovator in IP law and that the new global intellectual property regime involves expansions of both patent and copyright law.

Treaties and Conventions

According to the United Nations World Intellectual Property Organization (WIPO), the need for international intellectual property agreements was first felt in 1873, when foreign inventors refused to attend a convention in Vienna, fearing their creations might be misappropriated by inventors who would learn of their inventions at the convention and produce them in other countries.[20] These fears were addressed by the Paris Convention of 1883, the first agreement to give international recognition to something like patents, which it referred to as "industrial property," but its regulations were minimal and it did not set up technical criteria for international IP claims.[21] Soon after, the Berne Convention provided protection for artistic and literary works, and in 1893 this convention was merged with the Paris agreement to form the United International Bureau for the Protection of Intellectual Property (better known by its French acronym, BIRPI).[22] What appears to be the first effort at resistance to international IP agreements occurred in the 1960s, when African and Indian delegates argued that the folklore of developing countries should be protected by copyright under BIRPI "as a source of development income."[23] In a move that foreshadowed the exclusion of nonbiomedical treatments from patent protection, representatives of developed countries rejected these efforts, claiming that the Berne Convention was meant to apply only to individual authors. The Paris Convention was last amended in 1979 and can be understood as a more flexible predecessor to the WTO's IP agreement.

In 1970, another international instrument, the Patent Cooperation Treaty, was enacted. As the legal scholar Ikechi Mgbeoji observed regarding international intellectual property agreements, no "global" patent treaty "creates a so-called global patent" and the effect of the Patent Cooperation Treaty was to "streamline the administrative processes involved in filing a patent application in different countries."[24] Member states had the flexibility to shape their own IP laws under these early treaties, and although there are important flexibilities in the WTO's TRIPS agreement, TRIPS establishes a more uniform global system.

The circumstances that led to the development of TRIPS were different from those that gave rise to earlier agreements. The earlier treaties were enacted and enforced in international forums such as the United Nations, which "have a preponderance of numerically superior but economically weak states from the South."[25] Sensing their disadvantage because of their lower numbers in legislative debates, the more economically powerful Northern nations "relocated intellectual property functions from the UN agencies and forums to the framework of the WTO, where [they have] effective control of the agenda and norm-making functions."[26] The UN-affiliated WIPO, originally formed in 1974, continues to make policy recommendations and provisions, and developing countries prefer this forum because of its more democratic nature. This body is limited, however, to "exert[ing] moral suasion" on states and on the implementation of TRIPS.[27]

The more exclusive forum of the WTO made it possible for powerful corporate actors to shape an international IP agreement that suited their concerns and priorities. The intellectual property scholar Peter Drahos (1995) tells the story of how US business interests worked with the US government to implement TRIPS in the General Agreement on Tariffs and Trade (GATT) meetings, which led to the creation of the WTO. Other countries—including European countries and Japan—did not consider increased IP protections to be a priority in their negotiations, but US business interests were able to insert their IP agenda in the GATT negotiations.

To its supporters in the US Congress, US corporate leaders argued that stronger IP protections would grow US industry, create jobs, and restore the country to a more dominant position in the international balance of trade. The Advisory Committee for Trade Negotiations (ACTN), chaired by the CEO of Pfizer, provided the US government direct advice on trade policy and pushed for the international implementation of US-style IP standards. The United States also prepared the ground for the GATT negotiations on the bilateral level by putting countries it felt did not have appropriate IP standards on watch lists. Eventually an Intellectual Property Committee was formed, consisting of Bristol-Myers, DuPont, IBM, Merck, Monsanto, Pfizer, and other corporations with IP priorities, which was able to shape a consensus among key players in the GATT negotiations, especially Europe, Japan, and the United States. Drahos characterized these IP negotiations as an achievement of "cooperation and coordination between US business and the US state, which was aimed at preserving the central position of the US in the world economy" (13). India and Brazil registered their opposition to the GATT IP agenda, but TRIPS was eventually passed.

India's Patents Acts and a Burgeoning Pharmaceutical Industry

India did not appear to have any clear equivalent to intellectual property law prior to the colonial period. The early body of Sanskrit texts on jurisprudence known as the *dharmasastras* is often seen as a source of Indian precolonial legal principles. Though its principles come from what could be considered Hindu perspectives, the British used them during the colonial period as the native law of India. The *dharmasastras* address a variety of duties and principles, such as the nature and obligations of property, debt, contracts, and land tenure.[28] During the Mughal Empire, one of the most extensive political states of the Indian subcontinent, which lasted from the sixteenth to eighteenth centuries, laws based on Koranic principles were developed, and Mughal emperors employed jurists who would debate, interpret, and revise laws of the empire, which generally differed for Hindu and Muslim subjects. A concept akin to intellectual property, though, has not been observed in precolonial India.[29]

India developed its first copyright legislation in 1847, during the British colonial period, and the first patent law was implemented in 1856 in the parts of India that were under direct British control but not in the princely states that constituted much of the subcontinent. In the late nineteenth and early twentieth centuries, Ayurvedic, Siddha, and other indigenous medicines were widespread. Western biomedicine had been introduced by the British and was spread by other influences such as Christian missionaries and the United States–based Rockefeller Foundation, which funded projects to promote the use of biomedicine in India. The Indian biomedical pharmaceutical industry was small, producing only a fraction of the country's allopathic drug supply, most of which had to be imported. During World War II, a shortage in the drug supply from foreign companies led to a burgeoning Indian pharmaceutical industry. Cipla, one of India's first pharmaceutical companies—and one of the most nationalistic and defiant of the new patent regime—helped fill the WWII drug shortfall. Gandhi visited Cipla in 1939 and, according to the company, "inspired our founder to make essential medicines for the country, and strive for self-sufficiency."[30] See figure 1, showing Gandhi, the nationalist leader

Figure 1. Dr. Sushila Nayar, Mohandas "Mahatma" Gandhi, Dr. K. A. Hamied (founder of Cipla), and Sardar Patel, 1939. (Cipla 2015)

Sardar Patel, and the renowned public health advocate Dr. Sushila Nayar meeting with the Cipla founder Dr. K. A. Hamied.

Although not a champion of allopathic medicine, Gandhi was determined to see India become economically self-sufficient and free from its dependency on trade with Great Britain.

The ayurvedic drug industry emerged around the same time at the outset of the twentieth century, replacing a system where individual ayurvedic physicians sold medicines they made in their offices directly to patients. Early ayurvedic pharmaceutical companies, such as Arya Vaidya Sala and Dabur, also had the support of Indian nationalist leaders who wanted to revive an indigenous medical system that had been undermined by the British colonial rulers, who promoted their own Western medicine as superior to and more rational than the Indian systems. Interestingly, despite the alleged irrationality of Indian systems of medicine, the British and other Westerners have looked to these systems to discover new medications since the nineteenth century.[31]

After independence from British rule in 1947, the Indian government revised the colonial intellectual property laws to better fit the priorities of the new nation. In 1957, the government appointed Justice Rajagopal Ayyangar to lead a committee to assess the reigning patent law in the context of the country's poverty and mortality rate. In order to lower the price of pharmaceuticals and to end India's reliance on imported medicines, the committee recommended that *product* patents not be permitted for medicines or food on the grounds that such patent rights would interfere with citizens' right to life, which is guaranteed by the Indian Constitution.[32]

The committee was also quite prescient about the strategies of the pharmaceutical companies and international patent priorities. In discussing the reasons that foreign interests take patents in India and other countries, the committee reported: "These patents are therefore taken not in the interests of the economy of the country granting the patent or with a view to manufacture there but with the main object of protecting an export market from competition from rival manufacturers particularly those in other parts of the world."[33] Thus the committee recommended implementing patents only for the *process* of making food and medical products to encourage the growth of the local pharmaceutical industry and to lower costs through competition.

These recommendations resulted in the passage of the Patents Act of 1970, India's reigning patent law until the TRIPS-compliant Patents (Amendment) Act was passed in 2005, which this book refers to simply as the Patents Act of 2005 (though technically the new law is a modification of the 1970 Act). Under the 1970 law, one could patent only the process for making a drug but not the drug product itself. Multiple producers could make the same product if they could find different methods of doing so, a process popularly known as "reverse engineering." Reverse engineering involves examining a product to see how it is constructed in order to re-create it, and owing to a competitive business environment and the ability to draw from a workforce with training in science and engineering, Indian pharmaceutical companies became adept at finding ways to reassemble chemical compositions developed by other companies. For example, while fluoxetine was under patent in the United States under the brand name Prozac, a variety of Indian producers re-created this drug using their own processes and marketed it under their own brand names, such as Fluex, Barozac, and Depzac.

A key element of the Patents Act of 1970 was Section 5 of Chapter II, which specified:

5. Inventions where only methods or processes of manufacture patentable

(1) In the case of inventions
　　1. claiming substances intended for use, or capable of being used, as food or as medicine or drug . . .

no patent shall be granted in respect of claims for the substances them selves, but claims for the methods or processes of manufacture shall be patentable [sic]. (Government of India 1970, emphasis added).

The intellectual property specialists from the Indian pharmaceutical company Ranbaxy, Vijayaraghavan and Raghuvanshi, argue that this law accomplished the Ayyangar Committee's goals when they observe that "it is generally said, with justification, that the Patent Act of 1970 was the single most important factor that laid the foundation for the robust and thriving generic pharmaceutical industry that India has today" (2008:111). They add that the law:

resulted in the development of a highly competitive domestic pharmaceutical sector that was very fragmented, where the top player often had just about 5 per cent of market share. Being highly cost-competitive was an imperative for survival. This necessitated constant innovation and led to the honing of the now highly regarded chemistry skills of the workforce. Such honing happened without the need or availability of sophisticated research facilities; many such innovations happened on the shop-floor (112).

Contrary to the expectations of contemporary patent advocates, this law that was weak by WTO standards led to "constant innovation." Vijayaraghavan and Raghuvanshi add that today's stronger patent regime can help Indian pharmaceutical companies grow further (118). While India's patent law was often singled out for attention in media coverage of recent patent controversies, India was not alone in crafting a law with a special exception for pharmaceuticals: a 1998 study by WIPO found that forty-nine of the ninety-eight countries who were parties to the Paris Convention excluded pharmaceuticals from patent protection.[34]

In implementing a new international intellectual property regime, the TRIPS agreement mandates that all WTO member states enact *product* patent protections, guaranteeing exclusive market control to the patent holders. Thus the third page of the Patents Act of 2005 contains a brief statement that may turn out to have a major effect on public health in low- and middle-income countries around the world: "Section 5 of the principal Act shall be omitted."[35] These few words bring India's new Patents Act into conformity with TRIPS by eliminating the product patent exception for medicines and food, and they may, along with enduring conditions of poverty, keep important new medications out of the hands of numerous people with HIV/AIDS in India and Africa who have relied on India's cheap drug supply. Or, as we will see later, it may have a greater effect on access to medicine for poor people living in middle-income countries like Brazil and China. As the new patent regime emerges over time, it will become apparent which of these two scenarios is more likely to materialize.

Before 2005, Indian companies could reverse engineer and produce antiretroviral drugs that were under patent in other countries, since Indian law at the time allowed this. Thus Indian producers such as Cipla, Ranbaxy, Hetero, Aurobindo, and many others produced inexpensive versions of AIDS drugs, greatly bringing down the price of antiretroviral therapy. The Communist Party of India (Marxist) and other leftist allies with influence in the central government at the time—because they were needed by the mainstream Congress Party to help form a majority coalition—succeeded in implementing a grandfather clause in the 2005 Patents Act, which exempted most currently used antiretroviral drugs from the provisions of the new act. The leftist coalition also promoted Section 3d of the act, which prevents "evergreening" of patents and me-too drugs, a practice they saw in other countries where pharmaceutical companies extend protections for drugs whose patents are expiring by developing minor modifications on these medications and filing for a patent on the "new" product.[36] Genuinely novel medications, such as the ARV maraviroc, which is effective against resistant forms of HIV, have been patented under the new product patent legislation, but Section 3d has been used to block several patent applications.

Hundreds of drug companies set up shop in Hyderabad and in other metro cities, such as Bangalore, Delhi, and Mumbai, in the decades since India passed a Patents Act that was tailored to its national priorities. Cipla Pharmaceuticals has not only helped India become self-sufficient in supplying its own medicines, it has opened offices in Great Britain, the Netherlands, and Miami, Florida, joining the ranks of "multinational" pharmaceutical companies, and other Indian companies have followed suit. The Indian pharmaceutical sector has thus grown from a fledgling industry in the early twentieth century to a proliferation of companies that have mastered the ability to create copies of medications and deliver their products at a low price. In the wake of the new WTO patent rules that were imposed on India, these accomplishments and the benefits they brought for public health in India and elsewhere were not going to be easily conceded by legal and health activists and their allies in the Indian pharmaceutical sector.

2

THE NEW PATENT REGIME

The Activists and Their Allies

After India changed its patent laws in 2005, I sounded an alarm because I was concerned that the new laws could dry up the supply of inexpensive Indian pharmaceuticals that much of the world depends on.[1] Several activist groups had the same concern and rallied efforts to oppose these laws. Once the laws were implemented, they fought to ensure that public health interests were upheld in India and other countries under the current regime, often utilizing the flexibilities in India's Patents Act in their efforts.

An organization of Mumbai- and Delhi-based lawyers known as the Lawyers Collective undertakes public-interest litigation on behalf of marginalized groups to ensure access to HIV medications and engages in other projects on women's rights, drug policy, and LGBT discrimination. Founded in 1981 after the Indian courts began to allow third-party groups to move the court on issues of public concern, the Lawyers Collective has mounted what are known as "pre-grant oppositions" to drug patent applications at India's patent offices. The group has also promoted access to affordable medications in other ways, such as rallying opposition to an

India-EU Free Trade Agreement, which may further expand patent protections. Pre-grant oppositions can be submitted to the court by any public groups that wish to state their objection to the awarding of a patent before it is granted. A key figure in the Lawyers Collective, Anand Grover, served from 2008 to 2014 as the United Nations Special Rapporteur on the Right to Health, during which time he called attention to health inequalities and warned of the effect of the new patent regime on global health.

Patent oppositions have also been mounted by the Indian Network for People Living with HIV/AIDS (INP+), a group that was founded in the 1990s by twelve HIV-positive men and women and has since expanded and developed connections to international AIDS organizations. INP+ engages in advocacy, network building, and providing services for people living with HIV/AIDS, and it has been assisted in filing ARV patent oppositions in India by a US-based group of legal activists, the Initiative for Medicines, Access and Knowledge (I-MAK). Made up of a team of lawyers and scientists, I-MAK provides technical advice, prepares licenses, and intervenes in court cases to challenge inappropriate patents and ensure access to medications.

The well-known humanitarian aid organization Doctors Without Borders/Médecins Sans Frontières has also been involved on the international level, raising awareness about the dangers of the new patent regime and assisting in maintaining access to essential medicines through various efforts, including creating guides for governments and NGOs on the prices of ARVs from various sources and developing a patent opposition database that includes information on how to build legal challenges to patents.

Concerns about an increase in the price of drugs for treating HIV/AIDS are well-founded. Production by Indian companies under the previous patent law significantly brought down the prices of essential medications, including ARVs. It is difficult to assess, though, how much these prices have fallen, since much of the reporting on price reductions makes untenable comparisons, claiming, for example, that the price of ARV treatment has come down from the $15,000 per person per year that big pharma companies charge buyers in high-income countries to the $200 per person per year that Indian companies charge in low-income countries.[2] Such figures ignore the differential pricing system for different countries that big pharma and other foreign- and India-based pharmaceutical producers use in low-income countries. Indian company prices are generally around 20–25 percent less than the prices charged by big pharma—or more precisely the "originator" company that developed the drug and owns the patent—in those same countries, and sometimes they are higher. For example, GlaxoSmithKline sells the ARV abacavir in low-income countries for $636 per person per year, and India-based companies Aurobindo and Cipla sell the same drug for $429 and $456 respectively. In the case of ritonavir, Abbott Laboratories sells this drug for $83 per person per year in low-income countries, while Aurobindo and Cipla charge $336 and $313.[3] More importantly, it is competition from Indian companies that helped bring the prices originator companies charge in low-income countries down to these levels.

Comparisons that show dramatic decreases in prices brought by the Indian pharmaceutical sector also ignore the fact that the allegedly low cost "generic" prices are still too high for low-income countries. The involvement of Indian pharmaceutical companies did not so much make the drugs "affordable" as make them simply less expensive than before. Government programs, NGOs, and individual consumers in low-income countries cannot afford to provide ARVs to most people with HIV/AIDS at current prices.

The change from process patents to product patents, reflected in the change from India's 1970 Patents Act to the WTO-compliant 2005 Patents Act described in the previous chapter, means that companies can now hold exclusive rights to a drug product itself, not just to a method of making a drug. If, for example, Pfizer, Merck, or Gilead comes out with a new AIDS medication, Indian companies can no longer produce a copy through reverse engineering without permission from the originator. Rather, they would have to obtain a license from the patent holder and pay royalties to produce the medication. This, critics felt, would reduce competition and increase the price of medications, which would in turn lead to major public health crises in the countries that depend on lower price pharmaceuticals from India, such as AIDS treatment programs in sub-Saharan Africa.[4]

These effects would not be seen immediately, as the patent laws would affect only medications that come out after the new law came into force, though some applications have been in a patent "mailbox," which is basically a queue, for years, waiting for approval under the new law. As more and more people become infected with forms of HIV that are resistant to the first-line drugs, the price of treating AIDS may go up, since the first-line drugs were developed before India's new Patents Act, whereas the second-line drugs fall under the new regime.

Nine ARVs can be now be manufactured by generic producers through the United Nations' Medicines Patent Pool, which allows non–patent holders to make products under certain restrictions, and some ARV patents have been defeated in the India Patents Office, which may help keep the price of medications down for now. A key early example of pricing under the new patent regime makes it difficult to tell what will happen in the future. California-based Gilead Sciences has voluntarily licensed tenofovir, an important AIDS drug it developed, and several other products to Indian generic producers, and the price has come down dramatically because of the scale-up of production from the Indian companies. The defeat of the patent on tenofovir in India, which came in the midst of developing this program, may be a factor in the drug's accessibility. While the Gilead model of voluntary licensing has its limitations—as will be discussed in chapter 4—this drug is now available at a cost of $30 per person per year, a price that is relatively affordable, and this was achieved with all parties involved working within the new patent regime. This is an encouraging story that demonstrates the complexity and difficulty in predicting the effects of the new patent environment. Whether this scenario is replicable with other drugs has yet to be seen.

Efforts to oppose patents and otherwise make essential medicines affordable in the new patent regime were aided by certain flexibilities that existed in TRIPS, or that activists and government agents realized they could add to their TRIPS-compliant laws. The obscure-sounding and controversial "Section 3d" of India's 2005 Patents Act was key in this effort.

Section 3d, Me-Too Drugs, and Coalition Politics

After the implementation of TRIPS, the member nations of the World Trade Organization met in Doha, Qatar, in 2001 for further negotiations. Delegates concerned about the effects of TRIPS on drug access in low-income countries demanded that TRIPS should allow for public health priorities. This resulted in the adoption by the WTO of the Doha Declaration, which affirmed:

> We agree that the TRIPS Agreement does not and should not prevent Members from taking measures to protect public health. Accordingly, while reiterating our commitment to the TRIPS Agreement, we affirm that the

Agreement can and should be interpreted and implemented in a manner supportive of WTO Members' right to protect public health and, in particular, to promote access to medicines for all.

In this connection, we reaffirm the right of WTO Members to use, to the full, the provisions in the TRIPS Agreement, which provide flexibility for this purpose. (WTO 2001:1).

The various parties agreed that patents could be overridden—or in the words of patent law, "compulsory licenses" could be issued allowing a non–patent holding company to produce a medication owned by another corporation—in the case of a public health crisis. A follow-up declaration in 2003 stated that countries with little or no pharmaceutical manufacturing capacity could import pharmaceuticals through compulsory licenses obtained by manufacturers in other countries.[5] This became a crucial issue in the patent struggles in India because many countries in Africa that have been hard-hit by the AIDS crisis do not have their own production capacity and had been depending on exports of ARVs from India. At the same time, one of the main concerns of foreign-based multinational pharmaceutical companies regarding their patent interests in India has been the ability of Indian companies to export medicines to other countries.

Aware of flexibilities contained in TRIPS and bolstered by the mandate of the Doha Declaration, Indian lawmakers developed the now-controversial Section 3d of India's 2005 Patents Act, which attempts to prevent evergreening and me-too drugs, where small modifications are made to existing drugs and other strategies are used to obtain new patents. These include "metabolite switching," which involves patenting a drug and later patenting the metabolite the body makes from the drug as a new product when the expiration of a patent is approaching. For example, when the patent on loratadine (Claritin) was going to expire, Schering-Plough patented and put on the market desloratadine (Clarinex), which is the chemical created by the body when loratadine is ingested, initially at a lower price to encourage customers to switch to the drug with the new patent before older drug's patent expired. Other methods are also employed, such as changing the way a drug is absorbed by the body to create a new product.[6] Such products are marketed as new and improved, distracting consumers from the fact that an equally effective drug just became available as a generic because the patent has expired.

Section 3d has been important in defeating several patent applications on drugs that were awarded patents elsewhere, and its legality has been challenged by multinational pharmaceutical companies. The modification of the original Section 3d involved only a small change in wording, but the effects are significant. In the 1970 Patents Act, Section 3d read as follows:

> 3. What are not inventions
> The following are not inventions within the meaning of this Act . . .
> d. the mere discovery of any new property or new use for a known substance or of the mere use of a known process, machine or apparatus unless such known process results in a new product or employs at least one new reactant (Government of India 1970)

This was changed in the 2005 Patents (Amendment) Act to the following:

> In section 3 of the principal Act, for clause *(d)*, the following shall be substituted, namely:—
> *"(d)* the mere discovery of a new form of a known substance which does not result in the enhancement of the known efficacy of that substance or the mere discovery of any new property or new use for a known substance or of the mere use of a known process, machine or apparatus unless such known process results in a new product or employs at least one new reactant.
> *Explanation.*—For the purposes of this clause, salts, esters, ethers, polymorphs, metabolites, pure form, particle size, isomers, mixtures of isomers, complexes, combinations and other derivatives of known substance shall be considered to be the same substance, unless they differ significantly in properties with regard to efficacy." (Government of India 2005).

They key difference is the addition of the clause requiring "enhancement of the known efficacy" for any product that is a new form of an existing medicine or chemical entity.

The requirement to demonstrate increased efficacy to get approval for a slight modification of an existing drug is not present in US patent law. This provision has limited the approval of me-too drugs, representing an effort that should earn praise by critics of the pharmaceutical industry. In her exposé of the pharmaceutical business, the former editor of the *New England Journal of Medicine* Marcia Angell (2004) explains that there is little true innovation in commercial pharmaceuticals, since pharmaceutical companies mostly produce me-too drugs. Sometimes it is only the dosage that is changed. And of the few true innovations that result in New Molecular Entities (NME), most are derived from government or university research that is then licensed to drug companies. For example, from 1998 to 2002, only 14 percent of new drugs approved by the United States Food and Drug Administration (FDA) were "truly innovative," in Angell's view, while 86 percent were for already existing drugs. Seventy-seven percent of the newly approved drugs did not show any more efficacy than current standards of treatment. A major problem, Angell argues, is that the FDA only requires drugs to be *effective* against a placebo, not *more effective* than the existing standard of care. Thus me-too drugs can be patented and brought to market if they are merely as good as or even less effective than the standard treatment, as long as they beat the placebo. This was the case with GERD—an advanced kind of "heartburn"—treatment Nexium (esomeprazole), which Angell says is not as effective as the earlier Prilosec (omeprazole), and the several statins on the market that are slight modifications of Merck's original statin, Mevacor (lovastatin), which Angell says was truly innovative. Companies claim, however, that me-too products have advantages, and they are sometimes tested against the standard of care but not for the same uses.[7] This situation, Angell insists, highlights the poor enforcement of the requirement of novelty and non-obviousness in patent law in the United States.

If a provision like Section 3d were introduced into US patent law, it would eliminate the majority of pharmaceutical patents recently awarded and create more incentive for "true" innovations through finding NMEs or more effective modifications of existing drugs.

The story of the development of Section 3d is a complex one involving political maneuvering and eleventh-hour negotiations. The Communist Party of India (Marxist) [CPI (M)] and other left allies joined a coalition government in which the Congress Party, the mainstream party made famous by Jawaharlal Nehru and Indira Gandhi, was the largest constituent. While the communist parties of India are not in the political mainstream, they have millions of followers, and sometimes the Congress Party needs their support to form a government and get legislation passed. The leftists thought the language originally in the new Section 3d was overly friendly to multinational drug companies and that the government should raise the bar of patentability by including language that requires a new drug to show increased efficacy or by allowing patents only for new chemical entities. Mainstream members of the coalition government, however, thought this might deviate too much from the requirements of TRIPS, but since they needed the support of their leftist allies to get the bill through parliament, they allowed the bill to go forward with the language that required increased efficacy. As the *Times of India* explained, "Thus, the legislative breakthrough happened as a concession that a coalition government was forced to make. The history of Section 3(d) shows that if the ruling party had enough strength to push the Bill through Parliament, the government would have stuck to the MNC [Multi-National Corporation]-friendly scheme of the ordinance."[8] Thus one of the reasons the new patent regime has not had as negative an impact on global drug prices as anticipated is that leftist parties dug in their heels to preserve this change in legislation.

Section 3d is not the only legislative tool for limiting the applicability of patents in India. Certain other flexibilities exist in patent law based on earlier international treaties, such as the Paris Convention of 1883, which allows for the overriding of patents and awarding of compulsory licenses if a patent is not worked in a particular locality. This continues to apply in the contemporary patent environment. For example, in 2013 Indian producer Natco was able to obtain a compulsory license to manufacture and sell Bayer's anticancer drug Nexavar (sorafenib), since the courts decided Bayer was not working the drug—that is, it was not sufficiently making it available in India.[9]

The Activists and Their Oppositions

The Lawyers Collective has filed several oppositions to HIV drug patents, including an attempt by Novartis to patent a second-line protease inhibitor, atazanavir, in India. The opposition to Novartis's application claims that the compound is among those identified in an earlier patent and that the use of this compound as a protease inhibitor is obvious to anyone experienced in drug development. In addition, the Lawyers Collective argues that the knowledge that the protease enzyme can be used as a therapeutic agent in treating HIV, which is the basis of the effectiveness of this treatment, was discovered through research funded by the US government's National Institute of Allergy and Infectious Diseases (Lawyers Collective

2006: 5, citing the 1996 NIAID AIDS Agenda). Thus, according to the Lawyers Collective, Novartis cannot claim that the treatment using this compound is sufficiently based on the company's own innovative efforts, and the invention is not sufficiently novel to warrant a patent. The opposition also urged the court to take into account the negative effect on public health due to the high cost of this medication that would result if the patent were awarded.

In its arguments to the Chennai Patent Controller in charge of this case, the Lawyers Collective further advised that while India met its WTO obligations by passing the Patents Act of 2005, "India retains full sovereignty in determining the standards that must be met with respect to patentability" (4), urging that the patent be denied under Section 3d, which prohibits patents on "a new form of a known substance" (15). In this case, the Lawyers Collective works within the new patent regime to oppose patents by arguing that the innovation does not meet the standards of Section 3d and by defending India's sovereignty to determine such standards. Novartis eventually withdrew its application on atazanavir in the face of opposition to this patent.

Meanwhile, the Lawyers Collective and other groups have successfully opposed other patent applications on similar grounds. For example, the Initiative for Medicines, Access and Knowledge (I-MAK) assisted the nonprofit Indian Network of People Living with HIV/AIDS (INP+) and the Delhi Network of Positive People (DNP+) in opposing Gilead Science's application for a patent on tenofovir, which is both a second-line drug and a recommended less toxic first-line drug, on the same grounds. The opposition from INP+ and DNP+ states:

> Section 3 (d) sets out that a "*mere discovery of a **new form of a known substance** which does not result in the enhancement of the known efficacy of that substance*" does not amount to an invention and is not patentable under the Act. The 'Explanation' for s3(d) provides further clarification in that "*salts, **esters**, ethers, polymorphs . . . combinations and other derivatives **of known substance shall be considered to be the same substance**, unless they differ significantly in properties with regard to efficacy.*"
>
> 21. Based on a plain reading of s3(d), it is quite clear under that [sic] any new discovery of an ester for a known compound is not patentable as an invention. (I-MAK 2014a, emphasis in original)

Note how the opposition makes use of the language inserted at the behest of the left allies in the passage of the new Patents Act. The India-based pharmaceutical company Cipla also filed an opposition to tenofovir claiming the product lacked an inventive step and invoking Section 3d. This drug is already patented in the United States, but its application for an Indian patent was denied.

The Lawyers Collective in the atazanavir patent opposition was able to tap into the fact that the innovations claimed by the pharmaceutical companies had been discovered by government-funded research. Often drug development by pharmaceutical companies depends on knowledge developed from publicly funded research carried out by government agencies and universities. This legal strategy involves what the critiques of the myth of autonomous invention, mentioned in the previous chapter, point out: that invention is normally incremental and dependent on prior knowledge. What pharmaceutical companies often do is not so much invent new drugs but buy IP rights from innovators—such as university researchers and small companies—and scale up their discoveries into a marketable product. This includes investing money in clinical trials and the mass production of the product, which many innovators cannot do on their own. Some have critiqued pharmaceutical company claims that they need to recover profits from patents to invest in the discovery of new drugs, arguing that most truly innovative drugs come from publicly funded research.[10] Angell gives the examples of paclitaxel (Taxol), the anticancer drug that was developed by National Cancer Institute research at a cost of $183 million to US taxpayers and then licensed to Bristol-Myers Squibb, and Novartis's leukemia treatment imatinib mesylate (marketed as Glivec and Gleevec), which were based on the discoveries of university researchers in, respectively, Pennsylvania and Oregon.[11] In both cases, the company made significant investments in supplying and testing the drug, but the innovative steps came from public research. In the John Moore cell line case in the previous chapter, we also saw an instance of corporate licensing of a university innovation. UCLA doctors and the Regents of the University of California made an agreement with Sandoz and Genetics to market products based on cells from the body of UCLA patient John Moore. It seems that while corporations do not develop much in terms of innovation, they are trying to recover money for scaling up production and paying for clinical trials. Thus what patent law often protects is the transferability of intellectual properties rights, or the ability to buy someone's rights over their innovations and make that innovation into a marketable product. It does require a substantial investment of capital to bring a new drug to market. An often-cited study by a research group at Tufts University that has received funding from the pharmaceutical industry puts the price of research and development for a new drug (a real innovation in Angell's and the new Indian Patents Act's definition—a new chemical entity, not a me-too drug) at $802 million in 2000 (projected, in the 2003 article, to be $2.16 billion in 2012).[12] Other analysts, however, have critiqued assumptions used in the development of this figure and calculated the cost to be about one-tenth this amount.[13]

After opposition from the Lawyers Collective, INP+, I-MAK, and Indian pharmaceutical companies, some patents were defeated. In other cases, companies withdrew their applications. Novartis withdrew its application for atazanavir in 2007 in the face of opposition under Section 3d, and GlaxoSmithKline backed off its claim for the second-line ARV abacavir later in the same year after it was opposed by INP+ with the help of I-MAK and Doctors Without Borders. The application appears to have been withdrawn out of concern that it was a slight modification of an existing medication and would not pass the standard of Section 3d.[14] Meanwhile, patents have been awarded for compounds whose novelty does meet the standards of Section 3d, such as the second-line AIDS medication maraviroc, owned by Pfizer, and it is such patents that leave cause for concern about the future prices of second-line ARVs. Pfizer has announced in the UN Medicines Patent Pool its intention to license this product, allowing other manufacturers to produce maraviroc for low-income countries, but this drug has not been recommended by the WHO and no licenses have been issued so far.[15]

The standards for the approval of patents under India's new law is at the heart of a controversial case that went to India's Supreme Court. An Indian patent office denied Novartis's application for its anticancer drug imatinib mesylate (Glivec, Gleevec in India), which provides effective treatment for some forms of leukemia, since it found that the drug represents an incremental step, not a novel innovation. Indian pharmaceutical companies had been producing their own versions of Gleevec, selling the drug in India for $2,500 per person per year, while the cost of this treatment can be as much as $70,000 elsewhere.[16] Novartis sued the Indian government, claiming the 2005 Patents Act was overly restrictive and Section 3d contains an overly narrow view of innovation for modifications of existing chemical entities. On April 1, 2013, the Indian Supreme Court ruled against Novartis in this case, affirming that Gleevec "did not represent a true invention" and supporting Section 3d.[17] In commenting on this ruling, Anand Grover, a member of the Lawyers Collective who represented the Cancer Patients Aid Association in India in the Novartis case and who was at the time Special Rapporteur to the UN on the right to health, contrasted the effect of India's law to the patent system in the United States, where incremental changes are more easily patented: "'What is happening in the United States is that a lot of money is being wasted on new forms of old drugs.' . . . Because of Monday's ruling, 'that will not happen in India'" (Harris and Thomas 2013).

Large pharmaceutical companies claim that such a law restricts their ability to recover their research and development investments, which is necessary to invest in developing new medications. This is at least their rhetoric since, as mentioned earlier, most new drug products do not come from companies' own R&D, and the large financial outlays they do engage in are for clinical trials, compliance, marketing, legal fees, and other costs. Big pharma does have some sympathizers in India who feel that Section 3d of the Patent Law is an obstacle to better United States–India business ties and to Indian pharmaceutical companies' own transition to becoming innovators and not just generic producers. Because of Section 3d, the United States placed India on a watch list of countries considered to have inadequate intellectual property enforcement. The business journalist Arvind Subramanian suggests removing Section 3d of the Patent Law to boost India's stature in the eyes of the US trade office, and he proposes that in exchange the United States return to the WTO, a multilateral forum, to settle trade disputes.[18] In the last few years, the United States has been resorting to bilateral negotiations with individual nations, feeling that the WTO has too often ruled against US interests. The European Union has done so as well, pursuing an India–European Union Free Trade Agreement, which has stalled partly because of proposed patent extensions that favor EU-based pharmaceutical companies and go beyond the requirements of TRIPS.[19]

Scholars and activists have regularly depicted the WTO as the central, hegemonic power that dominates the global economy on behalf of powerful corporate and national interests that shape its agenda. While there is a lot of truth to this, efforts by the United States and European Union to avoid the WTO forum in trade negotiations and the effective use of Section 3d to oppose patents show that policies of the WTO are not seamless and all-powerful. The situation is somewhat ironic and shows that the deployment of global hegemony is not as straightforward as the shapers of the WTO agenda anticipated. Big pharma representatives probably did not foresee India introducing a provision like Section 3d when they framed the TRIPS agreement, which aimed to impose a pro-corporate, pro-IP agenda around the globe. They probably also did not imagine that they would have to go to court in India to change India's TRIPS-compliant patent law—or that they would fail in this effort.

Taking a position somewhere between the anti-patent activists and the business journalist Subramanian, two IP experts from an Indian pharmaceutical company, Vijayaraghavan and Raghuvanshi (2008), claim the new patent law will spur innovation in the Indian pharmaceutical sector, but they also strongly defend Section 3d as protecting against "frivolous inventions" whose "aim is not to protect a product but prevent anyone else from coming up with an alternative."[20] Section 3d is important and should be maintained because a rigorous patent standard returns patent practices to the fairer ideals of a temporary and balanced contract between innovators and society as described by James Boyle (2008), the legal scholar discussed at the outset of the last chapter, and advocated by others such as the Initiative for Medicines, Access and Knowledge (I-MAK).

Other actors involved in negotiating the new patent terrain include a variety of NGOs such as I-MAK, which disseminates information about patent cases around the world and, like the Lawyers Collective, intervenes in Indian cases to oppose what it feels are unwarranted claims, including several applications for patents on drugs that treat HIV/AIDS. I-MAK's general position on patents is similar to the position of this book and Boyle's perspective, finding merit in some of the basic premises of IP law but claiming that IP protections have been overextended. I-MAK explains that "the patent system was designed to balance innovation in medicines and the dissemination of new treatments to society" but feels that the system has gotten to the point where it "upholds private interests over the public good" (I-MAK 2014b). The staff at I-MAK worked successfully to oppose Abbott Laboratories' patent application for lopinavir/ritonavir, which the Clinton Foundation has been involved in procuring at lower prices. They were joined in the opposition by three Indian pharmaceutical producers, Cipla, Okasa, and Matrix.

The Indian Network for People Living with HIV/AIDS (INP+) is an organization that employs a variety of interventions to improve the quality of life of people living with this diagnosis in India. These have included joining in some of the legal oppositions to patents on ARVs mentioned earlier. Meanwhile, claiming that "the existing system of health care is not geared towards the needs of the majority of the people, the poor and the rural segments of our society," an organization of India-based doctors, researchers, and activists known as the Medico Friend Circle engages in research and advocacy on the connection between health problems and political and economic factors, and it has been involved in legal action related to drug pricing and patent policies.[21]

Other actors from outside India are also involved in fighting what they see as unwarranted patents in India and elsewhere. Doctors Without Borders/Médecins Sans Frontières established a website (patentoppositions. org) to facilitate patent oppositions by patient and civil society groups around the world, such as pre-grant opposition cases in India, and it regularly offers critiques of patent policies through mainstream media outlets. Gilead's application for a patent on tenofovir in India was opposed in court by INP+ and the Delhi Network of Positive People (DNP+). Later, the Brazilian Interdisciplinary AIDS Association (ABIA) joined another Indian NGO, SAHARA, in filing an opposition to the tenofovir application:

> because a patent in India would not only restrict generic competition in India, but would also directly impact Brazil being able to import and access affordable generic versions of the drug.
>
> The Brazilian activists were aware that, should the patent be rejected, local production would take some time to start. During this delay, if no other source were available, Brazil would still have to pay monopoly prices for a short time. (Patent Opposition Database 2014)

The Brazilian activists had met members of India's Lawyers Collective at the International AIDS Conference in Toronto in 2006, and the two groups shared their experiences with opposing patents. ABIA adopted some of the claims the Lawyers Collective had raised in their patent oppositions in India, and eventually the Indian tenofovir application was defeated, since, in the words of the patent office, it "does not constitute an invention as it lacks an inventive step" and it "does not result in the enhancement of the known efficacy of that substance," citing, respectively, section 2(1)j of the 1970 Patents Act and section 3d of the 2005 Patents (Amendment) Act.[22]

On visits to India in 2004 and 2005, I met with organizations and activists working on HIV/AIDS and learned about the problems that India, and in particular the state of Kerala, was confronting in trying to expand access to treatments for this disease. Drug prices and the emerging patent regime were very much on the mind of individuals working in these areas, such as staff members I met from the state-run Kerala AIDS Control Society and private NGOs. Tapping into my knowledge of drug access and drug prices from earlier fieldwork on mental health in Kerala, I published an analysis of the potentially alarming public health effects of India's 2005 Patents Act.[23] India and other "less developed" or poor countries have had trouble scaling up their AIDS treatment programs in part because of drug costs, and increases in prices for essential medicines could only make matters worse. In addition, programs that have been intervening in the international AIDS crisis, such as Doctors Without Borders, the US President's Emergency Plan for AIDS Relief (PEPFAR), and the Clinton Foundation, had been obtaining medications from Indian sources and would be negatively impacted by such increases.[24]

Certainly, factors other than the new patent regime are involved, and it is important that we not leave the context of poverty out of the picture. Blaming poverty is a double-edged sword, however, in debates about patent policies. Big pharma points to poverty as the culprit to explain problems of access to essential medicines. Pharmaceutical company representatives I spoke to also pointed out that many countries that complain about the price of drugs and problems of access to essential medicines choose to spend huge sums of money on military technology. Such accusations have the effect of obscuring the contribution of patent laws to these problems. The context of poverty, however, and the priorities of government spending in low-income countries cannot be ignored. As mentioned earlier, AIDS services in low-income countries are unable to obtain sufficient quantities of ARVs at current and pre-TRIPS "low" prices offered by India-based pharmaceutical companies. We need to take into account poverty, government spending priorities, and patent policies as we assess how best to promote access to essential medicines.

ARVs and Affordability

In an effort to increase access to second-line AIDS drugs under the new patent regime, the Clinton Foundation negotiated price reductions for some ARVs: for example, bringing down the cost of lopinavir/ritonavir, a key second-line treatment, from $1,000 to $695 per person per year for lower- and lower-middle-income countries, including India and China.[25] This is an important achievement, although, as will be discussed later, this price is more than the average annual per capita income in India. The Clinton Foundation is procuring lopinavir/ritonavir from Indian manufacturers Cipla and Matrix, which have been able to produce this drug since Abbott Laboratories was denied an Indian patent for the product in 2010.[26]

People in low-income settings cannot afford the price of patent-protected ARVs, and often generic ARVs are out of reach as well. Although multinational pharmaceutical companies offer reduced prices to developing countries, these prices are usually significantly higher than the reductions negotiated by the Clinton Foundation and the prices Indian generic manufacturers offer, and they are far out of the range of affordability for people living with HIV/AIDS in poor countries. Multinational pharmaceutical companies are not going to sell these drugs to 90 percent of people with HIV/AIDS in low-income countries regardless of patent enforcement. In India, the cost of antiretroviral therapy for HIV/AIDS using grandfathered drugs that are exempt from the patent regime has dropped from $795 to $23 per person per month.[27] This was a dramatic decline, but it is rarely acknowledged that even this "low" price of $23 per month is close to the total average monthly per capita income in India.[28] Most people in India who take ARVs get them free from government programs, and how many people the government programs can serve is dependent on the price of medications. Likewise, the price charged by Indian companies for the generic version of Novartis's anticancer drug Gleevec is also still out of range for almost everyone in India (Ecks 2008), so generally people do not have access to this drug unless they get it through a government or

NGO program or are among the thirty thousand in low-income countries who get this medication free from Novartis.

Multinational pharmaceutical companies are concerned about their public image in relation to these issues. Pfizer, Merck, and other companies prominently display their global access programs on their websites. Novartis devoted a substantial portion of its website to defending its position in its Gleevec/Section 3d lawsuit in India while also spending money on television ads in the United States to celebrate its programs to subsidize American consumers who are unable to pay for their prescriptions.[29] Medical anthropologist Stefan Ecks has tracked pharmaceutical company efforts to develop a positive image among the communities and customers they interact with.[30] This undertaking is known as "corporate citizenship," and it includes drug access and health programs aimed at underserved populations. While corporate drug donation programs and other corporate citizenship efforts do benefit patients, they also distract from profits made elsewhere, according to Ecks. In the case of Novartis's experiences in India—in its Supreme Court case and its Gleevec donation program—it was not Novartis's goal to make money off Indian consumers but to maintain their high prices in developing country markets by reducing the supply of inexpensive drugs made in India that may leak into markets in Europe and North America. They also aimed to reduce another kind of leakage that Ecks calls "information spillover," which refers to the awareness of the existence of lower-price drugs in these markets and how this may affect the willingness of people in high-income countries to continue paying high prices.[31] From speaking to pharmaceutical company representatives in the United States and India, as we will see in chapter 4, I too saw that the priority for multinational pharmaceutical companies was not so much to charge high prices in poor countries but to keep low-priced medications out of their more lucrative markets in middle-income and wealthy countries.

A Double Standard in the Concerns of Pharmaceutical Companies

A case of hypocrisy was overlooked in the media coverage of Novartis's challenge to Section 3d of India's Patents Act, and it is worthy of note since it encapsulates what some see as a key injustice of the new patent regime. At the time that Novartis led the legal challenge to make India's new patent law more amenable to what they saw as their intellectual property, this company was producing several products containing reserpine, a medication based on knowledge from ayurvedic medicine, India's largest indigenous medical system. The development of reserpine stemmed from ayurvedic knowledge about the antihypertensive and antipsychotic characteristics of the plant *Rauwolfia serpentina*, which ayurvedic doctors use in treating mental disorders. Ciba Pharmaceuticals originally patented the drug in the 1950s after isolating the active ingredient, reserpine, from *Rauwolfia serpentina*, and Ciba was later acquired by Novartis. The patent on reserpine has expired, and Novartis and several other companies continue to use this substance in a variety of products. However, no Indian entities ever received compensation for the insights that were the basis of this "invention." Novartis seems to hold a double standard about whose innovations are worthy of legal protection and whose should be available for free sharing and replication. The same could be said about Bristol-Myers Squibb, a subsidiary of which created early anesthetics based on indigenous South American people's knowledge of curare, and which, like all big pharma companies, actively defends what it considers its innovations in courts around the world.

Patent struggles in India thus take on an extra layer of complexity and intrigue because India is home to several indigenous medical systems whose products might potentially be patentable and which have already been an inspiration for new medical therapies and innovations in the West. The physician and anthropologist W. H. R. Rivers in 1924 presented a brief survey of what was known of the world's medical systems at the time. In discussing the native healing practices of many places, such as Australia, Africa, and the Americas, he is somewhat condescending, assuming that his own European system of medicine is far more advanced. In discussing India, however, his tone changes, and he says, "We find in India an extensive pharmacopoeia and a surgery from which that of Europe has taken more than one lesson."[32] He then explains that Europeans adopted the practice of rhinoplasty and of conducting surgery under hypnosis from India. Since then, other medical practices from South Asia have been adopted and also patented in Europe and the United States.

In my early investigations into the emerging patent regime in the late 1990s and early 2000s, there was concern about these forthcoming changes from interests other than AIDS activists and legal NGOs. The United States had granted a patent for the wound-healing properties of turmeric, and the European Union approved a patent for fungicidal uses of products from the neem tree, both "innovations" having their basis in knowledge of plant uses in India. Dismayed by these decisions, practitioners of India's indigenous ayurvedic medical system began to worry about the effect the new patent regime would have on their knowledge and practices. Under TRIPS, they wondered, could foreign entities patent products based on ayurvedic knowledge? If so, could such patents prevent ayurvedic doctors from using these treatments themselves? And did ayurvedic practitioners therefore need to compile information on the ayurvedic pharmacopoeia to defend against cases such as the patents on turmeric and neem?

3

Ayurvedic Dilemmas

Innovation, Ownership, and Resistance

In the mid-1990s, when India's new patent laws were on the distant horizon, I was conducting fieldwork on ayurvedic treatments for mental illness in Kerala. I had learned about inpatient procedures that featured spa-like treatments, such as the application of what I call medicated "mudpacks" to the heads of patients. Ayurvedic doctors who specialize in mental health had introduced me to theories of personality formation, their methods of talk therapy, and their pharmacopoeia, which involved distilling and processing medicinal plants into medications. They referred to medicinal plants by Sanskrit names, such as *shankhapushpi* and *serpagandhi,* and they explained the properties of these plants using ayurvedic terms for the functioning of the body and the effects of plant substances. I was familiar with many of the ayurvedic categories and terminologies, and I wondered if ayurvedic medicines and their effects could be explained in terms of Western, biomedical concepts of chemistry and biology, so I decided to visit the Tropical Botanical Garden and Research Institute, an Indian government research center in the lush foothills of the western

Ghat mountains in southern Kerala, an area that is home to an abundance of medicinal plants known to local indigenous people and to practitioners of Ayurveda.

The botanical garden is open to visitors and features a collection of plants used in Indian systems of medicine. To get there, I took the bus from Trivandrum, the muggy tropical city on the coast where I was living, to the cooler hill town of Palode, only an hour and a half away. After getting off the bus, as I was enjoying the cooler, drier air, I noticed a group of pepper plants that are native to this part of India growing along the side of the road. I pulled off some of the small green kernels that I knew would turn into black peppercorns once they were laid out in the sun to dry. I had seen families doing this with the pepper growing in their own backyards in Trivandrum, and I reflected on how this substance is so familiar in kitchens and on dinner tables in the West, yet many people who use black pepper in North America or Europe do not know where it comes from or what it looks like in its natural state. These ruminations prefigured what I would later learn about the exchange of plants and botanical knowledge between India and the West and the recent concerns that multinational companies will come "bioprospecting" for plant knowledge in India in pursuit of new commercial products. Even the Linnaean system of classification used in the West, and in the international scientific community, that employs Latin names to scientifically classify plants—such as *Piper nigrum* for black pepper—I later learned was based in part on the native system of plant classification in this part of South India.

I entered the botanical garden, took a quick walk through the collection, and headed for the main office in search of a researcher I had been referred to who had expertise on ayurvedic plants. Being naive at the time about the politics of bioprospecting and patent regimes, I asked my contact whether he could explain some of the characteristics and uses of plants in their collection. He replied, somewhat apologetically, that he was not at liberty to divulge this information because the government was still in the process of establishing policies under the 1993 Convention on Biological Diversity (CBD) to protect Indian knowledge systems from misappropriation. The CBD's goal was to preserve biological diversity while also ensuring benefit sharing for local communities for products derived from their biological resources. The WTO's TRIPS agreement had also recently been enacted. As a "less developed" country, India had until 2005 to conform to TRIPS, but the looming changes to intellectual property laws were already on the minds of many and the cordoning off of Indian medical knowledge was already under way.

The researcher I spoke to sounded apologetic when he refused to provide more information, because, I believe, the act of withholding knowledge comes unnaturally or is at odds with the ideals of scientific and intellectual exchange we are taught to believe in—perhaps because these ideals were developed under an earlier, looser patent regime. The Indian government did eventually develop protections to safeguard indigenous knowledge of biology and nature through a variety of measures such as the Traditional Knowledge Digital Library (TKDL), a database that was compiled to protect against unwarranted patent claims on insights that come from Ayurveda, yoga, or other practices and knowledge systems India now considers to be national property.

When I returned to India in 2004, the central government had passed the Biological Diversity Act of 2002, which set up state entities to approve commercial and research activity by "non-Indians and bodies with foreign equity" and to ensure the procurement of patent rights for products developed using India's bioresources.[1] India's TRIPS-compliant Patents Act was also soon to be enacted, and concern about the misappropriation of India's knowledge and resources was running high. Those concerned about "defending" Ayurveda were hoping that the benefit-sharing protections ensured by the Biological Diversity Act and the CBD could protect against threats from the TRIPS regime. Enclosure was increasing. Lines were being drawn around what knowledge could be shared and what was restricted.

It was unclear, however, what effect, if any, TRIPS would have on the practice of Ayurveda. While some ayurvedic *vaiyans* were up in arms about the possible exploitation of their knowledge and practices, others were unfazed by the coming changes, believing they would affect only the world of biomedical practitioners and producers. The intellectual property law expert Professor N. S. Gopalakrishnan of the University of Cochin, with whom I discussed the emerging patent environment, even anticipated that the new regime would be a boon to Ayurveda. He predicted that the patent laws would raise the price of biomedical drugs, which seemed likely if they reduced generic production in the Indian pharmaceutical sector. So surely, he told me, more people would then pursue ayurvedic therapy.

Following extensive discussions with ayurvedic activists and legal experts and after perusing the law itself, it was unclear to me whether the new law changed anything in terms of ayurvedic practice and the threat of biopiracy. Before TRIPS and the 2005 Patents Act, bioprospectors from multinational pharmaceutical companies could develop and patent a product based on ayurvedic knowledge, and after TRIPS they can still do this. Before and after the new patent regime, patents could also occasionally be defeated with proof of prior knowledge of the invention. The primary effect of the patent regime for India seemed that it would restrict the use of biomedical knowledge by the Indian pharmaceutical sector, since Indian companies could no longer reverse engineer patented drug products, while providing no additional protections for local knowledge systems such as Ayurveda. Put another way, in the past, Indian and Western producers could steal from each other—or share, depending on one's perspective—and now the stealing or sharing was becoming one-way.

If a multinational pharmaceutical company patents a therapy based on ayurvedic knowledge, this should not affect the ayurvedic use of the same insight from which the patented product is derived. Patents only protect the use of active chemical ingredients, which is the focus of biomedical pharmaceutical science, and not plant materials, which is the basis of ayurvedic pharmaceutical science. Ayurvedic producers cook, refine, and process natural plant materials in practitioners' offices or in factories, but they do not isolate active ingredients that may be present in the plants they use. In any case, patents based on ayurvedic or other "Indian" knowledge could be challenged in court, as were the US patent on wound-healing uses of turmeric granted to scientists at the University of Mississippi and a European patent awarded to the W. R. Grace company for fungicidal products derived from the neem tree.[2] Regarding the neem case, the high-profile scientist and activist Vandana Shiva explained, "It was pure and simple piracy. The oil from neem has been used traditionally by farmers to prevent fungus. It was neither a novel idea nor was it invented."[3] The opposition to the turmeric patent was also successful, as the "innovation" was based on prior knowledge from India about the uses of turmeric.[4] The yellow rhizomes of the turmeric plants are used in rituals, cooking, and both ayurvedic and home remedies. In addition to the antifungal uses in agriculture, the bark, leaves, and seeds of the neem tree are used in ayurvedic medicine to treat skin diseases and rheumatism.[5] While these two cases give cause for optimism in terms of challenging misappropriation, activists in India point out that the country has limited resources for fighting such legal battles in patent offices around the world.

In addition to the issue of injustice and misappropriation from "outside forces," such as US companies or the scientists at the University of Mississippi, who were of Indian origin and were basically patenting their home remedies in the turmeric case, some were also concerned that the new intellectual property environment could change the practice of Ayurveda. Ayurvedic producers could try to obtain patents on ayurvedic treatments, possibly leading Ayurveda to more closely resemble biomedicine in its epistemology and practice. The only thing that was clear from all of this was that the potential effects of the new patent law were unclear: there was no consensus in the ayurvedic community about whether and what kind of threat was posed by this new regime.

All of this raises problems of agency and resistance in this environment. The coming together of intellectual property law, biomedical science, and ayurvedic science, all under the umbrella of a global treaty, creates an environment where the threat from powerful actors—national, international, and corporate interests—is difficult to decipher and presents a challenge for determining what should be done to resist it or even whether resistance is appropriate. Aside from the threat of possible misappropriation and injustice, for those who want to embrace the new patent regime—by claiming their ayurvedic formulations as proprietary—how Ayurveda fits this style of ownership and invention is also ambiguous. Some clarity may be found as practices of pharmaceutical production unfold in the new environment. That is, as ayurvedic doctors and manufacturers produce new products and realign their practices, they will set precedents and thereby establish the parameters for property claims in Ayurveda. Others will, at the same time, challenge those new practices and claims as inauthentic and unfaithful to ayurvedic principles.

Sharing and Stealing between India and the West: The Story of *Hortus Malabaricus* and Reserpine

The history of sharing and stealing knowledge about biology and medicine between India and the West—that is, Europe and later the United States—dates back at least to the compilation of the botanical text *Hortus Indicus Malabaricus* in the seventeenth century. This twelve-volume work was compiled by Hendrik Adriaan van Rheede, an official of the Dutch East India Company who was stationed in Cochin, South India. The text describes and classifies plants from the Malabar region—now part of Kerala—based on ayurvedic knowledge and was compiled with the help of indigenous informants, primarily from the Ezhava caste, which is in the lower ranks of the social hierarchy in this part of India. This compendium was brought back to Europe, where, in the eighteenth century, it informed the binomial system of taxonomy that is attributed to Swedish botanist Carolus Linnaeus and that scientists around the world continue to use to classify plant and animal species. Linnaeus's work in turn influenced other European naturalists, including Charles Darwin. The historian Richard Grove (1996) observed that the *Hortus Malabaricus* and the Portuguese physician da Orta's compendium of Indian medical knowledge, *Colloquios dos simples e drogas e cousas medicinaes da India*

> tended to privilege strongly Ayurvedic and Ezhava medical and botanical (and zoological) knowledge, and to lead to effective discrimination against older Arabic, Brahminical and European Classical texts and systems of cognition in natural history. An inspection of the mode of construction of the *Coloquios* and, even more, of the *Hortus Malabaricus*, reveals that they are profoundly indigenous texts. Far from being inherently European works they are actually compilations of Middle Eastern and South Asian ethnobotany, organized on essentially non-European precepts (126).

Reddy (2006) adds that "Ezhava botanical classifications and medicinal garden schemes were recreated intact in [the botanical gardens of] Leiden. Indeed, Linnaeus is said to have directly incorporated both the order and the functional taxonomy originally provided by the Ezhavas" (169). Thus the development of biological science in Europe was shaped by not just "Indian"—that is, the usual associations with Brahamanical North India—but lower-caste Ezhava understandings of nature from the Malabar Coast. When, in 2003, University of Kerala scholars completed a translation of the *Hortus Malabaricus* from Latin into English, it was celebrated as a major contribution to Kerala's cultural heritage. The project also brought up anxieties about how the translation might enable bioprospecting. These concerns were validated when the Mayo Clinic College of Medicine in Rochester, Minnesota, announced that its digital bioprospecting research wing would explore the new translation for leads in developing new medications. Meanwhile, the Ezhava community in Kerala staked a claim of ownership in relation to this text since it was based on their ancestors' knowledge (170–172).

Another example of the appropriation of biological knowledge from the Indian subcontinent comes from a more recent period, this time between India and the United States and between ayurvedic and biomedical psychiatry. In 1958, the American psychiatrist Nathan Kline declared that psychopharmaceutical drugs were reducing the inpatient populations of mental hospitals for the first time in the history of mental health care in the United States. One of the principle drugs responsible for this change was reserpine, an alkaloid derived from the plant *Rauwolfia serpentina*, which, as Kline explained, has long been used in India in the treatment of mental disorders (Kline 1959).[6] Reserpine came into use in biomedical psychiatry after Nathan Kline tested it on patients at the Rockland State psychiatric hospital in Orangeburg, New York. In their textbook on psychiatry, Kaplan and Sadock (1995) describe reserpine as the first effective antipsychotic in the treatment of mental illness.[7] This medication continues to be prescribed, but now as an antihypertensive rather than an antipsychotic. It brings in hundreds of millions of dollars in sales for several companies, including Novartis, the Switzerland-based pharmaceutical producer that challenged what they saw as the restrictiveness of India's new patent law in the Indian Supreme Court. Novartis's subsidiary Sandoz produces reserpine in combination with other ingredients in two of its products, Serpasil and Adelphane, and this drug is contained in products made by thirty-three other pharmaceutical companies. Ciba, the company that isolated the reserpine alkaloid from the rauwolfia plant and from which Nathan Kline obtained the drug for his trials, was awarded several patents for this medication in the 1950s. This in spite of the fact that the only "innovation" involved was the act of isolating the ingredient from its plant source and then later modifying the compound for various purposes such as better absorption.[8] Ciba later became Ciba-Geigy and eventually part of Novartis. *Rauwolfia serpentina,* from which reserpine was derived, is still used by ayurvedic physicians, and it is popularly known in India by its Sanskritic name "serpagandhi." This is provocatively reflected in Sandoz's trademarked brand name for one of its reserpine products, Serpasil. Thus while the patent on reserpine has expired, a hint of the contribution from India lives on in a trademark, another form of intellectual property.

While Serpasil is a registered trademark, the Sanskrit name of the plant from which it derives, serpagandhi, remains in the public domain, a seemingly small distinction that is nonetheless symbolic of contemporary intellectual property relations.[9] Also significant is the fact that no Indian entities have received a portion of the profits that have been made from reserpine. Since it developed at a time when the knowledge upon which it was based was part of an open public domain, there is no benefit-sharing or royalty obligation, and reserpine is now generic.

This kind of bioprospecting is not limited to Ayurveda or India, and the legal scholar Mgbeoji (2006) goes so far as to say, "The development of industrialized agriculture, biotechnology, and pharmaceuticals in the advanced capitalist economies has been predicated on the systematic and continuous appropriation of plant genetic resources and traditional knowledge from areas that lie principally in the Third World" (87). He then lists a variety of medicines that were derived from such sources including reserpine, birth control pills, and treatments for malaria, diabetes, tumors and respiratory disorders (91–93).

Benefit-sharing measures included in the new defensive reactions to the contemporary global patent regime such as India's Biological Diversity Act might allow sharing of proceeds from new uses of ayurvedic and other local knowledge, although how and to whom the benefits should be distributed is ambiguous and problematic since it is difficult to determine who counts as the custodians and beneficiaries of the knowledge.[10] The Convention on Biological Diversity (CBD), which informs India's Biological Diversity Act, says benefits from the use of plant resources should go to local and indigenous groups from whom knowledge of these resources was derived, and a supplementary agreement to the CBD, the Nagoya Protocol, which was implemented in 2014, aims to provide "greater legal certainty and transparency" for benefit sharing related to the use of biological and genetic resources (Convention on Biological Diversity 2016). The original plan for providing benefit sharing was critiqued because local and indigenous communities might not agree to or value the commercialization of their knowledge. Some communities and advocates have proposed the creation of "traditional knowledge commons" (TKC) which aim to ensure that so-called traditional knowledge remain in the public domain through mechanisms such as creative commons licenses (Srinivas

2012). This may require that commercial producers leave the benefits of their product to common use. Krishna Ravi Srinivas, an intellectual property researcher for the New Delhi–based RIS policy think tank, points out that a shortcoming of TKC is that the concept "presupposes the existence of a community with shared values and objectives" (414). Nevertheless he is optimistic that with the passage of the Nagoya Protocol, TKC and biocultural protocols might ensure benefit sharing or appropriate uses of resources in the eyes of local communities.

There remains an additional problem that ayurvedic therapies are not generally attributable to specific local communities or indigenous groups in India. Benefits from the use of ayurvedic knowledge could go into the national coffers of India or to sectors of the government that manage and support Indian systems of medicine such as the Ministry of AYUSH (Ayurveda, Yoga and Naturopathy, Unani, Siddha and Homeopathy). Or the Indian government could require that any commercial biomedical product developed from an ayurvedic insight remain, along with the ayurvedic knowledge, in the public domain or in a knowledge commons such as the Open Source Drug Discovery Program (discussed in the conclusion).[11]

I asked Dr. Ravindran Nayar, who owns a small ayurvedic pharmaceutical company that produces classic medications—not novel, proprietary products—if there is a tradition of ownership of medical knowledge among ayurvedic physicians, and he explained:

If we are using a compound like *chyawanaprash* [a popular general health tonic], anybody can change the composition of *chyawanaprash*. That is free to the physician. Like that, every physician has their own type of secret. We don't believe in that [secrecy] generally, but here a lot of families [of ayurvedic practitioners] keep these secrets and most of them will become extinct if the physician dies without passing on this knowledge. In the ayurvedic tradition, this is not the discipline. Sometimes it will happen that somebody keeps a secret, but we cannot keep secret the basic principles.

When I commented that the basic principles are in the *Caraka Samhita*, he responded: "Only we can keep secret our combinations. I am not advocating this. All of the knowledge should be exposed to mankind."

Secrecy is the closest thing to knowledge ownership in Ayurveda according to Dr. Nayar, but he raises a concern about secrecy: when knowledge is protected by keeping it secret, the knowledge may die with the creator. Dr. Aravindan, an ayurvedic doctor who was opposed to the new patent regime, shared with me the same concern about secrecy and the disappearance of knowledge in Ayurveda. This, we may recall, was one of the justifications for the development of patent law: given that knowledge can disappear with the death of the inventor when the only means of protection is secrecy, the state should give the inventor a temporary monopoly on production in the form of a patent in exchange for which the inventor must publically disclose his or her invention. The knowledge behind the innovation will then be available for public benefit once the patent expires.

Thus both Dr. Nayar and patent advocates support the public disclosure of knowledge, as does Dr. Aravindan, who otherwise opposes the new patent regime. But the extension of property rights in the new patent regime and the resistance to this regime through protective claims on local knowledge—that is, both the offensive and the defensive tactics—have resulted in a problematic situation where knowledge is becoming increasingly partitioned and proprietary. My disquiet with this situation arises not so much from Novartis or Ciba or patients with psychopathology or hypertension benefitting from ayurvedic knowledge with the development of reserpine, or similar benefits that may develop from other Ayurveda-derived drugs, as it does from the restricting of Indian pharmaceutical companies from reverse-engineering products patented by multinational companies. The earlier system, where each "steals" from the other, seemed fairer. Similarly, there is a sense of an injustice in the minds of many who question the new patent regime due to a double standard where the defense of only Western, biomedical ideals of creation and ownership is enhanced. While in principle, as Dr. Nayar says, ayurvedic knowledge should be freely shared, when protections for biomedical knowledge are amped up, many feel that there should be a similar defensive response from the ayurvedic community.

Ayurvedic Medicine and Innovation

Because this discussion of concerns about biopiracy and the new patent environment revolves around India's indigenous ayurvedic medical system, a brief description of key features of Ayurveda will help show what is at stake and why it is difficult to reconcile the knowledge and practice of this medical system with patent law.

The Indian subcontinent is home to a variety of formal and informal healing systems, from the ritual healing of priests and shamans to institutionalized medical practices such as Unani, Siddha, and Ayurveda. The Ministry of AYUSH, which oversees Indian systems of medicine, devotes more of its attention to Ayurveda, often translated as "the science of long life," than to the other systems. In general, Ayurveda is the most widely practiced Indian system of medicine, receiving the most institutional support in terms of government and private funding of ayurvedic colleges, clinics, and hospitals. It also features a growing pharmaceutical sector, with annual sales over US$600 million.[12] A variety of other non-biomedical systems of healing are practiced in India and in other parts of South Asia including Unani medicine, which, like biomedicine, traces its origins to Greek humoralism; Siddha medicine, which is primarily associated with and practiced in the Tamil region of South India; homeopathy, which developed in Germany and is widely practiced in India; and naturopathy, which developed in Europe, the United States, and India and is influenced by a Gandhian ideology.[13]

Those who are not familiar with Ayurveda often expect it to be easily explainable or reducible to simple principles, but Ayurveda cannot be easily summarized, although many popular books, especially the numerous New Age–style guides that are available on the subject, reduce Ayurveda to succinct concepts and principles. To know how to practice Ayurveda, one needs to study in an Ayurveda college, and then, after an internship, one earns a degree (Bachelor of Ayurvedic Medical Science, or a more advanced degree) and is qualified to practice Ayurveda. Alternately, some train under an accomplished practitioner who uses a *guru-sisya* method, where the vaidya trains a student in a one-on-one apprenticeship. What one learns in an Ayurveda college or through one's physician *guru* are the basic principles of Ayurveda, which include the knowledge of the dynamic properties and substances that underlie the functioning of the body, such as the three *dosas*, (*vata, pitta,* and *kapha*). The dosas are often translated as "humors," which lead us to think of them as substances, but they are better seen as something like the essences of bodily functions. The terms have no direct English translations, but vata refers to something like wind or movement, pitta is fire or heat, and kapha is often translated as "phlegm" but can also be understood as the principle of slowness or viscousness. Food, behavior, lifestyle, and environmental influences can alter the functioning of the dosas and lead to disease, and food, medicine, and health regimens are used to correct the dosic imbalance. This seemingly simple system of dosic balance is central to ayurvedic theory, but a variety of other concepts and principles are essential and can complicate the relations between dosas, the environment, and the body. Students must learn about the *dhathus*, which are tissues and bodily substances such as muscle, fat, hemoglobin, and bone; the *malas*, or waste products of the body; the thirteen groups of *agnis* that are involved in digestion and are similar to the concept of enzymes; the *srotas*, which are channels of movement and circulation; and many other categories of physiology. Some concepts are more abstract, such as *bala*, which is roughly strength or immunity, and *ojas*, which is similar to energy or vitality, whereas some learning requires rote memorization and attention to detail, such as getting to know the characteristics of medicinal plants and the ayurvedic pharmacopoeia.[14]

Although these concepts can be seen in classic ayurvedic texts and there is some continuity with the past, ayurvedic practices change over time, especially in relation to allopathy, or Western biomedicine, ever since this system became widespread in the Indian subcontinent. The medical anthropologist Jean Langford (2002) depicts contemporary Ayurveda as a reified constellation of medical practices that is fraught with debates and uncertainty about what is authentic. Ayurveda has in significant ways remade itself in relation to the practice of biomedicine and nationalist concerns in India about science and development. Practitioners frequently adopt practices, concepts, and technologies from biomedicine, and they have dropped some invasive procedures used in the past, such as surgical procedures, thus reinventing themselves as a gentler, more holistic alternative to biomedicine.[15] Ayurveda has also traveled beyond the Indian subcontinent, becoming a global medical practice, finding niches in Germany, the United Kingdom, and North America, and in the course of these travels, it has been endorsed by Hollywood celebrities and adopted by the cosmetics and food industries.[16]

While it is not possible to identify an authentic Ayurveda free of the influence of other medical systems, there are certain characteristics of ayurvedic practice in the contemporary period that can be productively contrasted to the practice of biomedicine.

First, compared to biomedicine, Ayurveda is more often in dialogue with its basic principles, such as the effects of the three dosas and other concepts mentioned above. In biomedicine, it is unclear whether there are basic principles, except for perhaps an unreflective pragmatism and an orientation to biological particularism, where the concern is with specialization and the efficacy of specific therapeutic procedures. Certainly, relations between food, the environment, and health are taken into account by biomedical doctors and scientists, but explicit principles are not taught, understood, and reflected on as such in biomedical training.

Second, ayurvedic vaidyans regularly engage with classic texts, including the *Caraka Samhita* and *Susruta Samhita,* which are over two thousand years old, and the *Astangahrdayasamhita,* which was composed around the sixth or seventh century C.E. Professors at Ayurveda colleges will fire passages from these texts back and forth at each other in Sanskrit in discussing ayurvedic therapies and will reflect on schools of philosophy such as *nyaya, vaisesika, samkhya,* and *yoga* that have informed Ayurveda. Although contemporary ayurvedic research journals report on new research and new treatments that are being developed, ayurvedic doctors regularly invoke the insights of Caraka and Susruta, preferring to rely on what they see as time-tested truths rather than constantly changing their treatments and beliefs as allopathic doctors do. Biomedicine, on the other hand, maintains no conscious or sustained dialogue with, say, Hippocrates or Galen. In fact, in biomedicine and in some histories of science, the ancient is perceived merely as a repository of wrong ideas that were corrected by later truths.

In 2004, I had a conversation about science and empiricism with Dr. Pramod Krishnadas, a physician at the Government Ayurveda Mental Hospital in Malappuram District, Kerala. Dr. Krishnadas explained that there are two kinds of drugs in Ayurveda: those described in classic texts, which he calls "scientific" drugs, and those that are newly created, which are known as "patent drugs." When I asked why he called the drugs from classic texts "scientific," he explained that "they will be more valuable, more reliable," which led to a discussion of how reliability and validity, two central principles of scientific knowledge, are viewed in Ayurveda. Dr. Krishnadas explained that the scientific drugs were developed by vaidyans like Caraka and Susruta, authors of the *Caraka Samhita* and *Susruta Samhita,* the two most influential classical texts. These vaidyans, he explained, had more *sattva*—an ayurvedic term indicating a more balanced, robust, and truthful personality, less prone to lust and greed—than doctors do nowadays. "Today's doctors are businessmen," he said, while Caraka and Susruta had no profit motive. Dr. Krishnadas proceeded to describe four different forms of knowledge, which I recognized from Indian schools of philosophy such as Nyaya and Vaisesika: 1) perception, 2) logic, 3) inference, and 4) the knowledge of experts. Perception refers to direct sensory evidence, logic has the same meaning as logic in contemporary science, and inference refers to truths that can be reasoned though not directly perceived. Susruta, Dr. Krishnadas said, felt that knowledge from perception is less important than the other forms. The last category, the knowledge of experts, is something like wisdom, the knowledge of an expert or a teacher who has gained insight through extensive experience.

From this discussion, I understood that the difference Dr. Krishnadas was depicting between ayurvedic knowledge and what he called "allopathic science" (biomedical/Western science that has become the international "standard" science) is that Ayurveda assigns a greater prominence to the last of the four categories of knowledge, the wisdom of experts such as Caraka and Susruta, than biomedicine does. He was also depicting ayurvedic science as being more balanced between the four kinds of knowledge, while biomedical researchers rely more on their perceptions, the form of knowledge that had the least value. Dr. Krishnadas furthermore depicted ayurvedic science as reliable because it focuses on truths that are unchanging. From this perspective, biomedicine is less reliable in that it is constantly producing new ideas, new treatments, new understandings of the body, while old views are discarded. Thus biomedicine—perhaps Western science as well—appears as if it lacks a central truth or a stable base of knowledge. If treatments and ideas once believed to be true are regularly thrown out in favor of new discoveries or truths, what can one rely on? How do we know present truths and forms of treatment, or the latest scientific discovery, will not be thrown out by future research? Ayurvedic physicians see their classic principles as having stood the test of time and that therefore they must be more real than new insights. But this does not mean new treatments cannot be developed by modifying therapies or building new techniques based on classical knowledge.

The emphasis on novelty in patent law thus reflects the biomedical preference for newness and innovation and limits the prospects for the patenting of ayurvedic treatments, which are based on adherence to or coherence with time-tested fundamentals. Nevertheless, practitioners have come forth claiming to have developed novel "proprietary" ayurvedic medicines based on modifying classical formulations. Ayurveda's relation to its past may change as ayurvedic practitioners develop new proprietary medicines and a fetishization of the new emerges along with the new patent regime.

In Ayurveda, plant materials are processed and refined in factories, the end result being a pill or syrupy tonic that often resembles a biomedical product. Thus, ayurvedic drugs are mass-produced using industrial processes just as with biomedical pharmaceutical production. Ayurvedic medications are, however, produced from raw plant materials, whereas biomedical pharmaceutical practice involves isolating active chemical ingredients. The race for developing new drugs and new patents in the biomedical pharmaceutical sector focuses on the development of New Chemical Entities (NCEs), which are sometimes derived from raw plant materials, and it is these NCEs' effects on particular illnesses that are patentable. In this way as well, intellectual property law conforms to biomedical concepts and practices.[17]

Ayurvedic practitioners and ayurvedic pharmaceutical companies could isolate active chemical ingredients from the medicinal plants they use, test these in placebo-controlled studies, and, if they are found to be effective, patent them. The patented product, however, would not be "ayurvedic," because in ayurvedic therapies the so-called "active" chemical ingredients are seen as working along with other properties of a plant product, which is often mixed with other medicinal plant materials and administered along with other aspects of a treatment regimen, such as modifying diet or behavior.[18] The turmeric and neem cases discussed above show that knowledge of plants can be used to defeat a patent by proving prior use of these biological materials, but ayurvedic uses of plants based on ayurvedic knowledge do not appear to be patentable.

Another salient difference in contemporary ayurvedic and biomedical practice that impacts intellectual property law and anthropological understandings of medical and scientific systems relates to what we could call the agents of innovation, which are communal or individual. The nature of the agent of innovation is in turn connected to the issue of novelty.

In patent law, creation is perceived as being either communal or individual, and it is the latter type of invention that is protected. Individual innovation is more of an ideal than a reality, however, because innovation is generally communal and incremental. In research in Kerala on ayurvedic treatments for mental illness in the 1990s and on innovation in Ayurveda in the 2000s, I observed a range of styles of invention that subvert the expectations of anthropologists and legal scholars who have examined intellectual property. These scholars have come up with the dichotomy of individual invention, which is associated with modern science and capitalism, and oppose it to communal knowledge, which is attributed to places deemed "traditional" or "indigenous."[19] Although there is some truth to this dichotomy, it conceives of non-Western forms of knowledge as somewhat homogenous—as if individuals in such societies never broke out of the social mold and developed their own innovations—and it confuses claims of individual innovation, the legitimating ideology, with the actual practice of creation in corporate settings.[20] Although patent claims are based on the archetype of the lone genius in the laboratory, biomedical innovation is, in fact, communal in the sense that research is carried out by teams of workers, in corporate or university settings, and the community must agree on a new treatment before it becomes part of practice through the approval of journal reviewers, professional boards, and government regulators. Indeed, the very name "corporate" speaks to the communal nature of the work of a corporation, which is nevertheless recognized as an individual by law. Furthermore, since patent rights are transferable and can be sold to investors that were uninvolved in the creation of the patented product, medical innovations are often developed by small companies, which then sell patent rights for their products to large corporations who bring these products to market.[21] Thus legal fictions fill the gap between the romantic myth of the individual innovator and the practices of patent ownership.

A certain type of individual innovation is, meanwhile, a common—one could even say a "traditional"—feature of ayurvedic medicine. Ayurvedic vaidyans often alter a standard prescription, tailoring medications to a particular patient's problems, although this practice appears to have become less common since ayurvedic pharmaceutical companies began mass-producing ayurvedic medicines in standardized forms.[22] Rather than working with standardized drugs intended to heal diseases, which are themselves standardized according to disease categories, as in biomedicine, ayurvedic doctors feel that each patient experiences an illness in a unique way. Each patient has a distinctive constellation of symptoms affected by his or her dominant bodily processes (which are due to the activity of the dosas), and medicines should be created that are specially suited to an individual's symptoms and constitution. Many doctors continue to use this practice, writing a prescription in the form of a recipe. The patient or her family members are then expected to buy raw plant ingredients at an ayurvedic pharmacy and prepare the medicine in their own kitchens following the doctor's directions. This is an informal and routine type of innovation, and vaidyans do not claim ownership of these intellectual products, although some who mix medications in their offices keep the ingredients of particular formulations secret.

A doctor may also create medicines for an institution in which he or she works, although these products are not necessarily owned by the individual or institution. Dr. K. Sundaran, now retired from the Trivandrum Ayurveda College and the Government Ayurveda Mental Hospital in Kottakkal, developed several of the drug combinations now in regular use at the Mental Hospital. These "inventions," however, are based on basic insights of ayurvedic medicine regarding the *dosas*, the *dhatus*, and other characteristics of the body. They developed from Dr. Sundaran's own contribution, but they are not exactly novel in the sense that the combinations of ingredients are anticipated by the basic principles and earlier insights in ayurvedic texts.

In his ethnography of medical practices in Bengal, Stefan Ecks profiles an ayurvedic doctor who worked for a state-run pharmaceutical company that produces allopathic and ayurvedic drugs. Although in his private practice Dr. Sengupta preferred to make his own medicines for his patients, he also turned "Ayurvedic recipes of this father and grandfather into medicines for mass manufacturing" at East India Pharmaceutical Works.[23]

The anthropologist Gananath Obeysekere has described what he calls the *samyogic* method of experimentation in Ayurveda, wherein practitioners add or delete ingredients from standard prescriptions according to ayurvedic principles and depending on the condition of a particular patient. It is in situations where ayurvedic principles provide no clear guidance that physicians invent medications. Obeyesekere profiles a Sri Lankan vaidyan, Dr. Fernando, who combines three plant ingredients to create a remedy for a patient with intestinal cancer. Dr. Fernando chooses ingredients that heal different kinds of growths and that treat abscesses in the stomach and colon.[24] The invention of medicines by Dr. Sundaran and Dr. Fernando involved concocting and rearranging materials according to principles set down in ayurvedic treatises. The inventions are both new and yet dependent on earlier knowledge. Biomedical innovation also depends on common scientific insights and the work of earlier researchers, but this connection is more readily overlooked in biomedical perspectives on invention.

When I spoke with Dr. K. T. Aravindan, an ayurvedic physician I met with in Kerala who was concerned about the new patent law, and asked how novelty is defined in Ayurveda, he explained:

> Ah, novelty, that's the problem because if you are finding one drug, one particular drug that has anti-rheumatic properties, you say it has these properties. Or with modern research methods I find out this fact, and so I apply for this patent license. And what happens, actually, is that it is from certain ayurvedic classics, *Caraka Samhita* or *Susruta Samhita*, but it is not based on the modern research background. These are ancient findings. So we have nothing to produce before the patent office to challenge your application.

Dr. Aravindan notes that the methods of "modern research" align with patent laws. However, his juxtaposition of modern research with knowledge based on ayurvedic classics oversimplifies the situation. It is possible to oppose a patent, but not to get a patent issued, based on knowledge in the *Caraka Samhita* or other classic texts. Also, some do apply "modern research" to Ayurveda, by developing new treatments, conducting clinical trials, and looking for ways of making ayurvedic products proprietary. "Proprietary" is a frequently used term for ownership claims for ayurvedic products, but it does not have the same meaning as "patent." In Maarten Bode's study of the commercialization of the ayurvedic pharmaceutical sector, the manager of an ayurvedic manufacturer, Dabur, explained, "Our products are not novel in the sense that they meet international criteria for patented medicines. Therefore the word 'proprietary' much better covers the state of affairs in Ayurveda. Government rules and regulations make it possible to protect investments made in designing and marketing of an ayurvedic product" (58).

This representative invokes a key rationale of patent law for corporate interests—protecting investments—and ties it not to the ideal of novel innovation but to investment in design and marketing. As chapter 2 showed, the investments biomedical companies are protecting are also connected to design and marketing more than developing novel treatments, but they emphasize that they are protecting investments in research and development. The cost of bringing an ayurvedic drug to market is much smaller than that of a new chemical entity produced by a big pharma corporation, but it is not that far from the cost of producing a generic formulation for an Indian biomedical pharmaceutical company. Ayurvedic producers must comply with Good Manufacturing Practice regulations promulgated by the Indian government and must contend with the rising cost of medicinal plant materials—and, like biomedical companies, they spend money on business consultants and advertising.[25]

The Dabur representative Bode met with then gave the example of his company's brand of chyawanprash, the classical formulation Dr. Nayar also referred to above. In protecting investments in this company's version of chyawanprash, the proprietary claims actually resemble a trademark more than a patent: though Dabur did not invent chyawanprash, Dabur's chyawanprash has a reputation they are trying to protect much as other companies try to protect their trade symbols and the reputation of products associated with them through trademark enforcement.

In an effort that predates the new patent regime but is made more significant by this new environment, many have been conducting research into Ayurveda using Western/international scientific methods, merging the two orientations to science and medicine and producing new research and treatments. At the same time, relations to classical texts and principles remain vital and coexist with this orientation to newness. For example, a contemporary work on *pancakarma* therapy—a multistep treatment that uses purgatives, enemas, nasally administered medications, and other procedures to detoxify patients and treat illness—features a chapter entitled "Recent Advances in Panca Karma Therapy."[26] This chapter reports not on new methods of pancakarma, but on recent tests of existing methods to evaluate their effectiveness on various diseases.

Much of the research reported in contemporary ayurvedic journals, such as *Aryavaidyan, Nagarjuna, Ayush Tomorrow, International Journal of Ayurveda and Alternative Medicine,* and the *Journal of Research in Ayurveda and Siddha*, also attempts to test treatments from classical texts using international scientific methods. For example, Srikanth et al. (2001)

in *Aryavaidyan* report on the effectiveness of using treatments known as *nasyakarma* and *ghritapana* in the management of migraine headaches. The authors say that because of the lack of effective treatments for migraines today, they have explored "alternative solutions hidden in classical texts" (170), claiming that 80 percent of patients they treated got some relief. Seema and Sapan (2013) report in the *International Journal of Ayurveda and Alternative Medicine* on *haridra khanda* and *anu tail nasya* in treating allergic rhinitis and say the treatment is safe and effective. The use of anu tail nasya, a nasally administered medication, is based on Caraka's recommendation of this treatment in his classic treatise for certain conditions, which led the authors to think it would be useful for allergic rhinitis. A similar research orientation was seen among students I met at the Trivandrum Ayurveda College who were working on graduate degrees. For example, one student was attempting to determine the physiology of *bala*, a term that means something like strength or vitality in Ayurveda, through clinical research. The library at the college is full of student theses that are contemporary clinical studies of ayurvedic concepts and therapies.

The interest in testing ayurvedic therapies through clinical trials has even entered the world of mainstream biomedical research in North America. A team of researchers at UCLA, the University of Washington, and other institutions completed a double-blind, controlled pilot study of an ayurvedic treatment for rheumatoid arthritis. The researchers found the ayurvedic treatment to be as effective as the standard of care, methotrexate, and to have fewer side effects.[27] This may augur a future of more biomedical, and big pharma, interest in ayurvedic therapies.

When I asked Dr. Shyam, a practitioner in southern Kerala, whether ayurvedic doctors invent new medicines or alter treatments from classic texts, he explained, "Here, most of the people are doing simple modification of traditional medicines," adding that creating new medicines takes hundreds of years. Dr. Shyam was pursuing an advanced degree at the Trivandrum Ayurveda College and conducting research on his own modification of a classic treatment. The Indian government operates an institution called the Central Council for Research in Ayurvedic Sciences, which is responsible for "development and promotion of research on scientific lines" in Ayurveda. In listing their accomplishments in clinical research, they take credit for the "validation and development of formulations" for a variety of ailments.[28] While this group says they "developed" formulations, they do not use the terms "invented" or "created." The choice of the terms "develop" and "proprietary" demonstrates the ambiguity of Ayurveda's relation to the tenets of novelty and innovation in patent law.

In an apparently successful attempt at staking an ownership claim over an ayurvedic medication, Dr. Nair of Pankajakasthuri Herbals India, an ayurvedic pharmaceutical company, "experimented with and reformulated combinations from the ayurvedic texts for respiratory ailments," developing a treatment for asthma, which was awarded a "proprietary patent" by the Kerala state drug controller.[29] Although a kind of proprietary protection was awarded, I do not know whether the "reformulating" Dr. Nair did was significantly different from the kind of modifications reported in the research journals mentioned above, such as in the examples by Srikanth et al. and Seema and Sapan. Pordié and Gaudillière (2014) report that the ayurvedic Himalaya Drug Company has created two new proprietary formulations, Diabecon for diabetes and Menosan, which is a kind of hormone replacement therapy. All of these drug developments involve reformulating or modifying treatments from classical texts and target biomedically defined diseases. If the alteration of the classical prescription is determined to be significant enough, one may receive protection. The proprietary protections, however, are not true patents of the kind that would be awarded under India's Patents Act, but are more like trademarks.[30] Meanwhile, T. C. James (2014), who works for a central government–affiliated IP think tank, provides examples of several patents on ayurvedic treatments, as well as treatments from India's other major indigenous medical systems, Siddha and Unani. Most of these are for processes of producing medications but some are for new "compositions" (247–248).

The medical anthropologist Harish Naraindas (2014) examined the mixing of methods from Ayurveda and biomedicine in cases similar to those presented here, though not specifically in relation to proprietary claims. He refers to this as a *creolization* of Ayurveda. In so doing, he underlines the power hierarchy involved when biomedical scientific principles and criteria are applied to ayurvedic concepts or when ayurvedic treatments aim to treat illnesses as defined by biomedicine. Thus Ayurveda may be changing in a way that is deferential to biomedical methods and concepts as practitioners find ways to adapt to the patent system.[31] When

I say that practitioners are "adapting" to the patent system, I do not mean that they are all attempting to get their products patented, although some are trying to claim ownership. I refer to a more general trend of thinking of one's creative work as proprietary or as something that needs to be defended, since such sensibilities are growing in the new IP environment in India. Since ayurvedic production has been commercialized, which started several decades ago, some manufacturers are also seeking proprietary claims over their products to increase profitability.

In the examples presented here, current practices in ayurvedic pharmacology and production involve "validation," "development," and "modification" and, in the case of Dr. Nair's product, it involved "experimenting" and "reformulating" (though these are the words of the social scientist analyzing his work rather than his own). They all avoid the term "invention," as if that is something others are doing.

We can make further sense of the difference between innovation in Ayurveda and biomedicine by returning to the critiques of the myth of individual invention and authorship by scholars of the history of property, literature, and science. Regarding the development of copyright in the early 1700s—at the insistence of booksellers, not authors—the literary critic Mark Rose asserts that the idea that an author owns or individually created an artistic work that he or she produced is a modern one stemming from conceptions of property and innovation proposed by John Locke, the seventeenth-century English philosopher whose writings advocate the sanctity of private property. Through Shakespeare's time, writers borrowed stories and plots from each other in a way that, by contemporary standards, would be considered a violation of copyright. Current literary theory undermines the idea that the individual author is the sole creator of a work and reveals this premise to be somewhat fictional. "Texts permeate and enable one another," says Rose, as any creative writing contains contributions from other works that precede it and cultural influences that bear upon it, and the author always conveys more than his or her own individual input.[32] Similarly, individual scientific or medical invention is, to a great extent, the outcome of prior knowledge and innovation. In fact, the idea of the individual inventor was borrowed from the notion of the individual author in literature, and it "similarly obscures the collective or collaborative element in scientific invention and discovery."[33]

Even Einstein's theory of relativity, which is popularly perceived as a work of independent genius, was scaffolded on the insights of others and constituted part of a larger effort being undertaken at the time in physics.[34]

Belief in the autonomy of the inventor enables a belief in the novelty of invention. If we are aware that invention is dependent on ideas, practices, and texts preceding an invention, innovative ideas appear less new and novelty appears less spontaneous, and thereby less authentic. As shown in this chapter, ayurvedic physicians and researchers maintain a more explicit relation to the past. "New" treatments in Ayurveda are actually modifications on earlier treatments, but ayurvedic producers do not just acknowledge the connection to the past, they highlight principles from classic texts that relate to their work to give it credibility.

Biomedical innovation is also dependent on earlier knowledge as innovators often alter earlier treatments or discover new medications by modifying insights into biochemistry and physiology discovered by predecessors. This is why it has been relatively easy for legal activists in India to defeat some biomedical patents under India's patent law. They are simply debunking the myth of independent innovation by tracking down the prior knowledge that is the basis of the innovation, usually citing research in scientific journals that makes the inventive step claimed in the patent application possible. The key difference, we might say, is that ayurvedic practitioners are more forthcoming about their connection to their forbears. In Ayurveda, individual innovation exists but the emphasis is placed on continuity with the past and the communal nature of knowledge. The novelty that develops is downplayed.

This is not to say that ayurvedic and biomedical practices are the same once the myth of individual invention is revealed or that creations require no legal protection from misappropriation. For biomedicine, the connection is to the recent past, to previous research that made, say, someone's insights into the characteristics of retroviruses lead to the formulation by another scientist, or team of scientists, of a reverse transcriptase inhibitor to prevent AIDS, but this connection is downplayed in how we think and speak about scientific innovation to maintain a semblance of inventiveness. The relation to the past in Ayurveda is deeper, stretching back to the authority of Caraka and Susruta and to what are seen as basic principles that remain true, not just to recent developments in the discipline.

Thus patent law overlooks Ayurveda and protects biomedicine because Ayurveda lacks a fetishization of novelty and features a different set of priorities for establishing truth and reliability.[35] But Ayurveda may change in order to adapt to or profit from the new patent regime by deemphasizing connections to the past and developing claims of novelty.

The relation of Ayurveda to patent law is complex and ambiguous, seemingly offering both opportunities and threats of misappropriation. How should practitioners of ayurvedic medicine react to this situation? Does the mismatch between patent law and ayurvedic knowledge affect ayurvedic practitioners in any important way? Or does the new patent regime constitute a benign set of changes that does not affect Ayurveda unless practitioners engage the new system and make patent claims? These questions bring up problems that are as challenging as making sense of the principles and myths of innovation in Ayurveda and biomedicine. An assessment of the relation of the new patent regime to the practices of ayurvedic medicine requires a knowledge of Ayurveda, science, and law that few possess, and challenges our capacity to understand the potential effects of new global constellations of power such as the new international patent regime.

Reacting and Resisting

In anticipation of changes to patent laws, ayurvedic physicians and manufacturers developed divergent strategies to prevent problems they feared might arise, such as multinational pharmaceutical companies developing and patenting new medications based on ayurvedic knowledge. Yet some are doing nothing in relation to these changes. I suggest that the strategies I encountered in this context constitute a range of resistances, reactions, and inactions that are not normally represented in analyses of power, resistance, and globalization.

The first interview I conducted with an ayurvedic practitioner on this topic was difficult. I was referred to this individual, whom I will call Dr. Krishnan, by another ayurvedic specialist, because of Dr. Krishnan's knowledge of, and interest in, intellectual property issues.[36] This was in 2004, before the new Patents Act was to come into effect, and Dr. Krishnan was determined to do something to resist what he felt would be potential deleterious effects on Ayurveda, although he was despairing of what he could accomplish. Dr. Krishnan was willing to speak to me, but as we got further into the topic of the misappropriation of ayurvedic knowledge by drug companies, he appeared uneasy, and he declined my request to audiorecord the interview. Certainly this had to do partly with who I am, a foreigner he does not know, from a country that is a proponent, indeed the key proponent, of the intellectual property regime that concerns him. Dr. Krishnan's mood was alternately despairing of cataclysmic changes, wary of me, and friendly toward me. This seemed to be a sensitive, almost painful, topic for him. He appeared daunted by changes and ready to throw up his hands at what he sees as the rich world's crushing power to do what it wishes with these issues.

When I asked what he thought should be done about the looming changes in India's patent laws, he said "It's a shot gone from the gun," that it didn't matter because it was too late to stop. He later added, with a mixture of optimism and resignation, "All we can do is resist." He was at the time collecting textual sources regarding ayurvedic knowledge to contribute to the Traditional Knowledge Digital Library (TKDL), the national database that is being compiled to counter attempts to patent products based on Ayurveda and other Indian systems of knowledge and practice, such as yoga.

I pointed out that India had successfully defeated a US patent that was derived from Indian knowledge about turmeric's wound-healing properties. Dr. Krishnan said that that was true but that the effort cost India crores of rupees (millions of dollars). Ultimately, Dr. Krishnan felt that this patent struggle all came down to resources, to time and money. It would be possible for poor countries to defend their interests within the proposed laws, but they do not have adequate legal and financial resources to do so—an analysis others have concurred with.[37] At the end of our interview, I asked Dr. Krishnan if he would be willing to meet again, and he explained that he was far too busy.

I left Dr. Krishnan's office asking myself what I had gotten into. This was clearly a sensitive topic, and it felt awkward getting Dr. Krishnan to discuss how he and others would defend themselves against policies my government and US-based companies had lobbied for as proponents of the WTO intellectual property agenda. In my earlier research on a more politically benign topic, treatments for psychopathology in India, people in Kerala had always been eager to speak to me and invited me back to meet them again. This interview, however, had been awkward, and I could tell Dr. Krishnan was relieved when it was over.

After visiting Dr. Krishnan, I headed to the city's Ayurveda college to seek out a friend who works there and confess my concerns about how difficult this research might be. Walking through this college amid the modern concrete buildings and open-air corridors, I detected, as usual, the acrid and earthy scent of dried plants that are stored at the college for making medicines. Perhaps I was smelling some of the plants that are now codified in the TKDL. Meanwhile, on the nearby college library shelves sit studies undertaken by researchers that testify to the effectiveness of some of these plants, using laboratory analyses and clinical trials. While the TKDL is a reaction to the emerging sense that ayurvedic knowledge should be protected, the college library operates on the principle that knowledge of Ayurveda should be shared.

In the corridors of the building where my friend works, I met a professor of ayurvedic medicine who approached me and, out of the blue, struck up a conversation. This was not unusual, as foreigners are rarely seen in this setting, and he had mistaken me for a European researcher he met earlier. I explained I am an anthropologist who is doing research on Ayurveda, and he asked the topic of my study. After I warily told him, he responded that this project sounded intriguing, inviting me to join him in his office to discuss patent controversies.

My conversation with this professor and practitioner, Dr. Isaac Paul, could not have differed more from the experience of speaking to Dr. Krishnan. Rather than my having to work through connections to arrange an interview with someone who really didn't want to meet me, Dr. Paul approached me and invited me into his office. Dr. Paul's view of the proposed patent law changes, which he offered eagerly, were also quite different. He explained that although he had read and spoken to people about these issues, he was unconcerned about them. In fact, he felt the new intellectual property provisions would be good for Ayurveda, suggesting, "Because of patent laws, Ayurveda will get global access." And, he predicted, "Intellectual property laws will popularize Ayurveda in developed countries." He added that "Intellectual property law does not aim to *transfer* knowledge from our country to other countries." The knowledge would still be Indian and could still be used by ayurvedic practitioners. Moreover, in Ayurveda, in his opinion, the belief is that knowledge should be shared.

He spoke of intellectual property laws and Ayurveda largely as if they inhabited separate worlds: even if ideas were appropriated from Ayurveda, it would not stop ayurvedic physicians from continuing to practice their trade. Dr. Paul's only concerns were that Ayurveda should get credit for its contributions and that patent laws should not prevent people in India from continuing to grow medicinal plants for their own use.

I realized from speaking to Dr. Paul that I should not rush to assumptions about the kind of sentiments this topic engenders and I should not conceive of ayurvedic specialists as a single group collectively resisting the changes in the country's patent laws. Indeed, the ayurvedic professionals I spoke with subsequently reflected the diversity of perspectives and plans of action as well as the lack of concern hinted at in my interviews with Dr. Krishnan and Dr. Paul.

Like Dr. Krishnan, Dr. Aravindan, whom I spoke to in one of the private-sector ayurvedic institutions where he practices, was troubled by the new patent laws and believed in taking action, though he was wary of the forces he and others were up against. Dr. Aravindan seemed well informed on these issues as he spoke at length about the provisions of TRIPS—although how well informed one can be on this topic and whether anyone has the legal and ayurvedic medical expertise to anticipate the impact of the changes in IP law are key dilemmas in this situation.

Dr. Aravindan spoke of changes in India's patent laws from patents on processes to patents on products, and he considered what he saw as the pitfalls and complications in the applications of the new standards. He was concerned that if multinational drug companies were to appropriate a medical insight from Ayurveda they might also start consuming the same plant materials that ayurvedic manufacturers utilize and thereby drive up the price of materials for ayurvedic drugs: "They will come to Kerala or India, and canvass the farmers to cultivate this. Otherwise you [addressing the drug companies] will canvass the contractors, and they will collect it from the forest and from outside and give you it for a good price [a higher price], but such a price I cannot give. . . . So the price of the raw materials will increase. So we cannot afford that."

Dr. Aravindan was also thinking of strategies to prevent misappropriation, and he felt India could protect ayurvedic knowledge through a provision of TRIPS known as "geographical indication," which protects products whose reputations are associated with a particular geographic region. He explained, "It is a WTO agreement. It is already written. How can we stop that? But at that time itself, if the government is ready to make some preventative measures, they can speedily establish this under geographical indication." These sounded to me like thoughtful, informed strategies. However, since biomedical pharmaceutical companies produce medications by isolating active ingredients in laboratories, I did not see how they were going to require a large amount of raw plant material. In the case of reserpine, the antipsychotic and antihypertensive drug developed from ayurvedic knowledge, the active ingredient was produced in Ciba's laboratories in the United States. The anticancer drug paclitaxel (Taxol) was derived from the bark of the Pacific Yew tree, but it was then artificially synthesized in a lab to be produced as a medication. It is hard to expect actors to be more informed or concerned than Dr. Aravindan. He practices Ayurveda, he has learned about the new law, he has studied WTO provisions, and he is politically savvy. It is the complexity and intelligibility of this situation—the expertise needed in multiple specialties and the unpredictability of mixing together patent law with a medical practice it was not designed to support—that makes it difficult to figure out how to react.

Dr. Nayar, who owns a small ayurvedic drug company and whose comments on secrecy were presented earlier, echoed the concern Dr. Aravindan had about biomedical pharmaceutical companies buying up plant materials and raising prices. He cautioned, though, that at present we cannot know what will happen to Ayurveda as a result of the new laws and speculated that the patent controversy may even be beneficial:

> Actually in one aspect it may be good for Ayurveda. Here, Ayurveda is not much promoted by the government. Ninety-nine percent of the budget allocation goes to modern medicine, and only one percent of this goes to ayurvedic and indigenous systems. It is not adequate. I think the government and government people are not aware of the potency of Ayurveda. Now there is an awareness that Ayurveda has some goodness, and somebody's coming here to study Ayurveda and is ready to patent medicines. . . . In that aspect, we appreciate it because only globalization and these issues are giving more importance to Ayurveda.

Dr. Nayar is thus aware of issues involved in the new patent regime. He is uncertain, however, of how to react, since he concedes that we simply cannot know what will happen and considers possible benefits that may emerge with a rise in Ayurveda's public stature.

Another individual I spoke to offered an example of a different "wait-and-see" perspective, or what might be seen as a form of strategic inaction. I spoke to Dr. Prekumar Vijayan in his office at the headquarters of the large, well-reputed ayurvedic pharmaceutical company he works for. Near the administrative buildings where his office is located are the processing plants where his company mass produces ayurvedic drugs for Indian and overseas markets. I spoke to Dr. Vijayan about a year before the new patent laws came into effect. Despite the possible risk to his company if it were adversely affected by the new laws, he said his company is doing nothing in preparation for any upcoming changes. He explained that his company is planning to wait and see what happens as the laws change, but he said he was concerned and was urging others at the company to do something. Dr. Vijayan opposes such moves by the WTO that he feels make the rich richer and the poor poorer: "We should resist as they did in Cancun and Seattle," he urged, referring to anti-WTO protests.

Although Dr. Vijayan wanted to act, I am also interested in his company's inaction. This company may well have a plan they are keeping to themselves. Or maybe they are choosing inaction as a strategy. Perhaps they view the situation as somewhat akin to what Dr. Paul depicted. They may be hoping that changes in patent law will not affect ayurvedic practitioners using ayurvedic therapy and creating ayurvedic products. Perhaps they see these changes as unfolding in a parallel world of biomedical practice and marketing that coexists with, but does not significantly affect, Ayurveda. Or perhaps they are hoping to "lie low." That is, if they do not actively resist—which would make them more visible and legitimize the new rules of property—these changes will indeed happen in a parallel world and will pass right over them. Or perhaps they want people to think they are doing nothing. If their strategy is in fact to lie low, this company may prove to be wise about the vicissitudes of resistance; some researchers have shown how by resisting one can actually end up reaffirming or validating hegemonic positions.[38] Thus, if companies or institutions are trying to claim intellectual property rights and someone says, in opposition, "Look, I own these particular rights, I have prior knowledge," one is thereby affirming the principle of owning ideas, or intellectual property. One is, effectively, engaging in a game and by doing so consenting to the rules. According to a legal scholar I spoke with, Dr. N. S. Gopalakrishnan, not playing, or not resisting, may be an effective strategy

Dr. Gopalakrishnan teaches at Cochin University's School of Legal Studies, and he has studied the potential effects of TRIPS in India. A skeptical and rigorous analyst of legal and social changes who has published on controversies surrounding intellectual property, Dr. Gopalakrishnan pointed out what he saw as some of the paradoxes and pitfalls of the new patent regime and the efforts to resist it.[39] His analysis is grounded in an awareness of the indeterminate nature of the law and the contingent effects that may emerge in practice. Even though he tries to utilize this knowledge to anticipate what resistance in such a situation might accomplish, he explained that it is hard to be confident in such predictions. Dr. Gopalakrishnan explained in my meeting with him in 2004 that the Traditional Knowledge Digital Library would probably have no effect on the misappropriation of ayurvedic knowledge. In fact, in a claim that echoed the concerns that arose in Kerala around the translation of the *Hortus Malabaricus* a year earlier, Dr. Gopalakrishnan said it is more likely that the TKDL will *facilitate* the exploitation of ayurvedic ideas by outside corporate interests. This is because, Dr. Gopalakrishnan stressed, the new IP laws will protect isolated chemicals including those that exist in medicinal plants, but not the use of plants. The TKDL would then provide a list of plant sources that a pharmaceutical company could use for developing new drugs, essentially guiding pharmaceutical companies to the ayurvedic knowledge that might be of most interest to them. A researcher seeking to develop new biomedical products from the ayurvedic pharmacopoeia would not even have to look up textual sources or learn Sanskrit, the language of classical ayurvedic texts. All the information indicating which plants could be analyzed for potential new medications would be arranged in a digital library already translated to English at the expense of the Government of India.

This confused me because I recalled the case where India defeated a US patent on medicinal uses of turmeric by presenting documentation on the same use of turmeric in India. Couldn't the TKDL be used in the same way? Dr. Gopalakrishnan explained that that case was successful because it was a bad patent. It was vulnerable because it listed all therapeutic uses of turmeric.

R. A. Mashelkar, the director general of the Indian Council of Scientific and Industrial Research, which challenged the turmeric patent, was more optimistic about the implications of this victory. He proclaimed:

"This seems to be the first case in which the US patenting of traditional third world knowledge has been successfully challenged, sending signals that if patent cases are fought on well argued, well supported techno-legal grounds, then there is nothing to fear about protecting our traditional knowledge."[40] Of course, the problem remains of how much it would cost to mount oppositions repeatedly on "well supported techno-legal grounds" in courts around the world.

Dr. Gopalakrishnan followed up his comments on the TKDL by stressing that centralizing knowledge in this way makes it more vulnerable. If it is dispersed among people and localities, it is harder to misappropriate, change, or affect it in a significant way. Was this perhaps what Dr. Vijayan's company was doing by doing nothing? Perhaps they knew that by not describing and centralizing their knowledge, by not engaging directly in the intellectual property struggle and becoming more visible, they would be less vulnerable. Or is it possible that this situation is daunting and confusing, and they simply could not decide what to do?

When I spoke to Dr. Gopalakrishnan again in 2005 after the passage of the new Patents Act, he told me he thought the new act would bring more patients to Ayurveda. He brought up the concern mentioned in the previous chapter that Indian companies would no longer be able to produce generic versions of drugs patented by multinational companies, and he explained that more people would turn to Ayurveda because it would become relatively more affordable. Thus two possible benefits for Ayurveda from the new patent law were raised: Dr. Gopalakrishnan suggested more patients would come to Ayurveda because of a rise in the cost of biomedical drugs, and Dr. Nayar suggested that the new patent struggles may raise the public profile of Ayurveda. Perhaps this is what Dr. Vijayan's company was hoping for, that they did not need to resist or defend against the new patent laws because they thought they might benefit from them. Or perhaps they felt the possible risks and benefits were still unclear.

After the passage of the Patents Act, Dr. Gopalakrishnan informed me that the compilers of the TKDL decided that the database should be confidential. Had the legal and ayurvedic experts involved in compiling the TKDL developed a more informed strategy? Perhaps further study of the situation was yielding more effective strategies of resistance, yet the results of this effort are unclear. Currently, the TKDL is accessible through the Internet. One must register for a user name and password and agree to use the database only for research and educational purposes to gain access. Perhaps, as the creators of the TKDL hope, users of this database will be bound by this agreement, and patent officers around the world will examine the database to learn of prior knowledge related to pending patents, saving the Indian government the time and money required to defeat patents in foreign courts. T. C. James, who works on patent issues at the RIS research center in New Delhi, published a list of 108 patent applications that were withdrawn or amended because of the TKDL. Fifty-nine applications were withdrawn at the European Patent office, but this has happened only once in the US Patent and Trademark Office.[41] So the TKDL appears to be effective, but there may be patents, especially in the US office, that were not "caught" by the TKDL.

I did not speak to any representative of Dr. Vijayan's company since my original interview with Dr. Vijayan in 2004. I was not able to detect any change in the company's business model or public profile in visits to Kerala in 2012 or 2014, but this is not to say that changes are not happening behind the scenes or that concerns are not heightened in the company's offices. On its website, the company describes itself as manufacturing "classical formulations," which are time-tested remedies that the company does not claim to have created. This shows ayurvedic producers adhering to foundational principles rather than promoting innovation as both an ideological orientation and a business model. Their reputation and profitability is staked on how well they make their classic formulations. The reliability of the company, the adherence to classic principles, and the use of good manufacturing practices and quality ingredients are important to consumers, and this is what Dr. Vijayan's company claims to provide. The company website says that the company is licensed by Kerala state and has a Good Manufacturing Practice certification, but informal and word-of-mouth reputation about this company's products are equally important to their success.[42]

The threat to Ayurveda and what might be an appropriate reaction—or whether any reaction is necessary—remained difficult to discern as I studied the situation, although some light was shed over time. There was the strategy of direct coordinated resistance by Dr. Krishnan and others who were working on the digital library; there was a case of what I would call inaction out of a lack of concern on the part of Dr. Paul; and Dr. Vijayan's company presented a case of inaction that may have been more strategic.

While some were urgently compiling the TKDL, Dr. Gopalakrishnan warned it would likely have the opposite effect from what was intended. Still others, including R. A. Mashelkar, who was involved in challenging the turmeric patent, suggested Ayurveda *should* be a "search engine" for biomedicine, where ayurvedic knowledge would help researchers select plants to screen for new biomedical drug discovery.[43]

Dr. Aravindan, meanwhile, was hopeful that ayurvedic knowledge would be protected under the "geographical indication" section of the proposed new intellectual property laws. I examined the provision for geographical indication in TRIPS and had trouble seeing how such protections would emerge. The provision aims to protect products that are associated with a particular region: "Geographical indications are, for the purposes of this Agreement, indications which identify a good as originating in the territory of a Member, or a region or locality in that territory, where a given quality, reputation or other characteristic of the good is essentially attributable to its geographical origin."[44]

This applies to cases where the reputation of a product is tied to the region from which it derives. One example is French wine designations— Medoc wine gets its reputation and marketability from its being grown in the Medoc region of Bordeaux. "Geographical indication" protects against another wine maker referring to a wine as Medoc if it was not grown in this region. I had trouble seeing how this would protect ayurvedic medications whose identity or reputations are not generally tied to particular regions, unless we were to see Ayurveda as a whole as tied to India or South Asia as a place. Dr. Gopalakrishnan agreed with my skepticism. Although in some of his early work he considered this as a possible protective measure, he later decided that geographical indication would probably not apply to ayurvedic medications.[45]

Might it be possible to protect ayurvedic knowledge by isolating the active ingredients in ayurvedic medicinal plants and patenting the therapeutic uses of those molecules? Some ayurvedic practitioners I spoke to had also considered this possibility. Such a project would be quite expensive, though, requiring a lot of capital. Even biomedical pharmaceutical companies I spoke with are hesitant about using this method to develop new drugs because of the investment involved. In any case, the resulting product would no longer be ayurvedic and could serve only as a defensive measure to counter potential biomedical patents or as a source of profit if sold to a biomedical pharmaceutical company. Ayurvedic medical theory does not operate in terms of active ingredients, and as mentioned earlier some practitioners suggest that so-called "inactive" ingredients, or chemical properties of plants working in combination, may have a role in the therapeutic effect of ayurvedic treatments. In addition, medicines are usually given as a part of a regimen that may involve dietary, behavioral, and lifestyle changes—all of which are considered necessary for a therapy to be effective. Thus, such a strategy would not protect ayurvedic knowledge in ayurvedic terms.

So what, ultimately, is being protected in these various defensive strategies? Resistances to the patent regime, such as the TKDL, seem either to stop a biomedical version of an ayurvedic therapy from being made or ensure that profits are shared if such products are made. I could not help but think of Dr. Paul's comment that creating biomedical drugs based on the active ingredients in ayurvedic plants would not take anything away from Ayurveda. The patent laws thereby may not affect Ayurveda significantly. Ayurvedic doctors could continue to practice their trade unconcerned that a patent elsewhere based on an ayurvedic insight will interfere with their ability to make and use ayurvedic medicines. Given the double standard of the new patent laws, however, and the huge imbalance in global economic relations, it seems compelling that Indian entities should claim some share of pharmaceutical profits derived from ayurvedic insights.

When social scientists talk of agency, we refer to the willful, informed actions of human actors in society. We assume that individuals, although they are profoundly shaped by their sociocultural context, have some room to maneuver, some power to act on their own and to resist social conditions they object to or find oppressive. We usually assume as well that the system of power, the hegemony under which people live, can be deciphered and that groups can organize and devise a plan of resistance that can work toward the goals of the resistors.[46] In the situation I have described, it is challenging for actors to interpret the actions of the state and the WTO policies. In terms of the TKDL, it is hard to anticipate whether the efforts of actors will accomplish what they set out to do. While it is difficult enough to know how TRIPS and resistances to TRIPS will affect biomedical drug prices and the availability of essential medicines, ayurvedic producers face an additional level of complexity. For them, the problem is not just political and economic, it is epistemological, since they have to contend with how their concepts of pharmacology and treatment fit and do not fit with a set of laws that were designed to conform to the norms of biomedicine. Ayurvedic practitioners offer varying assessments of the situation. For some, the new patent regime means more biopiracy coming from multinational pharmaceutical interests, and there is a sense of urgency to protect Ayurveda. For others, Ayurveda does not need protection, because it is not directly threatened. And for still others, the new patent regime may bring more patients to Ayurveda and give it more recognition.

In addition, if ayurvedic producers find a way to fit their practices to the standards of intellectual property law as Dr. Nair of Pankajakasthuri Herbals, the Himalaya Drug Company, and others have attempted in developing new "proprietary" treatments, ayurvedic practitioners will have another dilemma to contend with. This may be seen as both a successful attempt to conform to the new patent regime and as a threat to Ayurveda, remaking Ayurveda in the image of biomedicine and threatening the identity of Ayurveda as a distinct medical practice.[47]

The exchange of medical knowledge between India and the West will no doubt continue but may slow down under the new patent regime because of defensive measures on both sides. Multinational companies that file patents in the US and European patent offices have amped up restrictions on knowledge-sharing through TRIPS, and practitioners and defenders of Ayurveda have attempted to do the same through the CBD and the TKDL. In some cases they have successfully defeated patent applications based on ayurvedic knowledge. These represent victories for the pharmaceutical companies and the defenders of local knowledge, but the situation must not be very satisfying for those, such as Dr. Paul, who believe in the ideal of sharing scientific insights.

Finally, how might we assess Dr. Gopalakrishnan's prediction in the mid-2000s that the price of allopathic drugs will go up, leading more patients to the doors of ayurvedic vaidyans? Even though ten years have passed, it is still too early to assess the general effect of the new patent regime on biomedical drug prices. Only a few medications have been patented under India's new law and, at least in the state of Kerala, biomedical pharmaceuticals are still free or available at low, subsidized prices at government dispensaries and clinics. The price of one medication that has received significant attention from the media and activists because of its importance as a treatment for HIV/AIDS, tenofovir, has actually come down under the new patent regime. Thus one "obvious" effect of the new patent laws, in the views of some researchers and reporters, has thus far not come to be, and the actions of pharmaceutical companies in the post-TRIPS environment are also not quite what were anticipated.

4

The Gilead Model and the Perspective of Big Pharma

Although the subject of patent controversies was a sensitive issue for ayurvedic producers, it was even more so for the biomedical pharmaceutical companies I attempted to speak with. I had followed the work of ayurvedic practitioners and legal and public health activists regarding the new regime for six years when I decided I should also seek the perspective of the multinational pharmaceutical companies that are involved in patent controversies. The biomedical pharmaceutical sector was the missing piece in this research, since ayurvedic practitioners and anti-patent activists were primarily reacting to what they saw as the interests of "big pharma." I also felt it was important to "study up," as some anthropologists have referred to efforts to examine powerful institutions that are normally viewed only from afar or indirectly via theories of power.[1] Multinational pharmaceutical companies could not remain the faceless hegemonic agents that others responded to if I was going to understand what was at stake in the new global patent environment. This, however, proved to be a challenging undertaking.

Pharmaceutical companies make substantial efforts to demonstrate to the public that they are concerned and are doing something about the health problems of the world's poor (see Ecks 2008, 2010 and website screenshots in figures 2 and 3), but it is hard to get them to talk about these wonderful efforts in person. I began my attempt at contacting pharmaceutical company representatives by examining the websites of companies located in the New York/New Jersey area, where I live and where several big pharma companies are based. The websites of Merck and Pfizer did not offer any clues about where to start. They depict amorphous, multinational entities with no clear port of entry for an outsider to directly access individuals in the organization. Figure 3, from Pfizer's website, is interactive, allowing one to click on the images across the globe to learn about Pfizer's corporate social responsibility programs. Elsewhere on its site, one can view project descriptions from the company's Global Health Fellows grantees, but the communication is all one-way. They tell the public about their programs, but getting them to respond to enquiries is challenging.

While I was skeptical that pharmaceutical company efforts to attend to the health needs of the underserved were as impressive as their websites made them seem, I also had reason to suspect there was something amiss in the depiction of these companies by journalists and researchers as all-powerful agents trying to make large profits off of poor countries.

Tiered Pricing and the Tenfold Increase

Much alarm was raised among researchers, the media, and NGOs about the coming change in the patent regime under TRIPS, because it was no longer possible for Indian companies to produce copies of drugs patented elsewhere. The radical changes in prices that were predicted, however, such as a tenfold increase in the cost of ARVs in poor countries, have not occurred.

While there are important critiques of pharmaceutical company practices to be made, these should be based on a context-sensitive assessment of pricing and access issues in the new patent environment. Jeff Madrick's 2014 editorial in the *New York Times*, which coincided with the release of his much publicized book, *Seven Bad Ideas: How Mainstream Economists Have Damaged America and the World*, offers salient critiques of

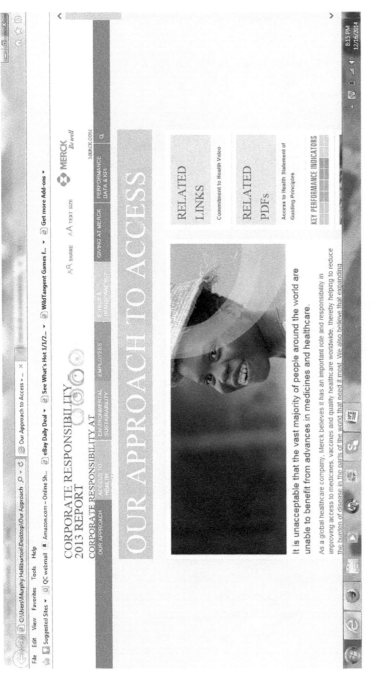

Figure 2. Excerpt from Merck's Corporate Responsibility Program regarding access to medicines.

Global Health

At Pfizer we strive to positively impact the health of people around the world. Our corporate social investment strategy focuses on leveraging the full range of the company's resources — people, skills, expertise and funding — to broaden access to medicines and strengthen health care delivery for underserved people around the world.

See where we're helping to make a difference:

Figure 3. Excerpt from Pfizer's Global Health Programs website, explaining their initiatives around the world.

free trade policies but says regarding the WTO's patent regime that "poor nations like India were forced to pay the same price for patented drugs as the rich West, because they were not allowed to make generic substitutes" (5). This imagines that drug prices in India had already shot up to high-income-country levels, which has not happened. Pharmaceutical companies know customers in low-income countries cannot pay the prices they charge in wealthy countries. These companies have been offering tiered pricing, making drugs available at significantly different costs in high- and low-income countries, and this was the case both before and after TRIPS and the implementation of India's new patent laws. The concern of the pharmaceutical companies in the new patent regime is not so much to make profits from customers in poor countries. Instead, they aim to prevent low-cost drugs from low-income countries from coming into wealthy countries and newly emerging middle-income markets and undermining the high prices they get there. In a way, the prices pharmaceutical products sell for in high-income countries—especially the United States—subsidize prices in low-income countries.

The *New York Times*, in covering the opposition to Gilead's application for a patent on the ARV tenofovir in India in 2006, explained that, at the time, tenofovir sold for $5,718 per person per year in developed countries, whereas the Indian pharmaceutical company Cipla was selling it for $600 per person per year without a license or a patent, as it legally could do up to that point.[2] This comparison made it seem like prices could go up ten times if a patent were awarded. We should have been told the price Gilead was charging in low-income countries at the time, which was $207 per person per year, according to Doctors Without Borders.[3] Cipla also engages in tiered pricing and was, according to the Doctors Without Borders pricing index, charging $195 per person per year for "Low Human Development Index" and $340 per person per year for "Medium Human Development Index" countries. So in the relevant context of prices charged in low-income countries, Gilead, the US patent holder, and Cipla, the Indian generic company, were charging the same price at the time this story came out. There was no clear basis to anticipate that prices in poor countries were suddenly to rise tenfold. A more significant problem was that $200 per person per year was not low enough to make these medications broadly accessible in low-income settings.[4]

The anthropologist Kaushik Sunder Rajan (2012), in an analysis of value in pharmaceutical markets, suggests that prices in poor countries could rise to high-income levels, though he offers only the example of Novartis' Gleevec (imatinib mesylate), which he concedes is also given away in charitable programs in developing countries. He notes that predicting pricing is complicated and acknowledges the use of tiered pricing, which he says is "extremely rare," whereas I would argue that, at least for ARVs, tiered pricing is routine.[5] Although I think it would be unlikely for drug prices in low-income countries to reach the level of developed countries, Sunder Rajan may be right that prices will rise significantly. The remainder of Sunder Rajan's theorization of value in the pharmaceutical industry is important, though, and I will engage it later in this chapter and the next.

I, too, raised concerns about rising prices under the new patent regime, also bringing up the case of tenofovir and citing the concern raised by

Doctors Without Borders that replacing stavudine with tenofovir, which is recommended by the WHO because tenofovir has fewer side effects, would increase the price of therapy from $99 to $426 per person per year.[6] Instead, the price went down 50 percent, largely because of voluntary licensing of this drug to Indian generic companies.

While waiting on the decision over its application for an Indian patent on tenofovir, marketed under the brand name Viread, Gilead issued voluntary licenses to several Indian pharmaceutical companies to produce this medication in return for a five percent royalty (recently reduced to three percent) on whatever price the Indian company decided to sell the product for. Gilead essentially handed over their right to produce this drug for a nominal fee, which was not anticipated by analysts, most of whom figured the post-TRIPS regime would center around *compulsory* licenses, where countries would seize on their right, guaranteed by the Doha Declaration addendum to the TRIPS agreement, to override patents in a public health crisis and produce a medication regardless of the wishes of the patent holder.[7] Gilead's voluntary licensing program and the mass production by Indian companies reduced the lowest available low-income country price for tenofovir from about $200 per person per year when the program started in 2006 to $48 per person per year in 2014, with Gilead's Indian licensing partner Strides currently offering the medication at $26 per person per year.[8]

Gilead's program, as one representative of an Indian pharmaceutical company told me, has at least improved the accessibility of an important medication and sown goodwill between this company and the Indian pharmaceutical sector. The Gilead model has its drawbacks, however, such as leaving middle-income countries off the list of places the licensee is allowed to sell to. Thus the Indian generic partners cannot sell tenofovir to China, Mexico, Brazil, Colombia, and several other South American countries that have significant populations living in poverty. This effort may also turn out to be the exception rather than the rule for multinational pharmaceutical engagement with Indian manufacturers since, being a mid-size company, Gilead does not have significant market prospects in the regions covered by Indian pharmaceutical distributors and Gilead's patent on tenofovir was not approved in India—although Gilead's program predates this decision. While this indicates success in reducing the price of a key AIDS drug in areas that greatly need it, it is not clear how much we can project from this example about solving the problem of access to essential medicines, and there remains a large gap between need and access to lifesaving treatments for people who have HIV/AIDS.[9] If, over the long term, the price of AIDS treatments goes up as new medications are developed for emerging, resistant strains of AIDS under the new patent regime, we may see a reverse in the gains of the last few years against AIDS mortality.

I support the critiques of journalists, researchers, and activists that have engaged pharmaceutical policies on access issues, but our assessment of pharmaceutical company policies and access issues needs more precision. The truth about the role of pharmaceutical companies in pricing and drug access lies somewhere between their self-presentation in their corporate social responsibility materials as saviors of the underserved and the depiction of them as ruthlessly seeking to reap profits off the poor.

Pursuing the Big Pharma Perspective

Because of the difficulty I encountered in attempting to meet with employees of pharmaceutical companies, I decided to follow Hugh Gusterson's (1997) suggestions for "polymorphous engagement" around the periphery of powerful, inaccessible institutions. This is an approach Gusterson developed in his ethnographic study of nuclear weapons scientists whose work was secret and whose laboratories he could not visit. He had to operate around these restrictions, meeting scientists in community settings and through other indirect engagements such as visiting the churches they attended and using media sources to supplement his work. My methods of attempting to get the pharmaceutical companies' perspectives on patent controversies involved tracking corporate actions in the media, doing content analysis of their self-presentations on the Internet, visiting their corporate offices to see what I could glean from the publically accessible areas, and speaking to representatives of companies' international access programs. I had decided, as a polymorphous engagement strategy, not to directly ask, say, a company lawyer about his or her position on patents, as I anticipated it would be hard to get access to such individuals and the topic might be too sensitive to speak about in any form other than a well-vetted press release. Instead, I choose to contact people in corporate philanthropic or social responsibility programs and ask how they balance their defense of patent rights and issues of access to essential medicines for the underserved, a problem I figured they must have reflected on. I also spoke to representatives of pharmaceutical companies in India that had direct business relations with United States–based companies.

The difficulty of deciphering the new patent system for ayurvedic practitioners stems from the unpredictable effects of the coming together of patent law, ayurvedic medicine, and the global political economy. For those concerned about access to biomedical products, the difficulty in assessing the new system stems partly from pharmaceutical companies' desire not to be studied and to control the message they give to the public.

The medical anthropologists Whyte, Van der Geest, and Hardon (2002) discuss Maarten Bode's research on the ayurvedic and unani pharmaceutical industries in India and remark on the apparent ease with which Bode was able to meet manufacturers. They conclude: "Probably the Indian [ayurvedic] companies hoped to gain recognition by allowing a researcher on their premises." They then add that "for the same reason [concern about their reputation] 'Western' producers of pharmaceuticals have done the opposite and closed their doors to social scientists. They have—to the best of our knowledge—never allowed anthropologists to study their companies" (136).

Having worked with both ayurvedic and biomedical producers, I concur in this observation, although I was able to make inroads into directly studying biomedical pharmaceutical companies. Since Whyte, Van der Geest, and Hardon made this point in 2002, direct contact with pharmaceutical companies by social scientists is still rare. There is burgeoning interest in the social analysis of the use of pharmaceuticals. Such research, which has been conducted in various parts of the world, including North America, West Africa, and India, looks at official pharmaceutical policies, how people perceive and use pharmaceuticals, drug marketing and advertisements, and circuits in which pharmaceuticals travel, providing important insights into a world where consumption of medications has surged.[10] It is not common, however, for researchers to gain direct access to pharmaceutical company employees.[11]

What direct information outside researchers do get from inside pharmaceutical companies comes in bits and pieces.[12] Likewise, my penetration of pharmaceutical companies met with limited success, yet my

discussions with employees at Gilead and Pfizer and two majo⸱
cal pharmaceutical producers in India yielded important insigʰ
Van der Geest, and Hardon suggested that "if the *raison d'être* of the ᴅᵣᵤᵦ
industry, profit-making, is so much in conflict with the ideal image of its
products, it is indeed wise to close its doors to inquisitive social scientists
who will certainly focus their attention on what the industry is not showing to the outside world."[13] Since the avoidance of scrutiny seems to be
an explicit strategy of pharmaceutical companies, I have chosen to make
pharmaceutical company obfuscation an additional focus in this chapter.

Pressing On with Pfizer and Gilead

In early October 2010, frustrated with my effort to contact big pharma
companies via information on their websites, I tried a new approach and
made my way in person to the world headquarters of Pfizer. This was easy,
since the headquarters on 42nd Street in Manhattan are only four blocks
off my commute to my office at the City University of New York Graduate
Center. Although I was not too optimistic about making contacts at Pfizer
through this method, I was aware of the serendipity that often occurs
in ethnographic fieldwork, and I felt rewarded when I came through the
main doors and saw the mural that adorns the lobby of Pfizer's headquarters. This mural speaks symbolically to the issues involved in the current
patent regime and to the history of sharing medical knowledge between
cultures, endorsing an ethic of sharing that would seem to contradict contemporary policies on intellectual property. East Asian and Arab figures
are featured in the mural along with an image of a nun, a man in a skull-
cap gazing into a microscope, and a European figure in eighteenth- to
nineteenth-century attire. Chemistry vials are superimposed over these images, which attest to different cultures' efforts to understand disease and
treat the ill. Observing a depiction of what seemed to be a traditional Chinese physician, I could not help thinking of the controversy over the new
patent provisions that allow multinational pharmaceutical companies to
patent a compound based on local medical knowledge in China or India
while blocking manufacturers in these countries from producing biomedical drugs developed by companies like Pfizer. More thoughts were coming
to mind, but one cannot stand staring at this mural for very long before

security guards approach to ask what you are doing. So I walked up to a receptionist at the security cordon, which resembled the check-in area of an airport, explained my research interests, and asked if he knew whom I could contact. The receptionist took my card and said he would try to help. I was pleasantly surprised when he called several days later with a name and number of a Pfizer employee he said could assist me.

After a couple of weeks of calling this person and waiting in vain for a response, I returned to Pfizer's website for further clues about how to reach someone on the inside. The site presents their Global Health Programs along with informational videos and descriptions of available grants but does not provide any information on individuals who work in this division or any contact information for the program. There are only two phone numbers available for all of Pfizer on the website: one for contacts for the press and the other for everyone else. Doubtless the hundred thousand employees of Pfizer have direct phones and their own emails, but these seem to be kept from the public. Several employee names are listed and their accomplishments described on the company website. In some cases, their biographies are presented, but contact information is never provided. Although one can easily find a work phone number or email this way for someone in academia and in many other professions, a Google search of an employee's name and the word "Pfizer" does not yield results. Like many corporations, Pfizer clearly does not want just any employee speaking to outsiders and possibly saying something that may conflict with official company policy. It was also interesting, however, that there seemed to be no portal through which an academic researcher could enter.

After my failed attempt to get my first Pfizer contact to return my calls, my next effort involved calling the one number listed for all of Pfizer on their website. I was told, however, by the person who answered the phone that they could not give me the number for any department of Pfizer, such as their Global Health Programs division, nor for any individual who worked in any department. They simply said they "do not know" any of that information. I followed their suggestion to fill out an online form with my inquiry, hoping to get someone's contact information, but I never received a response.

I called the main phone number again in November and heard the same explanation about not having any information and not being able to connect me with their Global Health Programs department. I thought how strange it would be if someone called the college where I teach and was told by the operator that they did not know the phone numbers for, say, the anthropology department or the provost's office and that they could not connect the caller to either department. I was again told to fill out the online contact form.

I then decided to try calling Pfizer's media relations number, the only phone number that was different from the main number on their website. I figured social science research, and especially the ethnographic work of anthropologists, was not that different from being a reporter. The website declared that the number was to be used by "media professionals only." Currently, the site is more explicit, warning, "Pfizer media contacts may ONLY respond to calls and emails from professional journalists." The person who answered the media number scolded me for not being from the media, but gave me the number of someone in a philanthropic division of the company. This helped me reach an individual I will call Rebecca, who asked me to send my request to speak with someone at Pfizer by email. Rebecca replied several days later—it was early December by this time—saying, "due to business constraints we are unable to participate in your project work at this time," and sent links to the Global Health Programs on Pfizer's website that, by this time, I knew well. I wrote back asking if Pfizer was sure they did not want to comment on their global health programs, adding that I would just like to speak briefly to someone about patents and global access issues. I explained that I planned to publish articles on this topic, that I had spoken to activists and interested parties in India and suggested that Pfizer might be missing out on an opportunity to give their position on these issues. I explained that I wanted to be sure, before I finally decided to leave them alone, that they did not want to be included. Rebecca finally responded, apologizing for her earlier response, and explaining that they get many requests from researchers and cannot respond to all of them. She then scheduled a phone meeting between me and two Pfizer employees. By this time, it was early 2011.

In my conference call with these two representatives, I found them to be well informed on public health and access issues. They described the international programs and grants run by Pfizer that provide free medications and research money to address public health problems. I was also informed that the Pfizer Foundation, a separate legal entity from the manufacturing side of the company, gave significant amounts of money to address public health interventions and preventative measures that did not involve any Pfizer products, an effort that can counter claims that Pfizer access programs merely promote awareness and consumption of their products. They gave the impression of a diverse and well-funded program that was hard to critique in any simple and straightforward way in terms of limitations, conflicts, or double purposes. The projects of the Global Health Fellows listed on their website also support this impression where, for example, Pfizer employee-volunteers developed an information system for healthcare workers in Kenya to distribute workers to underserved areas and conducted research on how gender disparities led to health inequalities in India. Topic-wise, these were not that different from the kinds of projects developed by PhD students in medical anthropology. Other projects did involve the direct use of Pfizer products, such as antimalarial drugs, which are utilized along with prevention measures in Pfizer's "Mobilize Against Malaria" campaign.[14]

The key issue, I figured, was whether a case could be made that these programs compensated for any loss of access to medications people in poor communities experienced or will experience due to TRIPS-related intellectual property laws that Pfizer supports. I had hoped to bring up this topic when we sat down for an in-person interview as these representatives agreed to do, but my requests for a meeting went unanswered.

I also had difficulty trying to arrange a meeting with Gilead Sciences. Whereas Pfizer is the world's largest pharmaceutical manufacturer, with tens of thousands of employees and a wide portfolio of products including several blockbuster drugs (such as Viagra and Lipitor), Gilead is a mid-size, California-based multinational corporation that focuses on a handful of infectious diseases, including HIV/AIDS and hepatitis. Their size and focus may affect how they approach international access issues. Gilead's administrators come "from the bench," according to one employee, referring to the scientific rather than managerial background of their directors. The three top executives in the company have PhDs in biochemistry or organic chemistry, and they focus on a few unambiguous diseases, such as AIDS and hepatitis, while many larger companies develop or acquire just about any drug that can expand their portfolio, whether for major illnesses or what some call "invented" illnesses or "disease inflation."[15]

Unlike the Pfizer website, Gilead's site did provide—at least in 2010—a separate phone number and email address for their "Developing World

Access" program. However, no one answered the phone or returned the emails or voicemails I left saying I was interested in learning more about these programs. This seemed a reasonable request since their site expressly invited visitors to call the number for more information. In 2016, there was no longer any contact information on their "Developing World Access" site, only an email address for persons interested in receiving their newsletter. Perhaps Gilead recently adopted the method of one-way communication that was seen in Merck and Pfizer's websites. The invitation to submit an inquiry to Gilead is no longer there, even though it did not produce responses when it was.

I followed up by calling the main number for Gilead's headquarters in Foster City, California, and was eventually able to reach a representative of the company's access programs who met with me in the summer of 2010 for an informal discussion about Gilead's international programs and its relations to pharmaceutical producers in India. This employee indicated that I would be able to have a more formal interview to discuss Gilead's practices at a later date. After several months of pursuit, I was told I would be able to meet representatives at Gilead's headquarters sometime in July 2011, but I could not get my Gilead contacts to respond to my request to set a meeting date as the weeks went by. Concerned that July was approaching, when I would be free from teaching and the Gilead international access team would have returned from meeting with their generic partners in India, I decided to go ahead and leave for California, hoping that my actually being there would help compel them to meet. After arriving in the Bay Area, I was still not able to secure a meeting, so in early August, I wrote to my Gilead contacts saying that I had made a good-faith effort to arrange an interview in which Gilead had said they were interested, that I was now giving up, and that I was disappointed because I think pharmaceutical companies should speak to researchers about these issues that activists and public health specialists have been addressing. I immediately received an invitation to meet two days later.

This meeting with Polly Fields and Clifford Samuel from Gilead's International Access Operations was productive and informative. Both were gracious and inviting, so different from the kinds of personas I imagined in my communications with evasive pharmaceutical representatives. Ms. Fields had come to Gilead from the Clinton Foundation, where she worked on their international health projects, and Mr. Samuel had previously worked for a big pharma company. We discussed Gilead's relations ı Indian generic producers, its licensing program, and its perspective on patent controversies.

The Gilead Model and Its Replicability

Since 2006, Gilead has entered into what are known as voluntary licensing agreements with Indian pharmaceutical companies. The Indian companies are allowed to produce Gilead's HIV products, and Gilead provides technology transfer, which means that they show the Indian company how to make the drug so that they will not have to undertake the expense of figuring it out themselves. The Indian companies decide on the final sale price, of which Gilead gets a five percent royalty, which was reduced in 2011 to three percent. Thus Gilead's program would potentially add only three to five percent to the price Indian pharmaceutical companies were offering for its drugs before the enactment of India's 2005 patent law. Because of the economies of scale provided by the Indian pharmaceutical producers to whom Gilead has given licenses, however, the price of tenofovir (Gilead brand name Viread) and the fixed dose combination of tenofovir and emtricitabine (Gilead brand name Truvada) has actually gone down by 80 percent. This system of licensing and scaling up of production I call the "Gilead model."

Gilead's Access Program began in 2003 with an effort "to sell ARV products at 'no-profit' prices in developing countries throughout the world," which meant making the drugs available for only the cost of manufacturing and distribution.[16] This involved shipping the medicines from Gilead's manufacturing facilities in Europe and North America and also from its South African partner, Aspen Pharmacare, to distributors in low-income countries. In the first year of the program, one hundred patients received Gilead ARVs, and tenofovir sold for $468 per person per year. By 2006, the program was serving thirty thousand people and the price had gone down to $207 per person per year.[17]

In 2006, Gilead restructured the program, and a key change was the addition of licensing agreements with Indian pharmaceutical manufacturers. Currently, there are sixteen Indian pharmaceutical companies producing generic tenofovir with a license from Gilead, the price has gone down to $48 per person per year, and six million people in low- and middle-income countries are now taking this medication, which is a WHO-recommended first- and second-line treatment for HIV/AIDS. The program does not generate profits, nor is it charity, according to Gilead. It is, they claim, a self-sustaining program maintained by the royalty.

The Gilead model is distinct, as no other companies have such extensive licensing agreements with Indian producers. Gilead was also the first company to participate in the United Nations' patent-sharing clearinghouse, known as the Medicines Patent Pool, and it provides more extensive access to its products through this effort than any big pharma companies that also participate in the Patent Pool. Pharmaceutical companies place patented products in the Patent Pool, and these then become available for any company to license and manufacture for a "fair royalty." Only six companies have placed products in the Patent Pool. Gilead, with six of its own, has the greatest number of products in the pool. The rest have one or two, and most companies taking licenses from the pool are based in India.[18]

Other producers, including Pfizer and Bristol-Myers Squibb (BMS), have been developing relations with Indian pharmaceutical companies, though of a smaller scale and for a different purpose. BMS, for example, voluntarily licensed its ARV atazanavir to India-based Emcure Pharmaceuticals in 2006. While it has other types of access programs, the relations with Indian producers did not proliferate like they did with Gilead.[19] Pfizer announced a partnership of a very different kind with Hyderabad-based Aurobindo, which is also one of Gilead's generic partners. In this deal, Pfizer acquired rights to sell a variety of products manufactured by Aurobindo in the US and European markets in order to grow the generics side of Pfizer's business.[20]

The science and technology studies professor Anne Pollock (2011) has argued that big pharma is not so omnipotent as many analysts claim. The world's largest pharmaceutical company, Pfizer, for example, is looking for ways to expand its revenue since patents have expired on some of its most profitable drugs while drugs in its pipeline have failed to come to market. She claims that critiques of pharmaceutical companies from science and technology studies have made these actors seem omnipotent and says that "many overestimated the pharmaceutical industry's ability to produce blockbuster after blockbuster."[21] This may be why Pfizer was turning to an India-based company to grow its generic line.

It is important to add that Gilead does not have a patent on tenofo- vir in India. With opposition from the Indian Network for People Living with HIV/AIDS and the Indian pharmaceutical company Cipla, Gilead's patent application was denied by the India Patent Office in 2009 because it was a known substance and studies did not indicate increased efficacy over other treatments.[22] The lower toxicity, which explains the appeal of the drug and why it is recommended by the World Health Organization, did not warrant patentability. The implications of this are unclear. It may well mean that opposing and defeating patents will keep prices low or make them lower, compelling companies to go into voluntary licensing with Indian companies. Gilead would point out that its voluntary licensing program started in 2003, years before the tenofovir patent decision, and would claim that the licensing program would have continued just as it has even if a patent were awarded. Gilead executive vice president Gregg Alton at one point warned that the program would be discontinued if their patent were refused, because the product would no longer be Gilead's property in India (Reuters 2007). Yet the program continued after the defeat.

Critics of TRIPS anticipated that one way to react to this new patent regime was to demand compulsory licenses, where a state can legally over- ride a company's patent rights in the case of a health crisis. A license is then given to a producer, allowing it to make another company's patented prod- uct, and a royalty to the patent owner is usually required. Also, the law requires companies first to pursue a voluntary license before applying for a compulsory license. The possibilities of extensive voluntary license partner- ships and successful opposition to patent applications were not foreseen in analyses of the effects of TRIPS.[23] Compulsory licenses are still available as an option, but as we will see in the next chapter, representatives from Indian companies I spoke to prefer to operate under voluntary licenses.

Tiered Pricing, Economies of Scale, and a Sustainable Access Program

In my meeting with Gilead access program employees, the issue of com- pulsory and voluntary licenses came up early on. In explaining Gilead's position, Clifford Samuel said, "If a country feels that they have to issue a compulsory license because there's a pandemic in their country and they need to address this pandemic for its citizens, fine, do it. However, our model, what we are trying to demonstrate, is how you can responsibly use intellectual property, and it's through a tiered pricing approach."

In a tiered pricing approach, he explained, you need to look at a country's ability to pay: "You look at the GNI [gross national income] per capita and the prevalence of this pandemic, and then you set the price . . . and then the voluntary licensing component where you say let's give this license to Indian generic partners. They have the option to sell product in a region hardest hit—and they can sell the API [active pharmaceutical ingredient] to each other—and we get a nominal five percent royalty, which we've just reduced to three percent."

Clifford Samuel and Polly Fields emphasized that their international access program is not philanthropy or what is known today as "corporate social responsibility," but a self-sustaining partnership. Ms. Fields explained that this is what makes their model successful: "It's a social contract piece, but it's different from CSR [corporate social responsibility]. Once again, it's not philanthropy for us. Our role is to advocate for the model, and you can't really advocate for it if it's not sustainable. The only way it's sustainable is for it to be financially viable." She brought up the Bill and Melinda Gates Foundation, which along with the Clinton Foundation has been one of the largest contributors to AIDS prevention and treatment programs around the world, and explained, "Donation programs are great, but that's not a long-term solution for anybody."

Clifford Samuel followed up on this comment with an illustration:

> Bristol Myers and those guys had a wonderful program called Secure the Future. Millions and millions of dollars went into it, and then it was stopped. The thing is with some of these initiatives that are well meaning, if the company starts going through some . . . like the financial economic crisis that we saw, when they start looking "where do we tighten the belt"? It's these types of corporate social responsibility programs that get slashed, to the detriment of people who need it most.

Therefore, he added, "The goal is to create something that is self-sustaining, a sustainable program. And therefore it can stand on its feet. It has legs. And it's not this welfare entity that you create because that's not viable in the long run."

Viiv Healthcare, "a global specialist HIV company" created by Glaxo-SmithKline and Pfizer in 2009 that develops new AIDS medications and tries to ensure access through pricing and licensing schemes, also claims to be sustainable in this way, so this practice is not unique to Gilead.[24] Viiv Healthcare was established several years after Gilead's access program began, and it has adopted similar methods.

Another explanation for why the partnerships with Indian companies developed is that Gilead could not produce the high volume of drugs for the people that could benefit from tenofovir, which did not have the severe, sometimes fatal side effects of the alternative drug stavudine. Clifford Samuel explained that they could not produce "branded" medications—that is, medications they produce themselves as Gilead brands—at low enough prices for them to be widely accessible. "The cost of goods alone would be so high," he said, "and when we looked at who was known for manufacturing around the globe at low cost, it's the Indian generic partners [that is, the companies that would become Gilead's Indian generic partners]. They're very good at it. They're good at low-cost, large capacity, and what they do have more than anything, they have the scientists that can do the BE [bioequivalence] studies and do all of the necessary work. So it was a natural move that we should seek Indian generic partners to assist."

An employee of a generic pharmaceutical company I met in Hyderabad affirmed this view when he explained in concise terms his company's business strategy: "Our game is only economies of scale." Other companies in India that are moving away from the generic model to pursue research and development in the wake of the new Patents Act still emphasize their capacity for low-cost production.

The price of tenofovir and the effectiveness of activists depict an encouraging scenario for access to essential medicine, but HIV/AIDS might be an unusual situation. Polly Fields explained that the Gilead program works well for HIV/AIDS because HIV is a "unique space," where "you have financing, you have guidelines, you have a lot of organized advocacy." She added that you need a variety of elements and actors to come together to make access work in underserved places:

> We do what we do well, but we need the other stars to align. We need the
> WHO to change guidelines [as it did in replacing stavudine with tenofovir].

We need the advocates to advocate for broader treatment access and with the highest quality drugs. We need the governments to mandate the national programs and really have the political will to work with the ministry of finance, work with the ministry of health to ensure that there are sustainable programs. So everyone has a role to play.

Sometimes, she said, they can convene these players, and sometimes others bring the various stakeholders together. But, she explained, "We don't shy away from being at the table in those discussions and don't shy away from the criticism."

An Indian producer I spoke with cited the same factors in explaining why the cost of tenofovir came down as much as it did. So it appears the stars aligned with tenofovir, but the situation might not be replicable without a similar convening of multiple actors and political will. With more neglected diseases, like malaria or dengue fever, that overwhelmingly affect those with the least capacity to pay for drugs, the challenge is greater. The Gilead representatives I spoke to are aware of this problem and say the issue comes down to finding an "economic engine" to address it:

> CLIFFORD: Those other neglected diseases, the reason why they are called "neglected" is because there is no funding there.
>
> POLLY: And no commercial opportunities.
>
> CLIFFORD: And no commercial opportunities. And the large pharma companies aren't going to develop something that can't be sold in the US and Europe where, from a tiered pricing perspective, is where they make their core dollars. I think that's the bigger challenge: how do you make an economic engine that can fund things like malaria and TB and dengue and some of these other neglected diseases?

These are important points to be considered when we assess the future impact of the new patent regime, especially since so much of the research and media attention around the effect of the new patent policies has focused on AIDS, a disease that affects rich and poor countries with a lot of political mobilization behind accessing treatment.

As Clifford Samuel observes, pharmaceutical companies make their "core dollars" in the United States and Europe, so if an illness affects only people in low-income areas, there will be little financial incentive to develop medications for such problems. Finding financial incentives for developing treatments for neglected diseases has been an ongoing concern. People like Thomas Pogge of the Health Impact Fund—a group that rewards innovators based on the health impact, rather than the sales, of their creations—have offered novel proposals to cope with problems of incentive in drug innovation. These programs will be discussed in the conclusion.

Voluntary licensing may have a role in expanding access when treatments are developed for neglected diseases, but this mechanism must be understood within the context of the goals of pharmaceutical marketing. Clifford Samuel explained that multinational companies are looking to "emerging market countries" for expanded business opportunities. He gave the example of the BRICS, an acronym that refers to Brazil, Russia, India, China, and South Africa. He also used the term to refer to pharmaceutical company interests in emerging markets more broadly, explaining that "Part of their whole ability to grow revenues in the next five to ten years will come from the BRICS, which includes Indonesia, India, China, Thailand, Cambodia, and some of these countries." Also, while tenofovir is available to the poor in Asia and Africa at low prices through Gilead's generic partners, Gilead sells its own branded products, which are more expensive but are adjusted for local economies in Latin America. The effect of voluntary licensing on the price of tenofovir is encouraging, but critics of this system have claimed voluntary licenses can be like "golden handcuffs" for Indian producers by limiting the sale of these drugs to the lowest income countries.

Patent Oppositions and the Limitations of Voluntary Licensing

As mentioned earlier, other companies have voluntarily licensed products: most significantly, Viiv Healthcare, the joint venture to produce HIV medications by GlaxoSmithKline, Pfizer, and Shionogi. Viiv focuses on licensing of pediatric formulations of two of their AIDS medications, but Gilead's program is more extensive.

One of Viiv Healthcare's drugs in the Patent Pool is abacavir, which is not patented in India. GlaxoSmithKline withdrew its application for a patent on abacavir in 2007 after the Indian Network for People Living with HIV/AIDS, with the help of I-MAK and Doctors Without Borders, challenged it under Section 3d of India's Patents Act.[25] What are we to make of the fact that two of the ARVs in the Patent Pool—two medications that are the basis of probably most of the voluntary licensing agreements, tenofovir and abacavir—were not awarded patents in India? A new, second-line ARV, maraviroc, was granted a patent in India in 2007, but Viiv Healthcare/Pfizer has not placed this product in the Patent Pool. I have not found evidence of any voluntary licenses involving this medication, though one has been requested by India-based Natco Pharmaceuticals.[26]

Voluntary licensing agreements may be serving as instruments for companies to continue something like a relationship of ownership to the product in the face of the nonrecognition of their patent claims. GSK withdrew its patent application on abacavir soon after Novartis withdrew a patent application on similar grounds earlier the same year.[27] Then GSK began to license abacavir voluntarily through Viiv Healthcare. In fact, Viiv Healthcare was created in 2009, soon after the withdrawal of this application, and it now voluntarily licenses several AIDS medications.[28] Gilead's extensive voluntary licensing program focuses mostly on tenofovir, which is not patented in India although the program began before the patent was defeated. This may mean that opposing patent applications in India can keep drug prices low (or lower). Or it may mean, as suggested earlier, that these pharma companies do not want to put too much of an effort into fighting for patents and making money through increased pricing in developing countries. They may be more interested in protecting markets in middle- and high-income countries and places with emerging economies. Perhaps they want people with HIV in low-income countries to have access to their medicines, as they all claim, as long as they can do this in a way that does not result in spillover into their higher-end markets.[29]

When a producer, such as an Indian pharmaceutical company, accepts a licensing agreement to manufacture a drug, such as Gilead's tenofovir, the agreement specifies the countries the company can export the drugs to, and the licensee is not allowed to export the drug to any countries not on this list. While acknowledging apparent benefits of Gilead's voluntary licensing program, Doctors Without Borders offers the critique that the licenses allow exports to "least developed countries" and some "developing countries" but do not permit exports to middle-income countries that have potentially lucrative markets, such as Brazil and China.[30] Gilead negotiates prices for middle-income countries on a case-by-case basis and sells its own Gilead-brand products in these places. This is consistent with its tiered pricing approach where prices are determined according to a country's gross national income. The problem may be that a country's gross national income can be misleading in representing a population's ability to pay for medications. For example, the concern of Doctors Without Borders is that although Brazil and China are "middle-income" countries, they have substantial populations that live in poverty.[31]

My examination of voluntary license agreements in the Patent Pool confirms that Brazil, China, and other middle-income countries are routinely left off the lists of countries that licensees are allowed to sell to. Of the eleven licenses posted on the Patent Pool website, nine show the list of countries where the licensing manufacturer can sell the drugs.[32] All of these licenses, which are for medications to treat HIV/AIDS, list between 73 and 112 countries where the medication can be sold, and none of these lists include China or Brazil. Most also do not allow sales in other middle-income countries in Latin America, such as Colombia, Mexico, or Venezuela, with the exception of Viiv Healthcare's (GSK, Pfizer, and Shionogi) licenses for the pediatric versions of abacavir and dolutegravir, which include Argentina, Chile, Colombia, and Venezuela.[33] When companies exclude China, Brazil, and other middle-income countries, several million people with HIV/AIDS do not have access to the products the Patent Pool makes available at low prices. The number of people with HIV/AIDS in these areas is hard to specify mostly because there is little information on HIV prevalence in China. Even if China were to have one of the lowest prevalence rates in the world, this could mean that several million people have HIV there. UNAIDS estimates that 610,000–1,000,000 people are living with HIV/AIDS in Brazil alone. Mexico, Colombia, and Venezuela, which are regularly left out of license agreements, have low rates of prevalence but, combined, have close to half a million people living with HIV/AIDS (UNAIDS 2015b).[34]

An executive for an Indian pharmaceutical company that produces products voluntarily licensed by Gilead—and has also produced medications under compulsory license—told me that one drawback of the voluntary licenses is the limitations on the countries where his company could sell these products. In his comments, he specifically highlighted the exclusion of Brazil. He added that it would be good to have access to the Brazilian market due to the large numbers of poor there. He also praised Gilead's voluntary licensing initiatives for sowing goodwill between the Indian and multinational pharmaceutical industries.

Pharmaceutical company policies have a major effect on drug prices and access, but they are hard to critique in a succinct and easily comprehensible way. In the case of Gilead, their access program was effective at lowering the price of a major ARV. Simple critiques, such as the suggestion that pharmaceutical companies want to charge developed-country prices and make profits off the poor, miss what is really at stake with these companies: protecting high prices in developed-country markets and their interests in emerging middle-income markets.

Again, the debate is tricky. Pharmaceutical companies would say that this is fair because countries pay according to what they can afford, which is hard to argue with as a general principle. The problems are whether a place that is "middle income" like Brazil has large segments of poor that are left out of pricing consideration and the fact that the lowest prices offered by multinational brand producers *and* Indian producers are out of reach for vast segments of the world's poor.

Defeating drug patents in the Indian courts seems to have an effect, with the caveats mentioned above. It would be nice to be able to say that the defeat of patents led to voluntary licensing, but the most significant voluntary licensing program, the Gilead model, began well before the significant ARV patent defeats. There does seem to be some correspondence between patent defeats in India and the drugs that are available for license through the Patent Pool, and voluntary licensing agreements and the ensuing scale-up of production have not occurred with drugs that were awarded patents in India. The difficulty of gaining access to pharmaceutical companies makes it challenging to know what is in store and what is at stake in some of these policies. These companies hold their cards even more closely to their chests than did Dr. Vijayan's ayurvedic pharmaceutical company and other interests in ayurvedic drug production discussed in the last chapter. This may be because, as Anne Pollock (2011) suggests, they are more vulnerable than we think they are, and because, as with my assessment of Dr. Vijayan's company, they are uncertain of what to do in the new patent environment. They move forward tentatively while glancing at the moves of other companies, governments, and courts.

Finally, while much of the analysis of pharmaceutical production focuses on big pharma, the Gilead model may indicate that pharmaceutical companies vary in relation to their size and the kinds of medical problems they address. A company that focuses on major, debilitating infectious disease such as AIDS and hepatitis may make different choices than a company that focuses on these kinds of diseases plus "lifestyle" problems and medicalized conditions, such erectile dysfunction and premenstrual dysphoric disorder, or anything that can add to a company's portfolio.

Also, size limits the production capacity and thus the ambition for market hegemony. The Gilead representatives I spoke to said they could not produce enough medications for even a portion of the potential market for tenofovir even if they wanted to. Similarly, an executive I spoke to from one of Gilead's licensees in Hyderabad said that Gilead has nothing to lose in its international access model, since it is not large enough to serve a potential market in the countries where the Indian companies are selling their products. This makes it easier to voluntarily license drugs, and the license protects leakage into Gilead's primary markets. Clifford Samuel claimed that it was not just size but the ideology of the company that is important, and he explained that he and others who had formerly worked in big pharma, and Polly Fields, who had worked at the Clinton Foundation, were attracted to Gilead because its priorities were different. "Sometimes it has to do with just the philosophy," he explained. "Many of us came from big pharma and wanted to apply a different approach. So, you know, you could start small and grow up and become big pharma in the sense of the mentality and approaches. We really looked at what we can do differently even in the way we manufacture a product." Most of the senior executives at Gilead are scientists who had a career in the lab, often in academic settings, although, as with any corporate policymakers, they have to answer to the venture capitalists who want to see a return on their investments. The senior leaders in Pfizer, by contrast, have backgrounds primarily in business and finance and less training in science.

The anthropologists Kaushik Sunder Rajan (2012) and Joseph Dumit (2012), who have examined the pharmaceutical and biotech industries, claim that pharmaceutical companies in the United States are driven by the goal of realizing "surplus health," a concept of health that involves maximizing the intake of medications and an effort to prevent future health problems. This is different from the idea of healthiness, which involves living a healthy lifestyle and taking medicines only occasionally.[35] Similar points are raised in claims that pharmaceutical companies are engaged in "disease inflation," which involves the medicalizing of experiences that were not formerly seen as pathological and the lowering of "diagnostic thresholds," and by critics who say that pharmaceutical companies are "selling sickness" by expanding illness categories.[36] These are all methods of increasing drug sales and bringing new medicines into the patent pipeline in an industry whose profitability is based on the need to generate new products constantly.

This signals the emergence of orientations to health that should be of great concern. The concept of health and business models, however, varies by the size and orientation of the pharmaceutical company and characterizes Pfizer better than Gilead. Gilead may yet find itself at a crossroads where its orientation to infectious disease (currently prioritizing HIV/AIDS and hepatitis, with a few drugs addressing cancer and heart disease) conflicts with the concerns of its investors, and they may be pushed to adhere more closely to the model of value described by Sunder Rajan. Indian pharmaceutical companies may also eventually adopt the surplus health orientation of United States–based pharmaceutical companies if the new Patents Act leads them to more research and development and a model of profitability based on the constant production of new medications.

5

THE VIEW FROM HYDERABAD

The "Indian" Pharmaceutical Industry and the New Patent Regime

The "Indian" pharmaceutical industry is not confined to India. India-based companies span the globe. In Hyderabad, the seat of a former empire and now a high-tech boomtown of southern India, pharmaceutical companies occupy slick new office parks alongside technology and financial companies around a large business development district known as HITEC City. Meanwhile, just south of New Brunswick among the many nondescript warehouses and office parks near the New Jersey Turnpike are manufacturing and distribution centers for India-based pharmaceutical companies. Mumbai-based Sun Pharma and Hyderabad-based Aurobindo operate manufacturing centers near Monroe Township, and in Princeton, facilities operated by Hyderabad-based Dr. Reddy and Delhi-based Ranbaxy can be found near other United States– and foreign-based pharmaceutical company offices in a corridor of pharmaceutical production that runs from New York City to Philadelphia. In this chapter, I analyze predictions about the future of the Indian pharmaceutical industry in the new patent environment along with the perspectives of pharmaceutical representatives I met in India on issues of production and research and development in the post-TRIPS period. The presence of these Indian companies in the United States illustrates, however, that categories and terms that are used to discuss relations between Indian pharmaceutical companies and foreign multinational companies are problematic and need to be analyzed and deconstructed before we can understand the experience of "Indian" companies in the new patent regime. Indian companies are not simply small, generic producers; nor are they mere victims of large "multinational" firms.

Categorizing Pharmaceutical Companies

Media coverage and academic research often depict an opposition between "big pharma," or "multinational pharmaceutical companies," and "Indian" companies, which are often described as "generic" manufacturers. We are led to imagine that Indian companies are relatively small producers confined to India whereas "big pharma" is multinational, dominating the global scene and buying up smaller companies. While certain big pharma companies, such as Pfizer or Merck, are bigger than any India-based pharma company, the presence of companies such as Sun Pharma and Dr. Reddy's in the New Jersey pharmaceutical corridor testifies to the fact that many India-based companies are large and multinational as well. Sun Pharma operates a total of eight facilities in the United States that supply chain drugstores and managed-care providers (see photo of Sun Pharma's facility in Cranbury, New Jersey, figure 4). This is in addition to their twenty-one facilities in India and their manufacturing centers in Bangladesh, Brazil, Canada, Hungary, Ireland, Israel, Malaysia, Mexico, Morocco, Nigeria, Romania, and South Africa. Aside from its Princeton facility, Hyderabad-based Dr. Reddy's Pharmaceuticals has offices in Japan and Mexico. Cipla, which has often made the news for defying the new patent regime, has its headquarters in Mumbai and offices in Belgium, the United Kingdom, and Florida. Hyderabad-based Aurobindo, which was identified among industry insiders I met as one of the most "Indian" of Indian pharmaceutical companies for being more independent of foreign investment, has two production and distribution facilities in New Jersey. They also sell their products in over one hundred countries and produce medications for a United States–based company.

Figure 4. One of Sun Pharmaceuticals' three New Jersey facilities. Photo by author.

More accurate terms for these companies might therefore be "multinational pharmaceutical companies based in the United States," or "based in Europe," and "multinational pharmaceutical companies based in India," although these are more ponderous than "big," "global," "multinational," or "Indian." I will not use these unwieldy labels but will highlight the terminology and use a variety of synonyms in this chapter.

India and China now provide 80 percent of the active ingredients in all drugs sold worldwide.[1] A pill that is assembled by a United States–based multinational and given that company's branded label in the United States often contains active ingredients made in India or China. Indian and other multinationals have become highly enmeshed in other ways. Multinationals from high-income countries have acquired companies and opened offices in India, but this does not yet augur a rampant takeover of India-based companies by non-Indian companies. Most significant was the acquisition of Ranbaxy by Japanese producer Daiichi Sankyo in 2008. Although seemingly an example of a takeover of an Indian company by a foreign multinational, the story of this acquisition and its aftermath upends the conceptual opposition between Indian and multinational companies in two ways.

First, Daiichi Sankyo acquired Ranbaxy in order to expand its own network since "global" Daiichi Sankyo had a *smaller* global network than "Indian" Ranbaxy.[2] After acquisition, Daiichi Sankyo used Ranbaxy's network to expand its access to markets in Africa, Europe, and Latin America.[3] Second, in 2014, Daiichi-owned Ranbaxy was acquired by India-based Sun Pharmaceuticals.[4] So what seemed to be a harbinger of takeovers by foreign multinationals was a takeover by a Japanese multinational seeking to expand its network through a more multinational Indian company. Then that Japanese-owned Indian multinational was acquired by another Indian multinational producer. And before Daiichi Sankyo even came into the picture, Ranbaxy had acquired the US company Ohm Labs in 1995 and German and French companies in 2000 and 2004.[5]

Though we are far from seeing the Indian pharmaceutical sector become simply a place for outsourcing for foreign multinationals, one practice that has emerged is the outsourcing of research and clinical trials to India through what are known as Contract Research and Manufacturing Services (CRAMS) and Contract Research Organizations (CROs). Although these organizations provide services mostly to foreign-based companies, Indian companies also use these services to develop their products and even outsource their clinical trials to other countries.[6]

The dichotomy of the Indian *generic* producer versus the foreign multinational is also problematic. Many Indian companies are involved in research and development to create new products, and some buy small companies to acquire their products that are in development, just as big pharma does. Meanwhile, several companies that focus on generic products are based in the United States and other high-income countries and are multinational, such as Israel-based Teva and United States–based Mylan, which bought the Indian generic producer Matrix. As was the case with the Daiichi acquisition of Ranbaxy, the foreign multinational benefited from the Indian company's global presence in Mylan's acquisition: "Ironically, Matrix will also give Mylan a global footprint including Europe and in emerging markets like China and Africa. Matrix is already present in Belgium, the Netherlands, and Luxembourg through its acquisition of Docpharma."[7]

Before the acquisition by Mylan, Matrix had also acquired a Chinese pharmaceutical producer. Meanwhile, a Hyderabad-based company has been producing medications for Pfizer's generic line of products.[8] Thus generic producers can be Indian or foreign-owned and multinational.

To complicate the picture further, some "Indian generic producers" have started engaging in research and development, and they do so in the same way as United States– and Europe-based companies, including relying on university research and adopting ideas from other medical systems. For example, Ranbaxy's Synriam was based on a new chemical entity (NCE), developed by a Swiss NGO dedicated to finding new treatments for malaria and US university researchers, which Ranbaxy combined with an already-existing drug and brought to clinical trials. The NCE itself was based on artemisinin, a plant-derived medicine that has been used to treat malaria in traditional Chinese medicine since at least the third century.[9] The Chinese scientist Youyou Tu isolated the active ingredient in *Artemisia annua,* which she read about in an early Chinese medical text, and in 2015 she received the Nobel Prize in Medicine for reviving this antimalarial.

Perspectives and Predictions for the Indian Pharmaceutical Sector

The reaction of Indian biomedical pharmaceutical producers to the TRIPS patent regime is, like the ayurvedic practitioners' reactions, marked by uncertainty. Arguably, the changes in the biomedical pharmaceutical industry are easier to decipher, though they still run counter to expectations—as, for example, with the feared rise in the price of drugs that has not yet occurred. It is important to remember that the problems examined here are emerging, that constellations of power, such as the new assemblage of law, medicine, and global economic forces, can have unpredictable results. India-based pharmaceutical producers are navigating this new environment, and they are facing a variety of opportunities and adversities. These include the possibility of developing new products and competing with other international producers and the prospect of being acquired by multinational companies for the outsourcing of pharmaceutical manufacturing.

In considering the future of Indian pharmaceutical companies in the WTO-compliant IP regime, the anthropologist Kaushik Sunder Rajan argues that Indian producers are in the process of becoming "outsourced manufacturing facilities for multinational pharmaceutical companies."[10] Referring to acquisitions of Indian pharmaceutical companies by Western- and Japan-based companies, Sunder Rajan says:

> These moves suggest the difficulties of surviving as a large Indian generics company in the post-WTO climate, where reverse engineering new drugs be- comes legally difficult or impossible, and where moving to a research and development–driven business model that involves competing with global pharmaceutical powers is strategically difficult. But they are also consonant with the move of the Euro-American research and development–driven in- dustry to focus increasingly on mergers and acquisitions rather than research and development to build their own capabilities and ensure their survival.[11]

Although there are issues here we need to attend to, for now reverse engi- neering and generic production are very much alive because of the defeat of patents and the proliferation of licensing agreements. Also, although mergers and acquisitions play a significant role in pharmaceutical com- pany strategies, this has many dimensions beyond the acquisition of Indian companies by multinationals as we saw in the previous section. Moving to a research and development model is a challenge to Indian companies, as Sunder Rajan rightly observes, but some of these companies have been un- dertaking new research and development, and several patented products developed in India have already been released.

If research and development does continue to grow in India, it is im- portant to consider another observation by Sunder Rajan. He divides the world of patients into "those who die due to a lack of therapeutic ac- cess; and . . . those who might die due to therapeutic excess," referring to the problems of lack of access to essential medicines for the poor and the therapeutic excess, or overmedication, that is promoted in the United States.[12] As the Indian pharmaceutical sector continues to develop new products, we should observe whether an orientation toward therapeutic excess, or "surplus health," develops among India-based companies and the higher income customers they sell to, such as the US customers they access through their distribution centers in New Jersey.[13]

For now, many people around the world suffer from a lack of thera- peutic access and remain far from a situation of therapeutic excess. There are also some who suffer from both a lack of therapeutic access and thera- peutic excess at the same time. As I have observed in Kerala, some people suffer from dengue fever, which affects low-income countries and has no pharmaceutical treatment, while at the same time they are saturated with antibiotics and psychiatric medications, which are liberally distributed at clinics, dispensaries, and hospitals.

Supporters of the new patent regime argue that the environment now provides an incentive for new research and development in India, and hopefully this will lead to more R&D for neglected diseases that affect low-income countries. The former Doctors Without Borders and Patent Pool official Ellen 't Hoen (2005) predicted that, contrary to such hopeful assessments, TRIPS would not lead to "adequate R&D in developing countries for diseases such as malaria and tuberculosis, because poor countries often do not provide sufficient profit potential to motivate R&D investment."[14] Other public health activists countered the claim that new patent laws will spur investment in R&D in poor countries with this same point.[15] The concern that R&D for diseases of the underprivileged will be meager may be borne out in the long run. However, early returns are more encouraging: the first pharmaceutical to be patented by an India-based company under India's new law was for an antimalarial drug, Ranbaxy's Synriam (arterolane maleate and piperaquine phosphate), patented in 2012 and launched in seven African countries in 2014. Ranbaxy considers the drug part of its corporate social responsibility efforts, and the Indian government contributed funds to developing the medication. Investors are not sanguine, however, about the development because it is only marketable in low-income countries.[16]

Viewed from the outside, the position of India-based pharmaceutical producers under the new patent system looks complex and intriguing, involving a number of unanticipated alliances and developments. From inside two pharmaceutical companies I visited in India, the perspective depends on the goals of each company, with one looking for new opportunities in the new environment and the other maintaining the same approach as it did prior to the new Patents Act.

The View from Hyderabad

Deciding that I needed to get the perspective of Indian pharmaceutical companies, because they were key players in these patent controversies and several were going into voluntary licensing partnerships with Gilead and other companies, I traveled to India in 2012 hoping to speak with representatives of Indian producers. Although these companies have manufacturing centers and corporate offices all over India, my main destination was Hyderabad, the southern Indian city that is the hub of the pharmaceutical sector. Making contacts with Indian pharmaceutical representatives was not much easier than arranging meetings with their counterparts in the United States. I began in March to try to arrange meetings for my visit in June. After numerous emails and phone calls to twelve different companies, which included sending them a copy of my letter of affiliation from the prestigious Centre for Policy Research in New Delhi, I had a few leads in Hyderabad and with Ranbaxy, in Gurgaon, a suburb of Delhi.

I was eager to meet with employees of Ranbaxy, since it is one of Gilead's largest generic partners and was producing several of Gilead's ARVs under voluntary license. After emailing the research and development and corporate communications departments at Ranbaxy on several occasions, I finally heard from someone who said he was willing to meet with me, but I had trouble getting him to agree to a date. As with my trip to visit Gilead, the day when I would have to depart was getting closer, but I was not able to confirm any meetings. I had received emails indicating only a general willingness to be involved in this research project. During earlier fieldwork, examining treatments for mental illness in Kerala, I had a much easier time setting up meetings and interviews. Healers readily discussed their techniques, patients shared their life histories with me, and I was invited to observe therapy sessions.

I decided to try the approach that ultimately worked with Gilead. I left the United States bound for India. My first stop was to be Delhi, and I alerted my contact at Ranbaxy, letting him know what dates I would be in town. When my flight touched down at Indira Gandhi International Airport on a late morning in June, the pilot welcomed us to India and said the temperature outside was 40 degrees (104°F). The first few days, I struggled to adapt to the heat while meeting with colleagues and researchers I knew. I did manage to reach my contact at Ranbaxy by phone, and told him I hoped I could meet him before I left for Hyderabad. He explained he was about to go to a meeting and would call me back when he was done. I waited by the phone in my hotel room in vain and was not able to reach him again. Once again, as in the United States, I was struck by the challenges of studying how corporate institutions operate in the contemporary environment, while academic or government experts proved much more open to inquiry. In New Delhi, for example, I had a fruitful meeting with researchers at a government think-tank that worked on intellectual property and was able to consult with a colleague at a university. The government researchers who had not fled to the hills to escape the sweltering weather were very accommodating, and we had an extensive discussion about the TKDL and concerns about biopiracy.

Still determined to reach Indian pharmaceutical representatives, I headed back to the airport for my flight to Hyderabad, hopeful that my contacts in the corporate sector there would be more fruitful. While I did not think I could go door-to-door trying to find a company that would speak to me if these connections failed, I felt that, being in a city with so many pharmaceutical headquarters, I could somehow learn about the Indian pharmaceutical sector's perspective on recent patent controversies. I eventually was able to meet with representatives of two companies I call Osmania and Kanaka Pharmaceuticals.[17]

When my plane from Delhi landed in Hyderabad in the late morning, the pilot said it was 22 degrees (72°F) outside. I thought I must have done the math wrong in converting Celsius to Fahrenheit, but because Hyderabad has some altitude up on the Deccan plateau and the monsoon had arrived, it was almost cool compared to Delhi. The climate in Hyderabad also turned out to be more comfortable for meeting with pharmaceutical representatives.

Hyderabad: Cyberabad and Pharmacity

Hyderabad is a major boomtown of the Indian subcontinent, rivaled only by Bangalore and Mumbai. Aided by the aggressive economic development policies of Andra Pradesh chief minister Chandrababu Naidu, this city has seen an explosion of high-tech industries in the last two decades. Currently the combined capital of the state of Andra Pradesh and the newly created state of Telangana, Hyderabad has been a cosmopolitan center of the subcontinent for centuries. A popular tourist attraction in Hyderabad is Golconda Fort, which is the original walled city that later expanded to become Hyderabad. Tourists can wander through the remains of residences, temples, citadels, and mosques of Golconda and experience a sound and light show depicting the age when the Qutb Shahi kings hosted visitors from other nations and empires, fought off invasions from neighboring kingdoms, and enjoyed the cosmopolitan life of the city from the 1300s to the 1600s. Modern India is a single nation-state, but for thousands of years the Indian subcontinent had been divided into many countries, nations, and empires. The region around Golconda and Hyderabad has long been a nation-state known as Hyderabad, which, like the Mughal Empire, was ruled by Persian monarchs, and this territory remained a semi-independent princely state until shortly after India became free from British rule.

In the late 1500s, Golconda was bursting at the seams. One of its rulers built the Charminar monument—a triumphal arch and mosque that is still the architectural icon of Hyderabad—to mark the center of a new, expanded city outside the walls of Golconda, which is now known as the old town. In the 1990s, under the auspices of chief minister Chandrababu Naidu, Hyderabad saw another major expansion around an area known as HITEC (for Hyderabad Information Technology and Engineering Consultancy) City or "Cyberabad," a modern sprawl that is home to a growing information technology and pharmaceutical sector.

When you arrive at Hyderabad's elegant new Rajiv Gandhi International Airport, it is hard to tell you are in a country with major problems of poverty and poor infrastructure. Heading to HITEC City on the highway, you pass billboards advertising new direct flights from Hyderabad to Kuala Lumpur, London, and elsewhere. Entering HITEC City, the urban landscape begins to resemble Los Angeles, with the fast-paced urban expansion around Gachibowli and the Jubilee Hills area. This part of Hyderabad, with its wide boulevards, office parks, and deluxe hotels, is home to software, pharmaceutical, biotech, and other businesses. High-end local and international chain restaurants, stores, and malls also line the boulevards. Unlike other Indian urban areas, where buildings and people are closely packed together and the roads teem with buses, bicycles, and autorickshaws, this area is designed for car traffic, with no public parks or walkable public roads.

The pharmaceutical sector and other high-tech industries are at the center of Hyderabad's rampant growth, providing the cash that the upper middle class spends at the Diesel, Steve Madden, and Tissot stores in the area and the pubs that serve Belgian beer—spaces of consumerism that most people in India do not have access to.

Thus the physical settings where Hyderabad and United States–based companies operate resemble each other, which is appropriate because in many ways India-based and United States–based pharmaceutical companies are not that different. Both are concerned about their image and about managing what they say to the public, and both are driven by the need to make a profit. Lest anyone think that Indian pharmaceutical companies are concerned only with marketing drugs for the poor, it should be noted that several blockbuster medications in high-income markets, including atorvastatin (Lipitor) and sildenafil citrate (Viagra), are also mass-produced by Indian companies. Two executives whom I tried, unsuccessfully, to meet at a particular company in Hyderabad earned $106 million and $20 million in annual compensation according to their Forbes.com profiles, and in India, prices for consumer items, real estate, and other products are a fraction of what they are in the West. Because of the low cost of scientific labor in India and economies of scale, Indian companies are able to sell medications at low prices while offering generous compensation among their higher ranks.

While workers at both Indian and United States–based pharmaceutical industries are concerned about profitability, many also take seriously the issue of drug access. India-based companies work on access issues as long as these do not interfere with getting what they think is an appropriate return on their investments, and, like United States–based companies, they also have corporate social responsibility programs to aid the underserved in ways that go beyond their low-price manufacturing. For example, Ranbaxy's Community Healthcare Society operates a fleet of vans in north India that provide healthcare services to the poor. The company says this effort has greatly reduced the incidence of infant and maternal mortality in the areas served. The corporate social responsibility section of their website also highlights their low cost ARVs and their new antimalaria medication.[18] Additionally, like foreign-based multinational companies, Indian companies are beginning to engage in biopiracy practices to develop new drugs—Ranbaxy's antimalarial, the first patented product developed in India under the new law, is based in part on a treatment from traditional Chinese medicine.

Economies of Scale, Research and Development, and Other Priorities of Indian Pharmaceutical Companies

When I visited Hyderabad in 2012, I stayed at one of the many new hotels in HITEC City and ventured out from there to meet with the employees I had contacted at pharmaceutical companies. The Aditya Sarovar was part of an Indian hotel chain, and the interior design of the building was cutting edge, with rooms full of new electronic gadgetry and trendy restaurants on the ground floor. I got to return to Hyderabad in 2014 for a conference at the Indian Institute of Technology and was put up by the organizers in another HITEC City hotel, another space of impressive design, featuring contemporary art and sculpture and high-end restaurants and bars. This was the India of the affluent new business class, and it felt quite different from the India I was familiar with from more long-term fieldwork. In Kerala, where I had worked with ayurvedic doctors and visited healing centers around the state, successive communist governments had created a society that lacked the boomtown atmosphere and wealth of the big metro cities like Hyderabad but also lacked the grinding poverty and profound social inequality that could easily be found in the metro cities. One had to hire a car to see that other side of Hyderabad from HITEC City, as the sprawling urban space is not conducive to walking and there are not many other ways to leave the area.

After pursing pharmaceutical company representatives by email and phone and achieving little success in making contacts, I was surprised when the vice president of Osmania Pharma responded to my request to meet. I had also received a response from an employee at Kanaka Pharmaceuticals indicating that he could arrange for someone to speak with me. The vice president of Osmania, Pramod Rajkumar,[19] was open to meeting and gracious in our email interaction. I was disappointed, though, when I arrived at the Osmania offices to hear that Mr. Rajkumar would not be available, but it turned out he had arranged for two other employees, Mr. T. K. Varma and Mr. Subin Fernandes, to speak with me. I was introduced to Mr. Varma and Mr. Fernandes, who showed me to a conference room where we engaged in an extended discussion about Osmania's experience producing medications, such as tenofovir, which they, like fifteen other companies in India, produce under license from Gilead, and on their prospects for research and development. Throughout our conversation, Mr. Varma took the lead and Mr. Fernandes, in what is a normal conversational style in India, provided brief verbal reinforcements and confirmations of what Mr. Varma was saying. I too participated in this kind of "backchanneling," as linguists call it, where verbal affirmations and repetition of key points show that you are engaged with and interested in your partner's narrative.

Early on in our discussion, I brought up the Gilead model and that company's voluntary licensing program, and Mr. Varma offered the same explanation I heard from the Gilead representatives of how an ideal combination of factors led to the dramatic decrease in the price of the AIDS drug tenofovir: "I think our efforts on tenofovir in reducing the cost of tenofovir, Gilead's openness in terms of trying out a new method of licensing, and the WHO's guideline change, which came in 2009, all three contributed in their own way to making tenofovir accessible to the entire world." He added that "all of these things happened at the right time" and they "put tenofovir where it is today in the world."

When I asked whether it is possible to continue producing tenofovir at a low price, Mr. Varma explained how tenofovir production was business and not charity, providing the same explanation as the Gilead representatives of its sustainability:

> It's an important initiative for us, but it's a business. We need to run it as a business. My firm belief is that the minute anything becomes charity, it's not scalable. Charity is never scalable. A business is scalable because a charity always has a limited budget. It cannot grow, and every year when times are bad, people start cutting their charity budgets. That's the same with what is happening in the world, when the United States is putting money in PEPFAR or the Global Fund is putting money into their grants. Countries which don't have money, when times are austere, they don't want to do charity. So for us, it's a business, but it's a business with a human face. We understand that it's not a business where we can make the same profits which we do in other parts of our business.

I then asked whether and how Indian pharmaceutical companies have changed after India's WTO-compliant 2005 Patents Act. Mr. Varma responded that they changed primarily in terms of how they look at the Indian market:

What happened in India before 2005 was, there were no patents.

> MURPHY: Right, only the process patents.
> MR. VARMA: Absolutely. Anybody could reengineer and launch a new drug in India. There were no restrictions to that. So people have had to change their ways of thinking because whatever new product came into the market in the US or whatever, people simply copied that and launched it in India.
> MURPHY: That was legal.
> MR. VARMA: That was legal, absolutely. [. . .] Earlier it was new launches [releases of Indian versions of drugs patented elsewhere] that were the focus, newer drugs were the focus, but now people have started focusing on how do we get more innovative, what do we do differently, which of our drugs are making money? Finally, it's a branded, generic market, India. So how do I identify the rank holder? Which drug should I hold in my portfolio?

But today, he explained, "People have done a lot of pruning. People have started looking at their portfolios more seriously. Earlier it was whatever came on the market, we launched that drug," referring to an earlier, almost exclusive focus on reproducing whatever were the big drug releases outside of India. Much of the media and research coverage of India-based pharma and this conversation with Mr. Varma focus on AIDS drugs or blockbuster drugs originated by big pharma, but much of pharmaceutical production in India has focused on common generic medications whose patents have long expired, such as amoxicillin.

Mr. Varma added that for companies that were focusing on generics and looking at the global market, things have not changed much since 2005. But some companies in India are now involved in developing their own new products. Before, innovators were reluctant to launch products in the Indian market because "ten Indian companies would come and crash the price." But since the 2005 law, "people [in the pharma sector] have become more open, people have started respecting patents," and now "people have started looking at innovators [getting involved in research and development] as a possible source of new business, and I think that definitely has changed in the past five to seven years." Virtually all companies in India were generic producers, but since 2005 some have been moving toward creating their own products.

I brought up Ranbaxy's new antimalarial and asked if a turn to R&D is going to result in more new drugs being launched by India-based companies. Mr. Varma said he thought this was probably not the case because the R&D for new drugs—New Chemical Entities (NCEs)—was too costly for India-based companies. If you look at big pharma, he explained:

> At the really big, big pharma, Pfizer or GSK, they have hundreds of molecules under development, and out of a hundred of molecules, even if three become blockbusters, the development costs of the other ninety-seven are justified. But I don't think any Indian company or for that matter Osmania has the scale in terms of the turnover to actually spend money on an NCE. Teva [an Israel-based generic company] has done that. Teva has one NCE, but I don't think there is any other generic company. . . . For example, Pfizer's Lipitor is bigger than Osmania.
>
> MURPHY: Oh, yeah. (Mr. Fernandes laughs.) I know. It's the biggest product in the world.
> MR. VARMA: Absolutely. It's maybe 10 or 12 billion dollars. Osmania is [less]."[20]

Other than Teva, Mr. Varma said, "I don't think any generic company has the scale to have a full-scale NCE program," and his claim has been echoed in the Indian media.[21] Mr. Varma went on to say that in the future we would not see "full scale" NCEs "but a lot of specialty developments like what Ranbaxy has done on arterolane and piperaquine." Elaborating on Ranbaxy's antimalarial he added, "It's an NCE, but those two products . . . Piperaquine is a new product. It was a product which was already available on the market. Arterolane is an artemisinin derivative. So they just combined the two, did some clinical trials, and said that this product works. So they are not NCE in the true sense."

Thus Ranbaxy's new product is not a true NCE in Mr. Varma's view because piperaquine was already existing. He calls it "new," referring to it being renewed, having come back after disuse.[22] Arterolane is a synthetic derivative of artemisinin, a plant source that was already known as a treatment for malaria going back to its use in traditional Chinese medicine. I pointed out to Mr. Varma that much, if not most, innovation by pharmaceutical companies, at least by United States–based big pharma, which Mr. Varma seemed to imply does regularly create genuine NCEs, uses similar methods, slightly modifying existing medications rather than creating truly novel entities. Mr. Varma agreed with this point, giving the example of the variety of statin products—whose over-proliferation Angell (2004) also criticized.

Mr. Varma's comments on Ranbaxy's "new" drug resemble other critiques that new products coming out of India are not truly innovative or truly Indian because they involved government funding, foreign and university research collaboration, or turned out to be minor variations on earlier treatments. Biocon's new biotech product for treating head and neck cancer was labeled as not completely Indian because it was based on a molecule licensed from a Cuban institution, and Ranbaxy's new antimalarial has been deemed wanting because of its dependence on foreign collaborative research.[23] These critiques suppose that companies elsewhere regularly develop truly novel chemical entities all on their own. As explained in chapter 2, most patents awarded in the United States to big pharma companies are for minor modifications of existing drugs, and genuinely novel innovations are often developed by university researchers with public funding and licensed to pharmaceutical companies. Therefore, Indian producers are thus far following what have become standard forms of research and development in the pharmaceutical industry. There is a perception in India, however, of an idealized autonomous creator of new medical products that is doing innovation correctly in relation to which Indian innovators are seen as deficient. Thus the romantic myth of the autonomous innovator emerges in how Indian pharmaceutical producers and journalists imagine the foreign pharmaceutical company and in the views of the courts and legal conventions when this ideal is juxtaposed to Ayurveda and other "traditional" medicines.

I asked Mr. Varma and Mr. Fernandes whether they thought there would be more R&D addressing diseases that affect low-income countries in the India-based pharmaceutical sector in the near future, and Mr. Varma said there would not be research on NCEs for these diseases, recalling the points we heard from Gilead representatives about the lack of financial incentives for addressing neglected diseases. He explained that

"More and more companies will start looking for niches in which they can compete. And this is an area where, again, companies will not be able to spend two billion dollars on R&D to develop a drug for TB or malaria because even if you launch it, it will be worth a few hundred million dollars or whatever maximum, or fifty million dollars or whatever." However, there are inventions outside of the realm of NCEs that Indian pharma may engage in in relation to neglected diseases, such as "a lot of dose titration, a lot of platform usage, maybe different dosage forms, new drug delivery systems, whatever, but I don't see too much NCE focus on these disease areas." When we think of R&D, we typically imagine it refers to the development of new drugs, probably because this is what the pharmaceutical sector emphasizes when it stresses the need to recover money through patent enforcement. But these comments show that there are other products, which Mr. Varma referred to as "generic R&D," that he thought Indian pharmaceutical companies would focus on, such as creating different dosage forms or new drug delivery systems. This can include, for example, making an inhaler or a transdermal patch for a drug that formerly was only available as an injection.

I then asked Mr. Varma and Mr. Fernandes whether there were any plans to use ideas from ayurvedic medicine to develop new drugs in the Indian pharmaceutical sector. I knew this was a concern among ayurvedic practitioners. Some in India had also advocated this as a strategy to develop new treatments (as mentioned in chapter 3), and I was curious if someone in the Indian pharmaceutical sector had considered this possibility. Mr. Fernandes explained that it is very difficult to pin down and extract the active ingredient in a medicinal plant that has therapeutic benefits and that few companies aim to do so:

MR. FERNANDES: That extraction part is difficult.
MR. VARMA: Finally who is doing it? Novartis did it for artemisinin [the antimalarial product from Chinese medicine], but I don't see a company of our size doing that.
MURPHY: Because that's too expensive?
MR. VARMA: It has to be two kinds of companies. One is an innovator who has got a huge R&D budget and who has got people on his rolls who are thinking in this direction.
MURPHY: Right, it's a way of thinking too.

MR. VARMA: Absolutely. This is maybe pure R&D. It's not applied stuff, which we do all the time. This is people who are paid to think. We don't have too many people who are paid to think.

MURPHY: It's more like theoretical R&D.

MR. VARMA: Or one of these boutique firms, small boutique firms, which is started by a scientist, like Gilead or something, who has got a lot of knowledge in that area. He works along with the innovator to do something like this.

Mr. Varma later said he is sure big companies like Pfizer and Novartis are utilizing this method of looking for active ingredients since "they are doing *everything* because their pipeline of new drugs is dwindling."

I thanked Mr. Varma and Mr. Fernandes for their time and told them I felt our conversation was very helpful in giving me a sense of how Indian pharmaceutical companies are reacting to the new patent regime. As I was heading to the elevator to leave Osmania, an assistant of Mr. Rajkumar, the vice president of the company who I was told was unavailable, hailed me and said that Mr. Rajkumar would be able to meet with me briefly before I left. I returned to the conference room where I had spoken to Mr. Varma and Mr. Fernandes, and soon after Mr. Rajkumar entered and greeted me. I was given the impression that this would be a brief, informal meeting, that he would say he was sorry he did not have time to meet me and would ask how my stay in Hyderabad was, so I did not ask if I could record our conversation. However, Mr. Rajkumar ended up speaking with me extensively and candidly in the conference room and then over lunch in the company's executive cafeteria. He was uninhibited in expressing his views about his company and the new patent scene. He even said I could use his actual name and his company's name in my research, but I opted to use pseudonyms because his colleagues wished to remain anonymous.

Mr. Rajkumar's outlook differed in one key respect from Mr. Varma and Mr. Fernandes's view of R&D in the new patent environment. While Mr. Varma and Mr. Fernandes thought new R&D would focus on non-NCE products such as drug delivery systems, Mr. Rajkumar thought that we would see new NCEs coming from Indian producers in the future, that it would happen despite the apparent cost.

Much of our conversation focused on the Gilead model and the use of voluntary licenses. Mr. Rajkumar said he is willing to work with either voluntary licenses or compulsory licenses, but he prefers voluntary licenses because the process is easier and there is more goodwill between companies. In speaking about the Gilead program of voluntarily licensing ARVs to Indian companies, Mr. Rajkumar said that overall this is a praiseworthy program. Although he was explicit about giving Gilead credit, he added that you also have to look at their motivation. He explained that Gilead was not involved in markets in Africa and other places where their drugs would sell under their voluntary licensing program so they were not going to lose out. A bigger company with a presence in Africa, he suggested, would have been less likely to issue licenses for drugs that would go to that market. In any case, he added, Gilead's program was important for improving relations between Indian and foreign multinationals.

As mentioned in the last chapter, the medicines placed in the United Nations Patent Pool for voluntary licensing by big pharma companies were put there after these medicines were denied patents in India. Gilead's tenofovir was denied a patent in India, but Gilead's licensing program began long before that decision. Perhaps Mr. Rajkumar's interpretation explains why Gilead was willing to go the route of offering voluntary licensing early on, figuring they could license drugs to Indian companies and the licenses would restrict the export of these drugs to sub-Saharan Africa and other low-income markets. While Mr. Rajkumar said he preferred to work with voluntary licenses, these came with restrictions on which countries they could sell to. Mr. Rajkumar specifically highlighted the exclusion of Brazil. He said he would like to sell tenofovir to Brazil because there are many poor people there, though he is prohibited from doing so by the license agreement. Mr. Rajkumar may also wish to sell to Brazil because of the profitability of a middle-income market, which is the same reason Gilead is protecting Brazil for its own branded marketing. And Mr. Rajkumar's company could probably make a profit selling tenofovir in Brazil at a price significantly below what Gilead could offer.

After my visit to Osmania, I went to Kanaka Pharmaceuticals, where I met with an executive, Mr. A. R. Biswas, and his assistant, Ms. Rekha Kamaladevi.[24] The Kanaka facility where I spoke with these individuals was a manufacturing center that also had a few business offices. While waiting for Mr. Biswas at the reception area, I gazed out at the large, drab buildings where Kanaka assembled their drug formulations and thought that these buildings held some of the low-cost drugs around which there was much controversy. Protestors in India, South Africa, New York, and elsewhere over the years rallied to keep factories like these producing generic medications against the looming threat of TRIPS.

Ms. Rekha brought me into a large conference room, and we chatted about differences in South Indian languages while waiting for Mr. Biswas. I was trying to see if I could perceive similarities between Malayalam, the language I had learned to conduct research in Kerala, and Telugu, which is the primary language in Hyderabad and Andra Pradesh state—although here as elsewhere in India, the business world is dominated by English. Both languages are part of the Dravidian family and are distinct from the Indo-European languages of North India. Ms. Rekha was surprised that a foreign visitor was interested in South Indian languages. Most visitors and many of the Kanaka employees themselves, who hail from various parts of India, speak English at the workplace. Foreign visitors coming to Kanaka on business, such as the corporate representatives that just preceded my visit to this company, have usually not even heard of the languages spoken by the hundreds of millions of people who live in this part of India.

After Mr. Biswas arrived, I explained my research project and my interest in the effect of TRIPS on the Indian pharmaceutical industry. In answer to my question about whether his company is involved in new R&D after the new Patents Act, Mr. Biswas said they were not pursuing R&D of any kind—not NCE, delivery systems, or other products. Mr. Biswas concisely explained his business strategy: "Our game is only economies of scale." Kanaka focuses only on bringing down costs of production and increasing sales, he said. Like many other India-based companies, Kanaka produces active ingredients that are contained in the products of other India-based companies and foreign-based multinational companies. Mr. Biswas did not seem to be preoccupied with the effects of the new patent regime, and it has not greatly affected the business model of his company. This would seem to confirm Mr. Varma's claim that Indian generic producers that are focused on the Indian market are not changing their business plan under the new Patents Act.

Though I did not specifically ask him about this, Mr. Biswas went out of his way to affirm that his company respects patents. Such a statement was not offered by the representatives of Osmania, though it may have been an implicit assumption, since that company is involved in R&D and plans to benefit from patent enforcement. Mr. Biswas may have also been distinguishing Kanaka from Cipla, the nationalistic pharmaceutical company described in chapter 1 that received a visit from Gandhi during the independence movement. Cipla has attracted attention by boldly defying the new patent regime, making some products without a patent or license. They seem to have recently changed course, though, having taken a voluntary license from Gilead to manufacture sofosbuvir, a new hepatitis-C product that has been criticized for its high cost in high-income markets.

I sensed that Mr. Biswas may nevertheless have been critical of the new patent regime, and I tried to convey that I was open to hearing critiques. He did not offer such comments, though, and seemed content to go along with the new patent environment, perhaps because it does not seem to greatly affect his business model. When I asked about the effect of the new patent laws on drug prices, he explained that there has not been any effect so far but said that in the future with the development of second- and third-line AIDS drugs we will see an increase in price.

Mr. Biswas provided additional useful information on his company, but to discuss those details here may reveal the identity of his company. Therefore, I worked additional observations from Mr. Biswas into the general comments on the nature of the Indian pharmaceutical sector earlier in this and the previous chapter.

From this meeting with Mr. Biswas and from my tracking of Osmania and Kanaka in the media, it appears that these two companies are reacting quite differently to the new patent environment. We might see Osmania as akin to Pankajakasthuri Herbals, the ayurvedic pharmaceutical producer mentioned in chapter 3 that was trying to adapt to the new patent regime and seek a way forward by advancing proprietary claims over ayurvedic products. Kanaka Pharmaceuticals more resembles Dr. Nayar's ayurvedic company, which was carrying on with little concern about the new Patents Act, though Mr. Nayar's optimism that the new patent environment may even be helpful to Ayurveda resembles the more opportunistic outlook of Mr. Varma and Mr. Rajkumar. A key difference between the biomedical and the ayurvedic producers was that the biomedical producers seemed more certain about how to navigate the new environment and saw clearer opportunities for growth.

Moving Forward: Toward Therapeutic Access or Therapeutic Excess?

There are two main implications in this analysis of the India-based pharmaceutical industry in the wake of the new Patents Act. First of all, the new environment has not greatly affected generic production so far. Although India-based companies can no longer legally reverse engineer patented products without permission from the patent holder, they are continuing to make these products via licenses, voluntary and compulsory. This was confirmed by Mr. Varma and Mr. Biswas and by the current business practices of Kanaka Pharmaceuticals. Second, the Patents Act has resulted in at least some R&D in the Indian pharmaceutical sector, including new pharmaceutical products. Among those that are engaging in R&D, some focus on NCEs and others focus on generic R&D such as drug delivery systems. How significant each of these is in the Indian pharma sector has yet to be determined, and we have seen divergent opinions within one company, Osmania, with Mr. Varma finding NCE development cost-prohibitive while his vice president thinks it is feasible. Even if NCE development does not become extensive, some products have already been released and some are in development.[25]

Ranbaxy's Synriam, a treatment for malaria, and Biocon's BIOMAb EGFR, a biopharmaceutical for head and neck cancer, are new products launched by India-based companies under the new patent law and represent the directional possibilities of future R&D in India. Ranbaxy's product treats a neglected disease that is prevalent in low-income countries, whereas Biocon's release treats diseases that are seen in low-income and high-income areas. Ranbaxy's new product was not greeted with enthusiasm by investors.[26] Right after Synriam was launched, the company's shares fell 1.8 percent on the Bombay Stock Exchange because, as a financial reporter put it, "anyone remotely connected to the business of medicine knows that malaria is not where money is."[27] To recover investments, Ranbaxy is looking to get Synriam placed in the Indian government's anti-malaria program, thus greatly increasing sales.

To interpret the implications of these new medical products, it is helpful to return to Sunder Rajan's (2012) observations on the global drug industry. Regarding the pharmaceutical market in the United States, Sunder

Rajan calls on the concept of "surplus health," explaining, "health itself becomes abstracted from healthiness and operates purely as potential for the generation of surplus value, in the manner that labor does when it becomes surplus labor in industrial capitalism."[28] He adds that "American patients get imagined as consumers who can grow markets if they just consume more drugs, leading to Americans consuming more and more drugs, and to their becoming, in the language of clinical trials, 'therapeutically saturated.' Given that drugs are, fundamentally, toxic molecules, this therapeutic saturation is not harmless."[29]

Sunder Rajan claims that pharmaceutical companies, at least in the US market, get patients to take increasingly greater quantities of drugs, seeing symptoms and future health risks as a source of value, a target for generating revenue. At the same time, in other parts of the world, people suffer because of the lack of treatment for neglected diseases. As pharmaceutical production continues to adapt to the new patent environment, we should observe which of these groups India-based pharmaceutical companies focus on.

If Biocon's product is the harbinger of the future, it may represent an effort to produce medications for problems that affect high-income populations. On the other hand, if Ranbaxy recovers some of its investment by getting Synriam adopted by India's national antimalaria program, in addition to selling it in African markets where it is already approved, this may encourage other pharmaceutical companies to develop therapies for neglected diseases. Even if this happens, it seems certain that India-based companies that can raise the capital to develop NCEs will also work on products to treat illnesses that affect populations in wealthy countries—or, to be more precise, they will create products to treat illnesses that *also* affect wealthy populations, since all of these illnesses affect people in low-income countries as well. Thus India-based pharmaceutical companies may go down both paths, finding some remedies for neglected diseases while also adding to the therapeutic saturation of patients in the United States, wealthy enclaves of India, and elsewhere.

All of this assumes, though, that pharmaceutical companies will continue to operate under the current system of financial incentives for drug development. While assessing how pharmaceutical production is changing in the new patent environment, it is worth considering models for drug development that have recently been proposed to offer alternatives to the current orientation toward maximizing profits and recovering investments. These offer incentives for drug development that are based on the health impact of new medications and that promise to share the benefits of drug discovery in more equitable ways.

CONCLUSION

In terms of dramatic effect, it would have been satisfying to have written a story of the global intellectual property regime that has unambiguous heroes and villains and clear solutions to inequalities in this sector of the global economy. In that story, big pharma would have pushed through the TRIPS agenda at the WTO, increased prices tenfold for AIDS drugs in poor countries, stolen ideas from Ayurveda, and taken over the Indian pharmaceutical sector for the outsourcing of pharmaceutical production. In fact, this is what many who know a little about these issues think has already happened. However, this study of the effect of the new global patent system on the control of medical knowledge and pharmaceutical production repeats a familiar refrain offered by social scientists when we study a social problem, which is, "It's complicated." In this story, Pfizer gets its way at the WTO, but Novartis gets turned down by the Indian Supreme Court, and ayurvedic producers are divided about whether there is a problem.

Sociocultural anthropologists tend to critique the prevailing knowledge and dichotomies produced by other researchers and the media and show

how they are misleading, but we do not put in their place other expl⟨ ⟩ tions that can account for these discrepancies. Our analyses often w⟨ ⟩ of the dangers of making premature generalizations and call for more research on the problem, which is a somewhat unsatisfying conclusion. Social, political, and economic issues, however, often defy explanations of them as coherent systems and belie predictions about their future. In this book, I have tried to consider social complexity in a productive way, offering an example of how an emerging constellation of power works on multiple levels over time and showing that if one looks closely and learns the details of patent agreements and the maneuverings of different stakeholders, it is possible to see where some of the problems lie.

At the same time, one of the most insidious problems with a global system like the new patent regime is that the workings of power are diffuse and obscure: one has to examine arcane details and the roles of multiple actors to decipher the problem, and this makes activism challenging. Thus, ten years into the new patent regime, I have shown how the crucial problems—which can be life-or-death issues in terms of access to ARVs— are in rather specific, hard-to-pin-down places, such as for the poor who live in middle-income countries. There are some heroes in this story, and it requires an awareness of the seemingly obscure sections of patent law and political negotiations to see that these are the leftist government representatives that dug in their heels to get Section 3d placed in India's new Patents Act. The heroes are not, as many think, the Indian pharmaceutical companies, which in fact behave just like what many think are the villains in the story, the foreign multinational drug companies. Fortunately, India-based companies are able to produce low-cost medications, but this is because of the low cost of scientific labor in India relative to other major centers of pharmaceutical production. India-based companies, like foreign multinationals, are concerned about giving a return to their investors, and they pay their executives generously.

Rather than describing a clash of heroes and villains, investigation of these issues often leads to a provocatively complex story. If we look at the case of Ranbaxy's antimalarial, where an India-based company created a drug for a neglected disease that affects low-income countries by using biopiracy (from Chinese medicine) and incentivized by a patent regime pushed by big pharma, we are challenged to see in this anything more definitive than a fortuitous development in a complex new global regime.

If there is a villain in this story, it is the overreliance on the profit motive for the development of new medications and the proprietary walls that are being placed around medical insights that limit the sharing of knowledge.

In the new patent regime, ayurvedic practitioners and producers must contend with uncertainty because of the different ideologies about science and creation governing ayurvedic drug production and patent protection. This makes it difficult to know what is secure and what is vulnerable and how much to be concerned about biopiracy and what to do about it. While the patent laws are not a clear threat to the practice of ayurvedic medicine, lack of compensation for their knowledge contributions is unjust, especially given the new environment of staking monetary claims over medical knowledge and given the history of the sharing of medical and scientific knowledge between India and the West. If ayurvedic producers decide to engage the patent system and make proprietary claims over their products, legal decisions on those efforts may bring more clarity about how Ayurveda fits, or does not fit, patent law. This process may also change the practice of Ayurveda.

Alternately, an effort could be mounted to change India's patent law to be more amenable to ayurvedic knowledge and practices. However, this would require allowing the patenting of the use of plants, which would pave the way for more property claims and set a precedent—so far avoided in patent law—in claiming ownership rights over products of nature.

Another problem with deciphering the meaning of a global process is that it is difficult to know how much needs to unfold before one is able to determine its effects. This book has presented a case study of the deployment of a political, economic, and legal regime and examined how multiple actors contemplate, interact with, and resist its effects. While efforts of hegemony and resistance produced results that are different from what was expected, predictions about the new regime that have not been borne out may yet come to fruition.

Concerns linger over prices and accessibility of essential medicines along with a sense of possibility in new pharmaceutical research and development coming out of India. Developments in the price of tenofovir are encouraging, but the alignment of several actors and conditions—activists, the WHO, economies of scale, and market prospects of pharmaceutical producers—was needed to lower the price of this major ARV. We have yet to see whether this can happen for neglected diseases. Ranbaxy's new antimalarial is encouraging, but we will have to observe how investors react over time to attempts to address neglected diseases and whether, in the long run, India-based companies will focus on products for higher-end markets.

My perspective on the current patent environment resembles the sociologist Nikolas Rose's analysis of emerging trends in biopolitics and power.[1] Rose argues that dire predictions about new developments in medicine and biology are misguided, and he suggests we turn our attention instead to the new meanings and orientations that are developing from new ways of thinking of bodies, selves, and life. For example, some have been concerned that the new genetics, including the decoding of the human genome and efforts at genetic modification, augurs a new eugenics. Rose argues that eugenics is a different kind of project, grounded in twentieth-century, nationalist, state ventures, which is not what we are seeing thus far in our ability to manipulate the genome. The new genetics does, nevertheless, merit our attention and concern in terms of new forms of subjectivity that are being developed, such as new ways of thinking of ourselves in relation to our biology and new forms of social control that may result.[2]

Neoliberalism, or the expansion of privatization and of policies that promote the interests of corporate actors, is a clear threat to the rights of the public, especially workers and marginalized people, and in the world of intellectual property its impact on the public domain is a major concern, but its trajectory is not straightforward and unstoppable. Big pharma companies shaped TRIPS to their advantage, but they do not completely control the current situation, which is made up of alliances between mid-size US companies, multinational Indian companies, and the activists that can use Section 3d to mitigate against these players. This has kept several important drugs in the public domain and upset large companies that have failed to defeat this provision in court.

I was among those who warned of the dire effects of the new patent regime on drug prices, but over the years since I first published on this topic, and now ten years after the WTO-compliant patent laws have been rolled out in India, I have had trouble finding clear evidence of major increases in drug costs. Is this because of foresighted provisions in India's new patent laws? Is it because those working within the regime have used such provisions to successfully oppose patents? Will the situation change in the future as more strains of HIV develop that are resistant to existing drugs and as Indian and foreign-based pharmaceutical companies develop products based on ayurvedic systems of medicine?

These issues are particularly salient as patent struggles take place in other regions of the world. India is the most significant locus of struggles over medical patents, although the issues involved, as this study has shown, are transnational, and what happens in India could affect drug prices and access to medicine in other places such as Brazil, China, and sub-Saharan Africa.

South Africa and Thailand have been involved in contentious, high-profile struggles with multinational pharmaceutical companies over patents on medications for AIDS and for cancer. Brazil, meanwhile, has emerged as another important site of struggles over the price of ARVs. Brazil conformed to the TRIPS agenda in 1997, eight years before India did, and in terms of maintaining an affordable drug supply, has been more at the mercy of multinational pharmaceutical companies than has India. Although Brazil has its own pharmaceutical industry that produces several ARVs that were developed before the new patent regime went into effect, four patented drugs—tenofovir, atazanavir, lopinavir/ritonavir, and enfuvirtide—have contributed to keeping the cost of AIDS drug regimens high. At first, Brazil's strategy was to threaten to issue compulsory licenses to allow local companies to produce patented drugs, which would result in foreign-owned patent holders offering these drugs at lower prices in Brazil. Then, from 2006 to 2008, Brazil actually issued compulsory licenses to produce some drugs locally at lower cost than what they were paying multinational producers. More recently, government agents and activists in Brazil have filed oppositions in court to the granting of patents, employing a method similar to that of the Lawyers Collective and other groups in India.[3] In cases where they were successful and a patent had been denied, Brazilian manufacturers began producing the medication and no licenses were necessary. Gilead's application to patent tenofovir in Brazil was defeated in 2009, the same year it was defeated in India, and in 2011 Brazilian pharmaceutical companies started producing this medication. The relation to Gilead was more adversarial in this context, however, and Gilead did not provide technology transfer to the Brazilian companies. Thus the two public-private pharmaceutical partnerships in Brazil that ended up producing tenofovir had to go through the long and costly process of figuring out how to make the drug. Because of this situation and lack of competition, the cost of Brazil-made tenofovir is much higher than the price charged by Indian producers, who are not allowed to sell their product in Brazil, and Gilead has appealed the patent ruling.[4] Atazanavir, which is in the Patent Pool available to be produced under a license that excludes sales to Brazil, is also available in Brazil at higher prices. In 2013, the cost in Brazil was $1,150 per person per year while Indian companies were selling it for $250 per person per year.[5]

Controversies over biopiracy of indigenous knowledge of medicinal plants have also emerged in Brazil, although these forms of medical knowledge and practice are quite different from Ayurveda. The Amazon has been referred to as a "treasure chest" of biogenetic resources, and various stakeholders in Brazil have been applying the Convention on Biological Diversity, the Nagoya Protocol, and benefit sharing agreements in the hope of finding a method for protecting local biological knowledge from misappropriation under the new patent regime.[6] It would be productive in the future to engage in a sustained comparison of the struggles over the control of medical knowledge, both in terms of access to biomedical medications and biopiracy of local knowledge, in India and Brazil.

New systems of incentives would help avoid some of the problems identified here related to biomedical patents, the affordability of medicines, and concerns about biopiracy by providing alternatives to the profit-driven model of drug development. In this context, two initiatives are worth considering: the Health Impact Fund and the Open Source Drug Discovery program.

Professors Thomas Pogge and Aidan Hollis developed the Health Impact Fund (HIF) as an alternative system of incentives for drug development. Through the fund, innovators would be financially rewarded according to the health impact, rather than the profitability, of their innovations. Pogge and Hollis feel this program, which would be supported by government and private contributions, will entice innovators to develop treatments for neglected diseases that affect low-income countries. An innovator would register a product with the HIF and agree that the product be sold at a price that would recoup only the cost of production. In exchange, the innovator would be paid by the HIF according to the product's health impact, which is the amount of disease and suffering it relieves as determined by the effect on Quality Adjusted Life Years (QALY).[7] While offering an incentive to develop treatments for neglected diseases, it could also reduce the level of "therapeutic saturation" and "disease infla-tion" in high-income markets. A team of researchers and policy analysts from China and India have even considered how traditional Chinese med-icine and Ayurveda might work with the Health Impact Fund to develop remedies that might offer affordable alternatives for treating diseases that affect low-income settings.[8] While this program is appealing, the chal-lenge will be in obtaining the necessary funding from government and other sources, which would require a major undertaking of political will.

Another effort, which has already resulted in a tuberculosis treatment currently under trial, is India's Open Source Drug Discovery program (OSDD). In 2008, India's Council of Scientific and Industrial Research (CSIR) established the OSDD, which is composed of an international net-work of scientists, companies, researchers, and students, working to de-velop new treatments primarily for diseases that affect poor populations. This is essentially a crowd-sourcing project where researchers collaborate online using shared portals and databases, and most of the focus has been on treatments for malaria and tuberculosis.[9] Collaborators in OSDD must accept an agreement that prohibits individual intellectual property claims on products that result from OSDD research. Any discoveries that develop from OSDD sharing, such as "the identification of drug-able non-toxic targets, in vitro and in vivo validation, in silico screening of molecules, lead optimization, pre-clinical toxicity and clinical trials," will constitute "Protected Collective Information," which will be publically accessible and available to generic producers without royalties.[10] This arrangement is the inverse of a patent. One commits, via license, to share research results and their benefits publically rather than claiming to own them. This obligation to leave one's contribution in the public domain resembles the "copyleft" agreements and Creative Commons licensing promoted by James Boyle, Lawrence Lessig, and other activist legal scholars that ex-plicitly entitle sharing and reproduction of artistic works. OSDD claims to have over eight thousand collaborators from 130 countries, and in 2014 a clinical trial began in India for a tuberculosis treatment developed by the collaborative.[11]

Knowledge from ayurvedic medicine led to the development of a bioenhancer—extracted from a plant known to Ayurveda—in a tubercu-losis drug that is being developed by the OSDD. This would mean that a public health benefit may be derived from Ayurveda, and the knowledge on which it is based must legally remain in the public domain. Another initiative that may be appealing to ayurvedic producers is the effort to develop "traditional knowledge commons" (mentioned in chapter 3). This is generally imagined as applying to the knowledge of indigenous communities, and it is based on the International Treaty on Plant Genetic Resources for Food and Agriculture and the Convention on Biological Diversity. It would involve placing plant resource knowledge in a commons—a repository of shared information—that would ensure the knowledge remains in the public domain and allow for benefit sharing for products derived from this knowledge. Traditional knowledge commons have the added benefit "that the values held by the communities are recognized and supported."[12] Thus ayurvedic practitioners may not have to go the route of adjusting their practices and epistemologies to fit private property claims, though some have already embarked down this road.

Some of what is happening within the pharmaceutical and government sectors under the new patent regime, however, is not so different from these alternative projects. Having just described the Open Source Drug Discovery program, it is hard not to recall the creation of Ranbaxy's Synriam. This medication treats a neglected disease, and its development was enabled by financial assistance from the Indian government and collaboration with the Malaria Medicines Venture, which is affiliated with the Open Source Drug Discovery project. In this case, however, Ranbaxy owns the marketing rights, whereas with OSDD, no group would have intellectual property rights.

While many are concerned about the effect on drug prices, a major loss has already been incurred by the new patent regime in terms of how we think about medical knowledge. The idea that medical insights can and should be owned has proliferated with TRIPS. Multinational pharmaceutical companies have increased protections for their intellectual property while ayurvedic producers and the Government of India, along with other groups around the world, are mounting property claims over their indigenous medical knowledge and other cultural knowledge and practices.

These changes represent a loss to the public sphere of knowledge and even to a broader spirit of sharing. When the compendium of South Indian botanical knowledge, the *Hortus Malabaricus*, was translated into English in 2003, K. S. Manilal, who led the project, said that the knowledge was not only Kerala's heritage but also belonged to all of mankind.

Kerala's Ezhava community countered that the knowledge was theirs and that Itty Achudan, an Ezhava who shared local botanical knowledge with the Dutch compilers of the *Hortus,* had made a mistake when he gave it away.[13] This contentiousness about community ownership is unfortunate, but it seems the Ezhava community is just adapting to the times in these claims about Itty Achudan's "mistake." They do not have many other clear choices, since international corporate interests upped the ownership ante by putting higher walls around their own knowledge. As the ayurvedic practitioner Dr. Krishnan said, TRIPS is "a shot gone from the gun." We cannot put it back where it came from, but perhaps we can make intellectual property law and enforcement adhere more closely to the original intentions of intellectual property as described by James Boyle and other legal scholars. This would involve finding a better balance between what the temporary monopoly innovators say they need in exchange for publically disclosing knowledge of their invention and society's right to benefit from these contributions while maintaining a robust public domain.

One of the basic principles of patent law is the requirement of *public disclosure* of an invention so that after the expiration of a patent or the inventor's death, the invention becomes publically available. Thus the public right to knowledge and the benefits of that knowledge is a central part of patent law, which is threatened by the increasing proprietary claims over knowledge that are invoked by TRIPS. The knowledge connected to a patent becomes part of the public domain after twenty years, but the increasing enforcement of patent rights is compelling people around the world to be more reticent to share their knowledge, and the expansion of copyright has taken much creative work out of the public domain. New forms of intellectual property such as data exclusivity, which makes data about efficacy and safety of a medication proprietary, would put new restrictions on access to and use of knowledge. Data exclusivity provisions were proposed and then later retracted in the not-yet-ratified India-EU Free Trade Agreement and have been inserted into the proposed Trans-Pacific Partnership agreement.

The right to knowledge is a more diffuse and abstract principle to defend or advocate for—compared, for example, to the right to essential medicines—but some have already undertaken this venture. The Access to Knowledge (A2K) movement is a dispersed coalition of individuals and interest groups that are concerned about access to knowledge in a world of growing copyright and patent protection. A2K includes individuals in the free software and access to medicines movements who engage in research, advocacy, and lobbying, and groups that use the A2K label interact with some of the other projects mentioned here, such as the Health Impact Fund.[14]

Although, up to this point, the new patent system has not brought the disasters we feared it would, it needs to be watched, and I have tried to show where to look and what to look for. This is a story about how actors struggled within a new regime of power and found ways to mitigate its effects, but it should not leave us complacent about future expansions to IP regimes.

Moving forward, the problems with the new intellectual property environment and other global constellations of power need to be approached from many angles and through attending to the details. We also need to consider how certain efforts—such as the "perfect storm" of activists, WHO policies, and pharmaceutical production capacities that made some ARVs more affordable and the efforts by leftist politicians in India to raise the bar for innovativeness—might offer models for a long-term project of improving access to medicines and sharing knowledge.

NOTES

Introduction

1. Collins 2011; Fish 2006; Liptak 2013; Sciolino 2008; WIPO 2006.
2. Kapczynski 2008; Kelty 2008.
3. Griffith 1945; Jayaraman 1997; Kline 1954; *The Hindu* 2005a.
4. Mgbeoji 2006, 92.
5. I am adopting here the terms "indigenous" and "traditional" as they are used in much of the literature on patents and biopiracy. These terms label forms of knowledge that are neither corporate nor biomedical, though these forms themselves are quite diverse. The terms have other limitations: "traditional" implies these are practices of the past that are unchanging, whereas Ayurveda is connected to the past but is also contemporary and changing. I additionally use labels such as "local" and "non-Western," which are less ideologically loaded, but these and all terms for the various practices that are not biomedicine have limitations. Thus I vary the terminology depending on context so as not to fix any medical practices to a specific label.
6. See Lang and Jansen (2013) for a detailed analysis of differences between ayurvedic and biomedical psychiatric diagnoses, and chapter 4 for more on characteristics of ayurvedic medicine.
7. Harris and Thomas 2013.
8. Silverman 2014. Even names that are more familiar to US consumers may be found on the label of medicines from India, as United States–based Pfizer, the world's largest pharmaceutical company, has contracted with an Indian company to produce medications for Pfizer's own generic line of products (Krauskopf 2009).

9. World Health Organization 2016, 1–3.

10. This should not be surprising in the case of law, but, as has long been observed in medical anthropology and science and technology studies, medicine and science are not outside the domain of culture but are profoundly shaped by their social context just like any other human endeavor (see, for example, Dumit 2004; Latour and Woolgar 1979; Martin 1987; Traweek 1988). Patent law aims to protect scientific innovation, but its creators imagined only one kind of science.

11. Jayaraman 1994.

12. Biagioli and Galison, eds., 2003; Brown 2003; Coombe 1998; Rose 1993; Woodmansee and Jaszi, eds., 1994.

13. The anthropologist Michael Brown warns of the danger to creative freedom that can result from an overly rigid definition of ownership, whether this comes from corporate interests copyrighting their products or local peoples making proprietary claims over what they see as their heritage:

> The fluid dance of imitation and contrast, reticence and disclosure is an essential part of social life in pluralist societies. It is suppressed only with difficulty and at some cost in creative freedom. To make this observation is not to defend commercial exploitation or gross insensitivity. Nor is it to claim that movement of cultural elements between the politically weak and the politically strong is equivalent to exchanges among equals. I wish simply to point out the risks of taking too rigid a view of cultural ownership, especially when technological and social changes are making cultural boundaries ever harder to identify (2003, 251–252).

14. Aragon 2012.

15. Whereas technically ideas cannot be owned and only expressions of ideas can become intellectual property in forms such as artistic creations or specific innovations, I would argue that the current patent environment has resulted in an effective restriction on the sharing of ideas because of, for example, the reluctance of scientists to share insights out of fear of patent infringement. Also, the defenses of indigenous knowledge that have developed in response to the new IP regime are not far from the hypothetical examples presented here about mathematicians obtaining rights to numerical concepts and Europeans paying royalties to China. Aragon's (2012) work has shown how Indonesia has claimed copyright ownership of classic myths, yoga postures are already inscribed in the TKDL, and a national cuisine has already been claimed as property (Sciolino 2008).

16. Foster 2012; Hayden 2011; Oguamanam 2008.

17. McCrea 2010; Wolf 1969.

18. Aspinall 2005; Gramsci 1992.

19. Scott 1985.

20. The rhizome metaphor originally comes from Deleuze and Guattari (1987).

21. Randeria 2007.

22. Ibid., 2.

23. Ibid., 26.

24. This is occasionally acknowledged, as in Ulrich Beck's (1992) analysis of what he calls our "risk society" of late modernity. Max Weber's explanation of rationalization as the driver of modernization no longer applies, Beck explains, to the present global phase of modernity. Rather, "in the risk society the unknown and unintended consequences come to be a dominant force in history and society" (22). Also, Sivaramakrishnan mentions in a tribute to the political scientist James Scott's work on power and resistance that Scott's analysis includes "a serious questioning of any easy relationship between ideas, coherent intentions, and

sociopolitical outcomes—be they in the context of petty class relations or the grand struggles of societies to forge new social orders" (2005, 324), but this relationship remains on the sidelines in this volume on Scott's work and other analyses of power, resistance, and globalization. Lazarus-Black and Hirsch (1994) attend to the varieties of forms of resistance, but the legibility of power is not a major focus even though they acknowledge that in "most struggles against domination . . . neither the ends of resistance nor the terms of hegemony are clearly articulated" (8–9). For more analysis on the intelligibility of power and an exploration of this issue in relation to perspectives from the field of science and technology studies, see Halliburton (2011).

25. The contributions to Biagioli, Jaszi, and Woodmansee, eds. (2011) look at the historical background and basic principles behind current principles of intellectual property as well as how contemporary technologies spur new terrains of IP claims. Mgbeoji (2006) and Oguamanam (2008) examine implications of the new IP regime for low-income and peripheral countries through a socially informed legal analysis. Contributions to Halliburton, ed. (2012) present case studies of struggles over "intangible" property—not limited to "intellectual" property—around the world and examine the breadth of objects, ideas, and practices that can now be claimed as property. Volumes such as Drahos and Mayne, eds. (2002) and Bellman, Dutfield, and Meléndez-Ortiz, eds. (2003) and the work of Shiva (1997, 2001) provide activist and applied interventions, offering policy analysis and social justice advocacy. Lessig (2004) and McLeod (2005) speak effectively to academic and popular audiences about limitations on freedom of expression, focusing on law, creativity, and the effect of digital technologies in a Western context. Finally, Hestermeyer (2007) examines the effect of the new patent regime on access to medicine by examining legal and economic sources.

26. Shiva's work (1997, 2001) is an important exception, having covered patent controversies in India, but from an advocacy perspective, and see Chaudhuri (2005). Hayden's (2003, 2011) research in Argentina and Mexico is an important ethnographic contribution to studies of IP issues outside the European and North American context.

27. Liptak 2013.

28. Halliburton 2009b.

29. Throughout this book, brand names of drugs will appear with the initial letter in upper case and generic names will appear in all lower case letters.

30. Nader 1972.

31. Gusterson 1997.

32. Halliburton 2009a.

1. The Invention and Expansion of Intellectual Property

1. Biagioli 2006; Boyle 2008, 6.

2. The first quote is from Angell (2004), cited in Light and Warburton (2011, 35), and the second is from Light and Warburton (2011, 35).

3. Lowie 1928, 554–556.

4. Hallowell 1955 [1943], 243, citing Seagle.

5. Brown 2003, 89.

6. Biagioli 2006; Sherman and Bentley 1999.

7. Biagioli 2006, 1143.

8. The Statute of Anne 1710.

9. Jaszi and Woodmansee 1994, 6.

10. Jaszi and Woodmansee 2003, 196.

11. Jaszi and Woodmansee (2003) claim that the link is direct, that the idea of individual inventiveness in science is borrowed from literary discourse.

12. Sherman and Bentley 1999, 16.
13. Jackson 2003, 127.
14. The points about the Patent Act are from Mueller 2009, and the quote is from 35 U.S.C. §112, cited in Mueller 2009.
15. *Diamond v. Chakrabarty* 447 US 303 (1980).
16. Mowery et al. 2004, 185.
17. Potts 1992.
18. Liptak 2013.
19. Boyle 2008, 54–82.
20. WIPO 2015.
21. Paris Convention 1979; Mueller 2009, 529.
22. Gorman 2011, 129.
23. Gorman 2011, 131. Gorman does not claim that this is the first instance of resistance by developing countries. This is my interpretation based on his and other chronicles of the development of intellectual property referred to in this chapter.
24. Mgbeoji 2006, 40.
25. Mgbeoji 2006, 43.
26. Mgbeoji 2006, 44.
27. Gorman 2011, 141.
28. Davis 2010.
29. Donald R. Davis and Shubha Ghosh, who have researched precolonial law in India, personal communication.
30. Chaudhuri 2005, 20–39. Mazumdar 2013, 18. Quote is from Cipla (2015).
31. Bode 2008.
32. James 2014, 243–245; Matthews 2011, 163–164.
33. Ayyangar 1959, 13.
34. Balasubramaniam 2003, 140, citing Mills 1985. See Hayden (2011) on the lack of recognition and enforcement of pharmaceutical patents in Argentina.
35. Government of India 2005.
36. Prasad 2007, *The Hindu* 2005b.

2. The New Patent Regime

1. Halliburton 2009b.
2. McNeil 2005, A11.
3. Médecins Sans Frontières 2007.
4. Abbott 2005; Balasubramaniam 2003; Halliburton 2009b; Havlir and Hammer 2005; Hestermeyer 2007; Satyanarayana and Srivastava 2010; Sharma 2005; *Economic Times* 2009.
5. Abbott 2005.
6. See Hitchings et al. (2012) on the various chemical modifications and combinations that can be used in evergreening. While drug companies claim there are advantages to such minor adjustments, critics claim that the therapeutic difference is not significant enough to warrant a new patent. In the case of tenofovir, which is considered extensively in this book, a minor chemical change resulted in lower toxicity for this ARV, which gave it an important advantage over the standard of care.
7. Angell also considers the case of Clarinex (mentioned above in relation to the Hitchings et al. study in note 5), which was promoted as an improvement on Claritin. While Clarinex (desloratadine) is simply the chemical the body creates when it metabolizes Claritin (loratadine), Schering-Plough markets the new drug as an improvement, since it is effective for indoor as well as outdoor allergies, but Angell claims that Claritin would have probably

been effective against indoor allergies if it has been tested for these. With the statins, some new products were promoted as more effective but only, Angell says, because they were tested against another product at a higher dose (75–82). See similar points about me-too drugs in Spector (2005) and Ornstein and Jones (2015).

8. Mitta 2013. The intellectual property lawyer and regular SpicyIP blogger Prashant Reddy (2013) critiqued Mitta's story in the *Times of India* in one of his blog posts, arguing that CPI(M) is taking too much credit for Section 3d, which is the result of the input of many interested individuals and groups involved in the negotiation. Who contributed what to the passage of Section 3d is hard to determine, but Reddy does credit the CPI(M) for applying "immense pressure" in advocating a higher bar for patents in the new law. In fact, he says the CPI(M) pushed for a ban on an incremental innovation, even those that result in enhanced efficacy, but this was not included in the final provision.

9. Vijayakumar and Rajagopal 2013.

10. Angell 2004; Light and Warburton 2011. In the film *Pills Profits Protest* (d'Adesky, Avirgan, and Rossetti 2005), which chronicles the global AIDS movement, James Love, who works on intellectual property and access to medicine issues for NGOs, also claims that truly innovative R&D comes from universities, government-funded projects, and small companies, not big pharma companies.

11. Angell 2004, 58–65.

12. DiMasi et al. 2003.

13. Light and Warburton 2011. Light and Warburton criticize assumptions that the DiMasi et al. (2003) study used, such as including the amount of money a company would have made from investing the money, in equities or bonds for a return of 11 percent, if they had not spent it on research as a research "cost."

14. Singh 2007.

15. Medicines Patent Pool 2014, and see chapter 4 for further discussion of licensing and the Patent Pool.

16. Harris and Thomas 2013. As pointed out elsewhere regarding similar claims of radical price reduction, this may be an incompatible comparison juxtaposing prices in high-income countries to prices in low-income countries. Novartis would point out that while Gleevec was expensive in high-income markets, it was giving it away for free in India and other low-income countries while the Indian producers were selling it for $2,500. The free drugs, however, were limited to 30,000 patients in low-income countries, so the issue may be whether the drug donations are significant enough to counter the pricing effects of a potential patent.

17. Harris and Thomas 2013.

18. Subramanian 2014.

19. The India–European Union Free Trade Agreement remains stalled as of June 2016 after sixteen rounds of negotiations (*The Hindu* 2016). The European Union has scaled back its demand for increased patent protection such as data exclusivity and patent term extensions and has instead proposed that drugs patented in the European Union and produced in India should not be allowed to transit through the European Union when being shipped to a third country (Dey 2015). With data exclusivity, safety information from drug trials would have been considered the property of the originator company that did the original safety testing of a drug. Had this provision been included, generic producers would not be able to use that data in getting approval for their own product, and would have had to run their own costly safety tests even though the safety of the drug had already been established.

20. Vijayaraghavan and Raghuvanshi 2008, 114.

21. Medico Friend Circle 2014.

22. Government of India 2013.

23. Halliburton 2009b.

24. Ironically, the George W. Bush administration, which implemented PEPFAR to provide AIDS medications to poor countries, advocated for the implementation of TRIPS provisions while at the same time sourcing drugs from low-cost generic producers in India to make its funding go further.

25. Dugger 2007, A9; MSF 2007, 29.

26. Radhakrishnan 2007; Indian Patent Office 2010.

27. Pachamuthu et al. 2006.

28. Balasubramaniam 2003, 138.

29. Novartis 2007. Novartis is still continuing its Glivec access program, but the corporate responsibility section of its website is now promoting the Novartis Access program, which enables low-price access to treatments for noncommunicable diseases in low- and lower-middle-income countries, and its Malaria Initiative, which it says has delivered 750 antimalarial treatments at no-profit prices (Novartis 2015, 12–13).

30. Ecks 2008 and 2010.

31. Ecks borrows the concept of "information spillover" from the economist Sudip Chaudhuri, who suggests that paralleling the concern about lower-priced drugs making their way to developed countries is the concern that the simple *awareness* of lower prices in developing countries may lead to a demand for lower prices in developed countries (Ecks 2008, 177–178). This is an intriguing concept worthy of further consideration, although I am uncertain about the significance of this at present, partly because drug companies openly advertise their tiered pricing policies in developing countries, showing there may not be great concern about information spillover. But perhaps these companies believe that knowledge about drug prices travels in different channels. Perhaps those who examine corporate policies and pricing on pharmaceutical company websites are distinct from patient groups in wealthy countries who may become aware of cheaper drugs in other parts of the world by other means.

32. Rivers 2004 [1924], 63.

3. Ayurvedic Dilemmas

1. Gabriel and Hariharan 2003, 54.

2. Kumar 1997.

3. *The Hindu*, 2005a.

4. Jayaraman 1997.

5. Sivarajan and Balachandran 1994, 169, 323.

6. In Kline's writings (1959), he refers to the use of *Rauwolfia serpentina* as coming from "Southeast Asia," which may have been a mistaken reference to what is usually known as "South Asia," the region of the Indian subcontinent. Specifically, he refers to a Dr. Vakil and "Indian" sources as bringing this treatment to the attention of the West.

7. Kaplan and Sadock 1995, 1989.

8. Schlittler and Mueller 1956; Schlittler 1960; Healy 2002, 101–107.

9. This study does not examine trademark issues. For critical social analyses of trademark disputes, see Coombe (1998) and McLeod (2005). As a political stunt, McLeod obtained a trademark for the phrase "freedom of expression." Thus the book cited here is *Freedom of Expression®*, and technically one must use the "®" symbol when using the phrase "freedom of expression®" to recognize McLeod's property rights (though not in all contexts). McLeod was critiquing the excesses of contemporary intellectual property law through this prank and at the same time conducting an experiment to see how far the US government would go in granting IP rights.

10. See Gopalakrishan (2002), Reddy (2006), and Srinivas (2012), who have discussed the problem of who should receive benefits.

11. A benefit-sharing agreement for a quasi-ayurvedic formulation was reached between Tropical Botanical Garden researchers in Trivandrum District and the Kani, an indigenous people in Kerala. Kani knowledge of the therapeutic plant *aarogyapacha (Trichopus zeylanicus)* was a key ingredient in a drug marketed by Arya Vaidya Pharmacy under the name Jeevani (Pordié and Gaudillière 2014, 70–71).

12. Based on figures reported in Bode (2008).

13. Kakar 1982; Jansen 2016.

14. More extensive discussions of Ayurveda can be found in Kakar (1982), Zimmermann (1987), Obeyesekere (1982, 1992), Langford (2002), Wujastyk and Smith, eds. (2008), and Halliburton (2009a). These are primarily studies by social analysts examining Ayurveda. There are many other guides written by practitioners of Ayurveda.

15. Zimmermann (1992).

16. Selby 2005; Wujastyk and Smith, eds. 2008.

17. James (2014) makes similar points about how Ayurveda does not fit the premises of IP law, explaining that "it may not be possible to have a totally 'new' drug. . . . Ingredients of formulations may change but a totally new drug is rather difficult to come up with" (242). He adds that Ayurveda uses a multifaceted or "holistic" therapy rather than isolating chemical entities (243). See also Wolfgram (2012) on innovation and the interplay of knowledge, science, and texts in contemporary Ayurveda.

18. Banerjee 2008; Pordié and Gaudillière 2014.

19. For example, Posey (1990); Brush (1993, 663); Greaves (1995); Boyle (1996, 119–143); Napier (2002).

20. Wolfgram (2012) also critiques the individual versus communal/traditional innovation dichotomy and explains that ayurvedic practices that he observed do not conform to this model.

21. Sunder Rajan (2006, 23); Ugalde and Homedes 2006.

22. Bode (2008) shows how Ayurveda and unani medicine have changed because of industrial production. This, he reports, has led to a pharmaceuticalization of Ayurveda, where pills are the focus of therapy and other interventions are becoming neglected. Similar claims are made by Pordié and Gaudillière (2014, 63). The tailoring of ayurvedic medications to individual patients, which I describe in the remainder of the paragraph, may be more common in Kerala than in other parts of India.

23. Ecks 2014, 71.

24. Obeyesekere 1992, 170–171. See also Obeyesekere (1982).

25. This is my estimation based on my knowledge of production in these industries in India, the price of medications, and discussions in Bode (2008). See also Sharma (2000).

26. Singh 1992.

27. Furst et al. 2011.

28. Central Council for Research in Ayurvedic Sciences 2014.

29. Harilal 2011, 193.

30. Harilal 2009. Pordié and Gaudillière (2014) report that products claimed as "Ayurvedic Proprietary Medicine" are registered as trademarks (64).

31. See also Naraindas, Quack, and Sax, eds. (2014) on the asymmetrical relations between biomedicine and other healing modalities. Rarely is the need felt to translate biomedical concepts into terms of ayurvedic physiology. This asymmetry predates the current patent climate, but the new standards of innovation and truth supported by the new IP laws further entrench this hierarchy.

32. Rose 1993, 3.

33. Jaszi and Woodmansee 2003, 197.

34. Holton 1973.

35. Wolfgram (2012) has attempted to show how what he calls "value," which is similar to what I am calling "truth" and "reliability" in this context, is created in Ayurveda via "entextualization"—roughly, the deployment of texts—which marks a domain of value that diverges from that of IP law.

36. I have used pseudonyms for informants to conceal their identity, but one exception is the legal scholar Dr. Gopalakrishnan, whose real name I preserved in this section since he has publicly commented and published on the issues he addressed in conversations with me. In addition, although he is an informant, his commentary takes the form of a scholarly analysis of the issues involved, for which he deserves recognition.

37. An article in the Indian business magazine *Business Today* on the defeat of the US turmeric patent argues that the main problem for India is that it is too costly and time-consuming to fight such cases on a regular basis (Bakaya 2002, 102). Randeria (2007, 9) makes the same point in her analysis of the opposition to a patent on a means of processing products of the neem tree.

38. For example, Foucault 1978, Nandy 1983, Abu-Lughod 1990.

39. In addition to the critiques presented here, see his contribution to the effort to develop an equitable means of protecting "traditional knowledge" and benefit sharing among custodians of that knowledge in Gopalakrishnan (2002).

40. Kumar 1997, 724.

41. James 2014.

42. I am not providing the citation for this website to preserve the anonymity of the representative I spoke with.

43. Patwardhan, Vaidya, and Chorghade 2004; Patwardhan and Mashelkar 2009.

44. WTO 1994, Part II, Section 3, Article 22, 328.

45. As testament to the importance of maintaining attention to process in examining such emergent constellations of power such as the new global patent regime, in Gopalakrishnan (2002), he considered geographical indication to be a possible means of protecting traditional knowledge, but in conversation in 2005 he was not optimistic about this as a protection for Ayurveda. See also Gopalakrishnan and Agitha (2012).

46. Sivaramakrishnan 2005; Das and Poole 2004; Aspinall 2005; Halliburton 2011.

47. Pordié and Gaudillière (2014) explain that ayurvedic producers base their proprietary formulations on plant materials rather than on isolated chemical entities, and thus, unlike producers of Chinese medicine, who have patented active ingredients, Ayurveda retains "a critical alterity to biomedicine" (67).

4. The Gilead Model and the Perspective of Big Pharma

1. Nader 1972; Gusterson 1997.

2. Gentleman and Kumar 2006. See also Shiva (2005), who says "patents on medicines increase the cost of Aids [*sic*] drugs from $200 to $20,000 and cancer drugs from $2,400 to $36,000, for a year's treatment" (23).

3. Médecins Sans Frontières (Doctors Without Borders) 2007.

4. See Cullet (2003) and Halliburton (2009b) on the problem of affordability of "low-cost" generic drugs.

5. Sunder Rajan (2012, 334 and note 25). Tiered pricing for ARVs, which has been at the forefront of concerns about pricing and access, is offered by Abbott, Gilead, Merck, Bristol-Myers Squibb, Roche, GlaxSmithKline, and others (Médecins Sans Frontières 2007, 2014).

6. Halliburton (2009b, 519). This claim by Doctors Without Borders must have been based on prices of tenofovir in 2003. If its 2007 pricing guide used the prices it reported from

2006, the anticipated increase would have been less—from $100 ppy to $270 ppy (Médecins Sans Frontières 2007). See also the concerns of Balasubrmaniam (2003) and Cullet (2003) about the effects of TRIPS and the impact on drug prices.

7. For example, Cullet 2003; 't Hoen 2005; Hestermeyer 2007.

8. Gilead 2014; Médecins Sans Frontières 2014.

9. From 2013 to 2015, the number of people on antiretroviral therapy increased by one-third, from 12.9 million to 17 million. Still, the majority (54 percent) of the 37 million people around the world who have HIV/AIDS do not have access to this therapy, and around one million people die of AIDS every year (World Health Organization 2016, 1–3).

10. For example, Whyte, van der Geest, and Hardon 2002; Petryna, Kleinman, and Lakoff, eds. 2006; Ecks 2014; Peterson 2014.

11. Important insights about the culture and social practices of scientists have been gained in anthropological and sociological studies of work in scientific laboratories, though this has not been undertaken at pharmaceutical companies (Latour and Woolgar 1979, Traweek 1988, and Rabinow 1996).

12. For example, the medical anthropologist Roberto Abadie (2010), in his study of "human guinea pigs," who make a living as participants in clinical trials, wanted to get input from pharmaceutical companies regarding clinical trials, but because of the "traditional secrecy surrounding the pharmaceutical industry," he was not able to get very far. He did have a productive conversation with a researcher from a large pharmaceutical company about risk and compensation in clinical trials but was not able to meet with this individual again (163–164).

13. Whyte, van der Geest, and Hardon 2002, 139.

14. Pfizer 2014a, 2014b.

15. The first phrase is from Angell (2004, 85–87) and the second is from Gabriel and Goldberg (2014). Angell (2004, 85–87) gives the examples of "Premenstrual Dysphoric Disorder" (which became the new purpose for Lilly's Prozac, renamed Sarafem, once the patent ran out) and "acid reflux disease" (formerly "heartburn"), while Gabriel and Goldberg (2014) show how pathologizing behaviors and decreasing diagnostic thresholds create markets for pharmaceuticals where they did not exist previously.

16. Gilead 2011, 2.

17. Médecins Sans Frontières 2007, Gilead 2011.

18. Medicines Patent Pool 2015.

19. Bristol-Myers Squibb 2014.

20. Krauskopf 2009.

21. Pollock 2011, 107.

22. Prasad 2009, Initiative for Medicines, Access and Knowledge (I-MAK) 2014, and see chapter 2 on tenofovir and other patent oppositions.

23. For example, see the concerns of Balasubramaniam (2003), Cullet (2003), and Halliburton (2009b).

24. Viiv Healthcare 2013.

25. Singh 2007, I-MAK 2014c.

26. Natco requested a voluntary license from Pfizer for maraviroc in 2010, and media reports anticipated this was the prelude to a request for a compulsory license (one must first request a voluntary license and be denied to initiate a request for a compulsory license as Natco did in being awarded a compulsory license for Bayer's anticancer drug Nexavar [sorafenib]) (Singh 2011). There is nothing in the media, however, since this time on the result of this request or any further steps taken toward obtaining a compulsory license.

27. Singh (2007), and see discussion of this and related oppositions in chapter 2.

28. This relates to the reemerging problem of the scrutability of power. Related to my claim that pharmaceutical companies do not want to be read—by direct research and

preferring one-way communication—it is difficult to assess whether the emergence of Viiv Pharmacare, which focuses on ARVs, relates to the defeat of a key ARV patent case by one of its founders. One can read on Viiv's website about the culture, values, and mission of the company, but the company does not connect its creation and its emphasis on voluntary licensing to the relative difficulty of obtaining patents on certain drugs under India's 2005 Patents Act.

29. See Ecks (2008) and chapter 2 regarding spillover.

30. Médecins Sans Frontières 2007.

31. Butler 2009.

32. For two licenses, this information is missing. The licenses this review is based on are:

Patent holder	Medication
Merck Sharp and Dohme	pediatric raltegravir
AbbVie	pediatric lopinavir/ritonavir
Gilead	tenofovir
Gilead	cobicistat
Gilead	elvitegravir
Viiv Healthcare	pediatric dolutegravir
Viiv Healthcare	pediatric abacavir
Viiv Healthcare	adult dolutegravir and abacavir
Bristol-Myers Squibb	atazanavir

Available at Medicines Patent Pool (2015).

33. While Mexico is excluded in all lists, South Africa is included in most. Both are middle-income countries, though Mexico has a very low prevalence of HIV, whereas South Africa's is very high. This would seem to indicate, as Clifford Samuel said above, that companies take into account both per capita income and the impact of the AIDS epidemic in determining their pricing and policy.

In all but one license, India is included as a country where the licensee can sell the licensed medication. India is on the border between low-income and middle-income country classifications, and it is likely that India was included because almost all of the licenses have been taken by India-based pharmaceutical companies. While India is sought after as an emerging market by multinational corporations, it may have been considered politically impossible or inappropriate not to allow Indian pharmaceutical companies to sell licensed medications in India.

34. This analysis does not include all middle-income countries. Others in Latin America, the Middle East, and Asia are left out of licensing agreements.

35. Precisely, Sunder Rajan's analysis is of multinational pharmaceutical companies based in the United States or other wealthy countries and how they approach developed-country markets like the United States as well as how they interact with "Indian" pharmaceutical companies. As we will see in the following chapter, these pharmaceutical companies are hard to label—"multinational," "Indian," and "US" are all inadequate. Sunder Rajan (2012) describes a context that fits this and the next chapter when he refers to his work as focusing "on contemporary global pharmaceutical economies, with an empirical focus on the United States and India" (321). Sunder Rajan's concept of surplus health is borrowed from Joseph Dumit's (2012) work on pharmaceutical consumption in the United States.

36. Gabriel and Goldberg 2014; Moynihan and Cassels 2005.

5. The View from Hyderabad

1. Harris 2011.

2. *The Toronto Star* 2008.

3. *The Financial Express* 2009a, 2009b.

4. *Business Standard* 2014.

5. Brandl and Mudambi 2014, 139.

6. Sunder Rajan 2010, 60; Sariola et al. 2015. The antimalarial drug Synriam, developed by Ranbaxy, underwent clinical trials in India, Bangladesh, Thailand, and Africa (Das 2012).

7. *The Times of India* 2006.

8. Krauskopf 2009.

9. Tu 2011; Damodaran 2012; and see chapter 3 and Angell's accusation that pharmaceutical companies are not as inventive as they claim, because they often simply license new chemical entities that are discovered by government and university researchers.

10. Sunder Rajan 2012, 334.

11. Sunder Rajan 2012, 335.

12. Sunder Rajan 2012, 339.

13. According to Joseph Dumit (2012), "surplus health" is the "capacity to add medications to our life by lowering the level of risk required to be at risk. . . . Surplus health research aims to constantly increase the total number of medicines we consume" (17). Dumit is concerned about the growing trend whereby millions of Americans are being put on drugs such as statins, often for life, not because they are ill but in order to counter risk factors that may lead to disease.

14. 't Hoen 2005, 205.

15. Kapczynski 2008, 850. See also Chaudhuri 2005, 153–79.

16. Damodaran 2012; Das 2012; and *Political and Business Daily* 2014. Although India's *Political and Business Daily* calls the drug "indigenously developed," the situation was more complicated. It was developed by Ranbaxy working with a European consortium on malaria, and it is a synthetic molecule based on insights into the effects of a plant known to traditional Chinese medicine. At the time the drug was developed, Ranbaxy was owned by a Japanese pharmaceutical firm, but it was since acquired by another Indian company.

17. While pharmaceutical companies are identified by their real names elsewhere in this book, the Indian companies where interviewees worked were given pseudonyms because they opted to have their names and workplaces concealed.

As a testament to the vast size of the pharmaceutical sector in India, it was challenging to come up with pseudonyms for these companies. Every Indian name I could think of, whether Hindi, Dravidian, Sanskritic, or Persian-derived, already had a pharmaceutical company named after it—seemingly every Hindu deity, every common surname, every Sanskrit term from religion or philosophy was already the name of a pharmaceutical company somewhere in India. To the best of my knowledge, there are no pharmaceutical companies called Osmania or Kanaka in India or elsewhere.

18. Ranbaxy 2015.

19. This and other names here are pseudonyms.

20. Mr. Varma specified the value of his company, but I have excluded this information here in case it might help identify the company. In terms of being worth less than Lipitor, this applies to many India-based companies.

21. Mandavilli 2007.

22. This is my interpretation of Mr. Varma's statement. The "newness" of piperaquine is unclear. Mr. Varma says it is new, already on the market, and yet not an NCE "in the true sense." A scientist quoted in a report on Synriam calls it "a completely new drug" (Das 2012), whereas an article in a scientific journal says piperaquine has been around since the 1960s, used extensively in China and Southeast Asia (Davis et al. 2005). Another article says it has been in use for three decades (Ahmed et al. 2008), while a report on a clinical trial identifies arterolane as novel, though acknowledges that it is a synthetic derivative of artemisinin,

which has long been used in China (Valecha et al. 2010). I include this here to qualify Mr. Varma's statement, and it is a good illustration of the indeterminacy of novelty that has been reencountered in this book. It may be that since it was used in China and Southeast Asia, piperaquine is not well known to researchers elsewhere. Where drugs were tested and used most likely has an effect on whether they are known to exist or considered effective.

23. Mandavilli 2007; Damodaran 2012.

24. Mr. Biswas chose to remain anonymous and opted not to have the interview audiotaped so I use pseudonyms for him, his assistant, and his company and took handwritten notes on our conversation.

25. Mandavilli (2007) estimates fewer than one hundred are being developed.

26. Das 2012; Krishna and Ahmed 2012.

27. Das 2012, 1.

28. Sunder Rajan (2012, 326), drawing on Dumit's (2012) concept of surplus health.

29. Sunder Rajan 2012, 327.

Conclusion

1. Rose 2006.

2. Paul Rabinow and Nikolas Rose (2006) have likewise challenged the depictions of power in the work of the influential Italian political philosopher Giorgio Agamben (1998) and the political analysts Michael Hardt and Antonio Negri (2001), who depict current regimes of power as based on the threat of punishment, death, and forms of banishment. Rabinow and Rose argue that the present is marked instead by productive and consensual engagements with power. Bringing in philosopher Michel Foucault, they claim that power today is not primarily based on forbidding and punishing. Power tells us what to desire and what to pursue—an orientation that is coercive and in its own way.

3. Brazilian and Indian activists were using these methods around the same time and influenced each other to a significant degree (Patent Opposition Database 2014, Veras 2014). Other information in this paragraph is from Marques, Guimaraes, and Sternberg (2005) and Nunn (2009).

4. Veras 2014, 97–98.

5. Chaves et al. 2015; Médecins Sans Frontières 2013.

6. Conklin 2002; Filoche 2013.

7. Health Impact Fund 2015; Ladikas and Chaturvedi 2014.

8. Chaturvedi et al., eds., 2014.

9. See www.osdd.net.

10. OSDD 2015a; OSDD 2015b, 2.

11. Creative Commons 2015; OSDD 2015c. I am grateful to T. C. James of Research and Information System for Developing Countries, New Delhi, for calling my attention to OSDD when I speculated whether anything like copyleft efforts might be undertaken in the development of new medicines.

12. Srinivas 2012, 413.

13. Reddy 2006, 170–172.

14. Kapczynski 2008; Krikorian and Kapczynski 2010.

References

Abadie, Roberto. 2010. *The Professional Guinea Pig: Big Pharma and the Risky World of Human Subjects*. Durham, NC: Duke University Press.

Abbott, Frederick. 2005. "The WTO Medicines Decision: World Pharmaceutical Trade and the Protection of Public Health." *American Journal of International Law* 99 (2): 317–358.

Abu-Lughod, Lila. 1990. "The Romance of Resistance: Tracing Transformations of Power Through Bedouin Women." *American Ethnologist* 17 (1): 41–55.

Agamben, Giorgio. 1998. *Homo Sacer: Sovereign Power and Bare Life*. Translated by Daniel Heller-Roazen. Stanford, CA: Stanford University Press.

Ahmed, T., P. Sharma, A. Gautam, B. Varshney, M. Kothari, S. Ganguly, J. J. Moehrle, J. Paliwal, N. Saha, and V. Batra. 2008. "Safety, Tolerability, and Single- and Multiple-dose Pharmacokinetics of Piperaquine Phosphate in Healthy Subjects." *Journal of Clinical Pharmacology* 48 (2): 166–75.

Angell, Marcia. 2004. *The Truth About the Drug Companies: How They Deceive Us and What to Do About It*. New York: Random House.

Aragon, Lorraine. 2012. "Copyrighting Culture for the Nation? Intangible Property Nationalism and the Regional Arts of Indonesia." *International Journal of Cultural Property* 19 (3): 269–312.

Aspinall, Edward. 2005. *Opposing Suharto: Compromise, Resistance, and Regime Change in Indonesia*. Stanford, CA: Stanford University Press.

Ayyangar, N. Rajagopala. 1959. "Report on the Revision of the Patents Law." Government of India, Ministry of Commerce and Industry. Accessed July 31, 2015. http://theipanalysts.com/resources/.

Bakaya, Abha. 2002. "Basmati, Neem, Turmeric . . . and Global Counsel." *Business Today,* July 21.

Balasubramaniam, K. 2003. "Access to Medicines and Public Policy Safeguards Under TRIPS." In *Trading in Knowledge: Development Perspectives on TRIPS, Trade and Sustainability,* edited by Christophe Bellman, Graham Dutfield, and Ricardo Melendez-Ortiz, 135–142. London: Earthscan.

Banerjee, Madhulika. 2008. "Ayurveda in Modern India: Standardization and Pharmaceuticalization." In *Modern and Global Ayurveda: Pluralism and Paradigms,* edited by Dagmar Wujastyk and Frederick M. Smith, 201–214. Albany: SUNY Press.

Beck, Ulrich. 1992. *Risk Society: Toward a New Modernity.* Translated by Mark Ritter. London: Sage.

Bellman, Christophe, Graham Dutfield, and Ricardo Meléndez-Ortiz, eds. 2003. *Trading in Knowledge: Development Perspectives on TRIPS, Trade, and Sustainability.* London: Earthscan.

Biagioli, Mario. 2006. "Patent Republic: Representing Inventions, Constructing Rights and Authors." *Social Research* 73 (4): 1129–72.

Biagioli, Mario, and Peter Galison, eds. 2003. *Scientific Authorship: Credit and Intellectual Property in Science.* New York: Routledge.

Biagioli, Mario, Peter Jaszi, and Martha Woodmansee, eds. 2011. *Making and Unmaking Intellectual Property: Creative Production in Legal and Cultural Perspective.* Chicago: University of Chicago Press.

Bode, Maarten. 2008. *Taking Traditional Knowledge to the Market: The Modern Image of the Ayurvedic and Unani Industry, 1980–2000.* Hyderabad: Orient Longman.

Boyle, James. 1996. *Shamans, Software, and Spleens: Law and the Construction of the Information Society.* Cambridge, MA: Harvard University Press.

———. 2008. *The Public Domain: Enclosing the Commons of the Mind.* New Haven, CT: Yale University Press.

Brandl, Kristin, and Ram Mudambi. 2014. "EMNCs and Catch-Up Processes: The Case of Four Indian Industries." In *Understanding Multinationals from Emerging Markets,* edited by Alvaro Cuervo-Cazurra and Ravi Ramamurti, 129–152. Cambridge, UK: Cambridge University Press.

Bristol-Myers Squibb. 2014. "Patents, Licensing, and Technology Transfer: Working with Generic Companies and other Partners." Accessed October 9, 2014. http://www.bms.com/responsibility/access-to-medicines/Pages/patents-licensing-technology.aspx.

Brown, Michael F. 2003. *Who Owns Native Culture?* Cambridge, MA: Harvard University Press.

Brush, Stephen. 1993. "Indigenous Knowledge of Biological Resources and Intellectual Property Rights: The Role of Anthropology." *American Anthropologist* 95 (3): 653–686.

Business Standard. 2014. "Sun Pharma Buys Ranbaxy from Japan's Daiichi." April 8. Accessed December 15, 2014. http://www.business-standard.com/article/companies/sun-pharma-buys-ranbaxy-from-japan-s-daiichi-114040700737_1.html.

Butler, Declan. 2009. "India Says No to HIV Drug Patents." *Nature*, September 3. Accessed October 17, 2014. doi:10.1038/news.2009.882.

Central Council for Research in Ayurvedic Sciences. 2014. "Clinical Research." Accessed September 12, 2014. http://www.ccras.nic.in/researchactivities/research_select.htm.

Chaturvedi, Sachin, Miltos Ladikas, Guo Lifeng, and Krishna Ravi Srinivas, eds. 2014. *The Living Tree: Traditional Medicine and Public Health in China and India.* New Delhi: Academic Foundation.

Chaudhuri, Sudip. 2005. *The WTO and India's Pharmaceutical Industry: Patent Protection, TRIPS, and Developing Countries.* New Delhi: Oxford University Press.

Chaves, Gabriela Costa, Lia Hasenclever, Claudia Garcia Serpa Osorio-de-Castro, and Maria Auxiliadora Oliveira. 2015. "Strategies for Price Reduction of HIV Medicines under a Monopoly Situation in Brazil." (Original Portuguese title "Estratégias de redução de preços de medicamentos para aids em situação de monopólio no Brasil.") *Revista de Saúde Pública* 49:86–96.

Cipla. 2015. "About Us—History." Accessed August 3, 2015. http://www.cipla.com/Home/About-Us/History.aspx?mid=1289.

Collins, John. 2011. "Culture, Content, and the Enclosure of Human Being: UNESCO's 'Intangible' Heritage in the New Millennium." *Radical History Review* 109:121–136.

Coombe, Rosemary. 1998. *The Cultural Life of Intellectual Properties: Authorship, Appropriation and the Law.* Durham, NC: Duke University Press.

Conklin, Beth A. 2002. "Shamans versus Pirates in the Amazonian Treasure Chest." *American Anthropologist* 104 (4): 1050–1061.

Convention on Biological Diversity. 2016. "The Nagoya Protocol on Access and Benefit-sharing." Accessed October 4, 2016. http://www.cbd.int/abs.

Creative Commons. 2015. "About the Licenses." Accessed April 9, 2015. http://creativecommons.org/licenses/.

Cullet, Philippe. 2003. "Patents and Medicines: The Relationship between TRIPS and the Human Right to Health." *International Affairs* 79 (1): 139–160.

d'Adesky, Anne-Christine, Shanti Avirgan, and Ann T. Rossetti, producer/directors. 2005. *Pills Profits Protest: Chronicle of the Global AIDS Movement*, DVD. USA: Outcast Films.

Damodaran, Harish. 2012. "Why 'Made in India' Is Just a Slogan." *The Hindu—Business Line*, May 8. Accessed October 29, 2015. http://www.thehindubusinessline.com/opinion/columns/harish-damodaran/why-made-in-india-is-just-a-slogan/article3397771.ece.

Das, Soma. 2012. "Blunting the Bite." *The Financial Express*, April 29. Accessed January 8, 2015. http://www.financialexpress.com/archive/blunting-the-bite/942953/.

Das, Veena, and Deborah Poole. 2004. "The State and Its Margins: Comparative Ethnographies." In *Anthropology in the Margins of the State*, edited by Veena Das and Deborah Poole, 3–34. Santa Fe: School of American Research Press.

Davis, Donald R. 2010. *The Spirit of Hindu Law.* Cambridge, UK: Cambridge University Press.

Davis, T. M., T. Y. Hung, I. K. Sim, H. A. Karunajeewa, and K. F. Ilett. 2005. "Piperaquine: A Resurgent Antimalarial Drug." *Drugs* 65 (1): 75–87.

Deleuze, Gilles, and Felix Guattari. 1987. *A Thousand Plateaus: Capitalism and Schizophrenia.* Translated by Brian Massumi. Minneapolis: University of Minnesota Press.

Devraj, Ranjit. 2005. Lesser-Than-Evil Patent Law Pleases Drugs Firms. Inter Press Service, March 24. Accessed January 12, 2006. http://web.lexis-nexis.com/universe.

Dey, Sushmi. 2015. "Fears over EU Plan for Strict Drug Patent Regime." *The Times of India.* April 14. Accessed September 27, 2016. http://timesofindia.indiatimes.com/india/Fears-over-EU-plan-for-strict-drug-patent-regime/articleshow/46914621.cms.

Diamond v. Chakrabarty. 1980. 447 *United States Reports* 303.

DiMasi, J. A., R. W. Hansen, and H. Grabowski. 2003. "The Price of Innovation: New Estimates of Drug Development Costs." *Journal of Health Economics* 22:151–185.

Drahos, Peter. 1995. "Global Property Rights in Information: The Story of TRIPS at the GATT." *Prometheus* 13 (1): 6–19.

Drahos, Peter, and Ruth Mayne, eds. 2002. *Global Intellectual Property Rights: Knowledge, Access and Development.* Houndmills, UK: Palgrave Macmillan.

Dugger, C. W. 2007. "Clinton Foundation Announces a Bargain on Generic AIDS Drugs." *New York Times,* May 9.

Dumit, Joseph. 2004. *Picturing Personhood: Brain Scans and Biomedical Identity.* Princeton, NJ: Princeton University Press.

——. 2012. *Drugs for Life: How Pharmaceutical Companies Define Our Health.* Durham, NC: Duke University Press.

Ecks, Stefan. 2008. "Global Pharmaceutical Markets and Corporate Citizenship: The Case of Novartis' Anti-cancer Drug Glivec." *BioSocieties* 3:165–181.

——. 2010. "Near-Liberalism: Global Corporate Citizenship and Pharmaceutical Marketing in India." In *Asian Biotech: Ethics and Communities of Fate,* edited by Aihwa Ong and Nancy Chen, 144–166. Durham, NC: Duke University Press.

——. 2014. *Eating Drugs: Psychopharmaceutical Pluralism in India.* New York: New York University Press.

Filoche, Geoffroy. 2013. "Domestic Biodiplomacy: Navigating between Provider and User Categories for Genetic Resources in Brazil and French Guiana." *International Environmental Agreements: Politics, Law and Economics* 13 (2): 177–196.

Fish, Allison. 2006. "The Commodification and Exchange of Knowledge in the Case of Transnational Commercial Yoga." *International Journal of Cultural Property* 13:189–206.

Foster, Laura. 2012. "Patents, Biopolitics, and Feminisms: Locating Patent Law Struggles over Breast Cancer Genes and the *Hoodia* Plant." *International Journal of Cultural Property* 19 (3): 371–400.

Foucault, Michel. 1978. *The History of Sexuality—Volume 1: An Introduction.* New York: Vintage Books.

Furst, D. E., M. M. Venkatraman, M. McGann, P. R. Manohar, C. Booth-LaForce, R. Sarin, P. G. Sekar, K. G. Raveendran, A. Mahapatra, J. Gopinath, and P. R. Kumar. 2011. "Double-blind, Randomized, Controlled, Pilot Study Comparing Classic Ayurvedic Medicine, Methotrexate, and Their Combination in Rheumatoid Arthritis." *Journal of Clinical Rheumatology* 17 (4): 185–192.

Gabriel, D. C., and Rajeshswari Hariharan. 2003. "Legislation Bids to Regulate Biodiversity." *Managing Intellectual Property* 127:54.

Gabriel, Joseph, and Daniel Goldberg. 2014. "Big Pharma and the Problem of Disease Inflation." *International Journal of Health Services* 44 (2): 307–322.

Gentleman, Amelia, and Hari Kumar. 2006. "AIDS Groups in India Sue to Halt Patent for U.S. Drug." *New York Times*, May 11.

Gilead. 2011. "Achieving Sustainable Access to HIV/AIDS Medicines in the Developing World." Accessed June 6, 2011. http://www.gilead.com/responsibility.

———. 2014. "HIV Treatment Expansion." Accessed October 1, 2014. http://www.gilead.com/responsibility.

Gopalakrishnan, N. S. 2002. "Protection of Traditional Knowledge: The Need for a *Sui Generis* Law in India." *Journal of World Intellectual Property* 5 (5): 725–742.

Gopalakrishnan, N. S. and T. G. Agitha. 2012. "The Indian Patent System: The Road Ahead." In *The Future of the Patent System*, edited by Ryo Shimanami, 229–275. Cheltenham, UK: Edward Elgar.

Gorman, Daniel. 2011. "Globalization, Intellectual Property, and the Emergence of New Property Types." In *Property, Territory, Globalization: Struggles Over Autonomy*, edited by William D. Coleman, 122–147. Vancouver: University of British Columbia Press.

Government of India. 1970. "Patents Act of 1970." Accessed October 15, 2016. http://ipindia.nic.in/patents.htm.

———. 2005. "The Patents (Amendment) Act, 2005." Accessed October 15, 2016. http://ipindia.nic.in/patents.htm.

———. 2013. "Decision. In the matter of Application no. 1135/del/2007." Patent Office, New Delhi. Accessed January 25, 2015. http://cdn.patentoppositions.org/uploads/patent_office_decision/user_uploaded_file/51e7e4854a0d620002000009/836fe780-d1d6-0130-ab15-1a4124cd25b9.pdf.

Gramsci, Antonio. 1992. *Prison Notebooks*. Translated by Joseph Buttigieg and Antonio Callari. New York: Columbia University Press.

Greaves, T. C. 1995. "Cultural Rights and Ethnography." *Bulletin of the General Anthropology Division* 1 (2): 1–6.

Griffith, Harold R. 1945. "Curare in Anesthesia." *JAMA* 127 (11): 642–644.

Grove, Richard. 1996. "Indigenous Knowledge and the Significance of South-West India for Portuguese and Dutch Constructions of Tropical Nature." *Modern Asian Studies* 30 (1): 121–143.

Grover, Anand. 2013. "Novartis Case: Supreme Court's Historic Decision on Section 3(d)." *The Times of India*, April 2. Accessed July 16, 2013. http://articles.timesofindia.indiatimes.com/2013-04-02/india/38217259_1_therapeutic-efficacy-chennai-patent-office-patent-oppositions.

Gusterson, Hugh. 1997. "Studying Up Revisited." *Political and Legal Anthropology Review* 20 (1): 114–119.

Halliburton, Murphy. 2009a *Mudpacks and Prozac: Experiencing Ayurvedic, Biomedical, and Religious Healing*. Walnut Creek, CA: Left Coast Press.

———. 2009b. "Drug Resistance, Patent Resistance: Indian Pharmaceuticals and the Impact of a New Patent Regime." *Global Public Health* 4 (6): 515–527.

———. 2011. "Resistance or Inaction? Protecting Ayurvedic Medical Knowledge and Problems of Agency." *American Ethnologist* 38 (1): 85–100.

———. 2012. "Introduction." (Intangible Property at the Periphery: Expanding Enclosure in the 21st Century—Special Issue) *International Journal of Cultural Property* 19 (3): 233–249.

Halliburton, Murphy, ed. 2012. Intangible Property at the Periphery: Expanding Enclosure in the 21st Century—Special Issue. *International Journal of Cultural Property* 19 (3).

Hallowell, A. Irving. 1955 [1943]. "The Nature and Function of Property as a Social Institution." In *Culture and Experience*, 236–249. Philadelphia: University of Pennsylvania Press.

Hardt, Michael, and Antonio Negri. 2001. *Empire*. Cambridge, MA: Harvard University Press.

Harilal, M. S. 2009. "'Commercialising Traditional Medicine': Ayurvedic Manufacturing in Kerala." *Economic and Political Weekly* 44 (16): 44–51.

———. 2011. "Growth, Transition, and Globalization of Traditional Medicine: Ayurvedic Manufacturing with Special Focus on Kerala." PhD diss., Jawaharlal Nehru University, Centre for Development Studies, Thiruvananthapuram, Kerala, India.

Harris, Gardiner. 2011. "China and India Making Inroads in Biotech Drugs." *New York Times*, September 19.

Harris, Gardiner, and Katie Thomas. 2013. "Low-Cost Drugs in Poor Nations Get Lift in Court." *New York Times*, April 2.

Havlir, Diane V., and Scott M. Hammer. 2005. "Patients Versus Patents? Antiretroviral Therapy in India." *New England Journal of Medicine* 353 (8): 749–751.

Hayden, Cori. 2003. *When Nature Goes Public: The Making and Unmaking of Bioprospecting in Mexico*. Princeton, NJ: Princeton University Press.

———. 2011. "No Patent, No Generic: Pharmaceutical Access and the Politics of the Copy." In *Making and Unmaking Intellectual Property: Creative Production in Legal and Cultural Perspective*, edited by Mario Biagioli, Peter Jaszi, and Martha Woodmansee, 285–304. Chicago: University of Chicago Press.

Health Impact Fund. 2015. "The Health Impact Fund: A Summary Overview." Accessed April 9, 2015. http://healthimpactfund.org/the-health-impact-fund-a-summary-overview/.

Healy, David. 2002. *The Creation of Psychopharmacology*. Cambridge, MA: Harvard University Press.

Hestermeyer, Holger. 2007. *Human Rights and the WTO: The Case of Patents and Access to Medicines*. Oxford, UK: Oxford University Press.

Hitchings, Andrew, Emma Baker, and Teck Khong. 2012. "Making Medicines Evergreen." *British Medical Journal* 345:18–20.

Holton, Gerald. 1973. *Thematic Origins of Scientific Thought: Kepler to Einstein*. Cambridge, MA: Harvard University Press.

India Patent Office. 2010. "In the matter of the application for Patent 339/MUMNpl200. Decision." Accessed June 27, 2014. http://www.i-mak.org/storage/339.MUMNP.2006_Decision%20copy.pdf.

Initiative for Medicines, Access and Knowledge (I-MAK). 2014a. "Our Cases—Tenofovir." Accessed June 27, 2014. http://www.i-mak.org/tenofovir/.

———. 2014b. "About I-MAK." Accessed June 27, 2014. http://www.i-mak.org/about-i-mak-mission/.

———. 2014c. "Our Cases—Abacavir Sulfate." Accessed June 27, 2014. http://www.i-mak.org/abacavir-sulfate/.

Jackson, Myles. 2003. "Can Artisans Be Scientific Authors?" In *Scientific Authorship: Credit and Intellectual Property in Science*, edited by Mario Biagioli and Peter Galison, 113–132. New York: Routledge.

James, T. C. 2014. "Traditional Medicine and Intellectual Property Policies." In *The Living Tree: Traditional Medicine and Public Health in China and India*, edited by Sachin Chaturvedi, Miltos Ladikas, Guo Lifeng, and Krishna Ravi Srinivas, 241–280. New Delhi: Academic Foundation.

Jansen, Eva. 2016. *Naturopathy in South India: Clinics between Professionalization and Empowerment.* Leiden, The Netherlands: Brill.

Jaszi, Peter, and Martha Woodmansee. 1994. "Introduction." In *The Construction of Authorship: Textual Appropriation in Law and Literature*, edited by Martha Woodmansee and Peter Jaszi, 1–13. Durham, NC: Duke University Press.

———. 2003. "Beyond Authorship: Refiguring Rights in Traditional Culture and Bioknowledge." In *Scientific Authorship: Credit and Intellectual Property in Science*, edited by Mario Biagioli and Peter Galison, 195–224. New York: Routledge.

Jayaraman, K. S. 1994. "India Set to End 'Gene Robbery'." *Nature* 370:587.

———. 1997. "U.S. Patent Office Withdraws Patent on Indian Herb." *Nature* 389:6.

Kakar, Sudhir. 1982. *Shamans, Mystics and Doctors: A Psychological Inquiry into India and Its Healing Traditions.* Chicago: University of Chicago Press.

Kapczynski, Amy. 2008. "The Access to Knowledge Mobilization and the New Politics of Intellectual Property." *Yale Law Journal* 117:804–885.

Kaplan, Harold, and Benjamin Sadock. 1995. *Comprehensive Textbook of Psychiatry: Sixth Edition.* Baltimore: Williams & Wilkins.

Kelty, Christopher. 2008. *Two Bits: The Cultural Significance of Free Software.* Durham, NC: Duke University Press.

Kline, Nathan. 1954. "Use of Rauwolfia Serpentia Benth in Neuropsychiatric Conditions." *Annals of the New York Academy of Sciences* 59:107–132.

———. 1959. "The Challenge of the Psychopharmaceuticals." *Proceedings of the American Philosophical Society* 103 (3): 455–462.

Krauskopf, Lewis. 2009. "Pfizer to License Generics from India's Aurobindo." Reuters, March 3. Accessed October 10, 2014. http://uk.reuters.com/article/2009/03/03/pfizer-aurobindo-idUKN0240167220090303.

Krikorian, Gaelle, and Amy Kapczynski. 2010. *Access to Knowledge in the Age of Intellectual Property.* Cambridge, MA: MIT Press.

Krishna, R. Jai, and Rumman Ahmed. 2012. "India Launches Novel Anti-Malaria Drug." *Wall Street Journal*, April 25. Accessed January 13, 2015. http://www.wsj.com/articles/SB10001424052702304811304577365641151741560.

Kumar, Sanjay. 1997. "India Wins Battle with USA over Turmeric Patent." *Lancet* 350 (9079): 724.

Ladikas, Miltos, and Sachin Chaturvedi. 2014. "The Health Impact Fund: Issues and Challenges." In *The Living Tree: Traditional Medicine and Public Health in China and India*, edited by Sachin Chaturvedi, Miltos Ladikas, Guo Lifeng, and Krishna Ravi Srinivas, 27–32. New Delhi: Academic Foundation.

Lang, Claudia, and Eva Jansen. 2013. "Appropriating Depression: Biomedicalizing Ayurvedic Psychiatry in Kerala, India." *Medical Anthropology* 32:25–45.

Langford, Jean. 2002. *Fluent Bodies: Ayurvedic Remedies for Postcolonial Imbalance.* Durham, NC: Duke University Press.

Latour, Bruno, and Steve Woolgar. 1979. *Laboratory Life: The Construction of Scientific Facts.* Princeton, NJ: Princeton University Press.

Lawyers Collective. 2006. "Pre-Grant Representation by Way of Opposition Under Section 25(1) of the Patents Act 1970 (39 of 1970) and Rule 55(1) of the Rules as Amended by the Patents (Amendment) Act, 2005. Re: Patent Application No. 805/ MAS/1997." Accessed November 5, 2006. http://lawyerscollective.org/lc_hivaids/amtc.

Lazarus-Black, Mindie, and Susan Hirsch. 1994. "Introduction—Performance and Paradox: Exploring Law's Role in Hegemony and Resistance." In *Contested States: Law, Hegemony and Resistance*, edited by Mindie Lazarus-Black and Susan Hirsch, 1–31. New York: Routledge.

Leslie, Charles, and Allan Young, eds. 1992. *Paths to Asian Medical Knowledge*. Berkeley: University of California Press.

Lessig, Lawrence. 2004. *Free Culture: The Nature and Future of Creativity*. New York: Penguin.

Li, Tania Murray. 2005. "Beyond 'the State' and Failed Schemes." *American Anthropologist* 107 (3): 383–394.

Light, Donald W., and Rebecca Warburton. 2011. "Demythologizing the High Costs of Pharmaceutical Research." *Biosocieties* 6:34–50.

Liptak, Adam. 2013. "Justices, 9–0, Bar Patenting Human Genes." *New York Times*, June 14.

Lowie, Robert H. 1928. "Incorporeal Property in Primitive Society." *Yale Law Journal* 37 (5): 551–63.

Madrick, Jeff. 2014. "Our Misplaced Faith in Free Trade." *New York Times*, October 5, Sunday Review section.

Mandavilli, Apoorva. 2007. "Reinventing an Industry." *Nature* 445:138–139.

Marques, Ubirajara Regis Quintanilha, Valeska Santos Guimaraes, and Caitlin Sternberg. 2005. "Brazil's AIDS Controversy: Antiretroviral Drugs, Breaking Patents, and Compulsory Licensing." *Food and Drug Law Journal* 60:471–477.

Martin, Emily. 1987. *The Woman in the Body: A Cultural Analysis of Reproduction*. Boston: Beacon Press.

Matthews, Duncan. 2011. *Intellectual Property, Human Rights, and Development: The Role of NGOs and Social Movements*. Cheltenham, UK: Edward Elgar.

Mazumdar, Mainak. 2013. *Performance of Pharmaceutical Companies in India: A Critical Analysis of Industrial Structure, Firm Specific Resources, and Emerging Strategies*. Berlin: Springer-Verlag.

McCrea, Heather. 2010. *Diseased Relations: Epidemics, Public Health, and State-Building in Yucatán, Mexico, 1847–1924*. Albuquerque, NM: University of New Mexico Press.

McLeod, Kembrew. 2005. *Freedom of Expression®: Resistance and Repression in the Age of Intellectual Property*. Minneapolis: University of Minnesota Press.

McNeil, Donald G. 2005. "India Alters Law on Drug Patents." *New York Times*, March 23.

Médecins Sans Frontières (Doctors Without Borders). 2007. "Untangling the Web of Price Reductions: A Pricing Guide for the Purchase of ARVs for Developing Countries, 10th Edition." Accessed November 28, 2007. http://www.accessmed-msf.org.

——. 2013. "Untangling the Web of Antiretroviral Price Reductions, 16th Edition." Accessed October 17, 2016. http://www.accessmed-msf.org.

——. 2014. "Untangling the Web of Antiretroviral Price Reductions, 17th Edition." Accessed October 17, 2016. http://www.accessmed-msf.org.

Medicines Patent Pool. 2014. "Patents and Licenses on Antiretrovirals: A Snapshot." Accessed January 27, 2015. http://www.medicinespatentpool.org/wpcontent/uploads/Patents_And_Licences_On_ARVs_Snapshot_web.pdf.

——. 2015. "Licenses in the Patent Pool." Accessed October 16, 2015. http://www.medicinespatentpool.org/current-licences/.

Medico Friend Circle. 2014. "Activities." Accessed June 30, 2014. http://www.mfcindia.org/main/activities.html.

Merton, Robert. 1988. "The Matthew Effect in Science, II." *Isis* 79:s606–23.

Mgbeoji, Ikechi. 2006. *Global Biopiracy: Patents, Plants, and Indigenous Knowledge.* Ithaca, NY: Cornell University Press.

Mitta, Manoj. 2013. "Evergreening Clause: Thank the Left for It." *The Times of India*, April 7. Accessed January 26, 2015. http://timesofindia.indiatimes.com/home/stoi/deep-focus/Evergreening-clause-Thank-the-Left-for-it/articleshow/19422636.cms?referral=PM.

Moynihan, Ray, and Alan Cassels. 2005. *Selling Sickness: How the World's Biggest Pharmaceutical Companies Are Turning Us All Into Patients.* New York: Nation Books.

Mowery, David, Richard Nelson, Bhaven Sampat, and Arvids Ziedonis. 2004. *Ivory Tower and Industrial Innovation: University-Industry Technology Transfer Before and After the Bayh-Dole Act in the United States.* Stanford, CA: Stanford University Press.

Mueller, Janice M. 2009. *Patent Law—Third Edition.* New York: Aspen.

Nader, Laura. 1972. "Up the Anthropologist: Perspectives Gained from Studying Up." In *Reinventing Anthropology*, edited by Dell Hymes, 284–311. New York: Pantheon Books.

Nandy, Ashis. 1983. *The Intimate Enemy: Loss and Recovery of Self Under Colonialism.* Delhi: Oxford University Press.

Napier, A. David. 2002. "Our Own Way: On Anthropology and Intellectual Property." In *Exotic No More: Anthropology on the Front Lines*, edited by Jeremy MacClancy, 287–318. Chicago: University of Chicago Press.

Naraindas, Harish. 2014. "Nosopolitics: Epistemic Mangling and the Creolization of Contemporary Ayurveda." In *Medical Pluralism and Homeopathy in India and Germany (1810–2010) (Medizin, Gesellschaft und Geschichte—Beiheft 50)*, edited by Martin Dinges, 105–136. Stuttgart: Franz Steiner Verlag.

Naraindas, Harish, Johannes Quack, and William Sax, eds. 2014. *Asymmetrical Conversations: Contestations, Circumventions, and the Blurring of Therapeutic Boundaries.* New York: Berghahn.

Novartis. 2007. "Information Center: India Glivec Patent Case." Novartis website, Newsroom section. Accessed 16 July 2007. http://www.novartis.com/newsroom/india-glivec-patent-case/index.shtml.

——. 2015. "Corporate Responsibility Performance Report." Accessed September 28, 2016. https://www.novartis.com/sites/www.novartis.com/files/novartis-cr-performance-report-2015.pdf.

Nunn, Amy. 2009. *The Politics and History of AIDS Treatment in Brazil*. New York: Springer.

Obeyesekere, Gananath. 1982. "Science and Psychological Medicine in the Ayurvedic Tradition." In *Cultural Conceptions of Mental Health and Therapy*, edited by A. Marsella and G. White, 235–248. D. Reidel Publishing Co.

———. 1992. "Science, Experimentation, and Clinical Practice in Ayurveda." In *Paths to Asian Medical Knowledge*, edited by Charles Leslie and Allan Young, 160–176. Berkeley: University of California Press.

Oguamanam, Chidi. 2008. "Local Knowledge as Trapped Knowledge: Intellectual Property, Culture, Power, and Politics." *Journal of World Intellectual Property* 11 (1): 29–57.

Ong, Aihwa, and Stephen Collier, eds. 2008. *Global Assemblages: Technology, Politics, and Ethics as Anthropological Problems*. Malden, MA: Wiley.

Open Source Drug Discovery (OSDD). 2015a. "Collaborative Innovation Platform." Accessed April 9, 2015. http://www.osdd.net/about-us/how-osdd-works.

———. 2015b. "License." Accessed April 9, 2015. http://www.osdd.net/about-us/osdd-policies/access-policy.

———. 2015c. "Annual Report 2013–2014." Accessed April 9, 2015. http://www.osdd.net/news-updates.

Orstein, Charles and Ryann Grochowski Jones. 2015. "Vying for Market Share, Companies Heavily Promote 'Me Too' Drugs." *ProPublica*, January 7. Accessed February 28, 2017. https://www.propublica.org/article/vying-for-market-share-companies-heavily-promote-me-too-drugs

Pachamuthu, B., S. Shanmugam, K. Nagalingeswaran, S. S. Solomon, and S. Solomon. 2006. "HIV-1 Drug Resistance among Untreated Patients in India: Current Status." *Journal of Postgraduate Medicine* 52:183–186.

Paris Convention. 1979. "Paris Convention for the Protection of Industrial Property, 1883, last amended 1979." World Intellectual Property Organization Database of Intellectual Property—Legislative Texts. Accessed July 18, 2013. http://www.wipo.int/export/sites/www/treaties/en/ip/paris/pdf/trtdocs_wo020.pdf.

Patent Opposition Database. 2014. "Success Story: The Case of TDF in Brazil." Accessed October 7, 2014. http://patentoppositions.org.

Patwardhan, Bhushan, and Raghunath Anat Mashelkar. 2009. "Traditional Medicine-Inspired Approaches to Drug Discovery: Can Ayurveda Show the Way Forward?" *Drug Discovery Today* 14 (15/16): 804–811.

Patwardhan, Bhushan, Ashok D. B. Vaidya, and Mukund Chorghade. 2004. "Ayurveda and Natural Products Drug Discovery." *Current Science* 86 (6): 789–799.

Peterson, Kristin. 2014. *Speculative Markets: Drug Circuits and Derivative Life in Nigeria*. Durham, NC: Duke University Press.

Petryna, Adriana, Arthur Kleinman, and Andrew Lakoff, eds. 2006. *Global Pharmaceuticals: Ethics, Markets, Practices*. Durham, NC: Duke University Press.

Pfizer. 2014a. "Global Health Programs. Global Health Fellows." Accessed December 17, 2014, http://www.pfizer.com/responsibility/global_health/global_health_fellows.

———. 2014b. "Global Health Programs. Mobilize Against Malaria." Accessed December 17, 2014. http://www.pfizer.com/responsibility/global_health/pfizer_malaria_partnership.

Political and Business Daily. 2014. "Ranbaxy Nod to Launch Synriam in African Nations." December 15. Accessed January 8, 2014. http://www.lexisnexis.com.queens. ezproxy.cuny.edu:2048/lnacui2api/api/version1/getDocCui?lni=5DVH-R3V1-JDKC-R26D&csi=270944,270077,11059,8411&hl=t&hv=t&hnsd=f&hns=t&hgn=t&oc =00240&perma=true.

Pollock, Anne. 2011. "Transforming the Critique of Big Pharma." *BioSocieties* 6 (1): 106–118.

Pordié, Laurent, and Jean-Paul Gaudillière. 2014. "The Reformulation Regime in Drug Discovery: Revisiting Polyherbals and Property Rights in the Ayurvedic Industry." *East Asian Science, Technology and Society* 8:57–79.

Posey, Darrell. 1990. "Intellectual Property Rights and Just Compensation for Indigenous Knowledge." *Anthropology Today* 6 (4): 13–16.

Potts, Jeffrey. 1992. "Moore v. Regents of the University of California: Expanded Disclosure, Limited Property Rights." *Northwestern University Law Review* 86:453–496.

Prasad, K. V. 2007. "Defend Indian Patents Act: Says CPI(M)." *The Hindu*, Feb. 3. Accessed July 16, 2013. http://www.hindu.com/2007/02/03/stories/2007020305131200. htm.

Prasad, R. 2009. "India Rejects Patent Claims on Two HIV/AIDS Drugs." *The Hindu*, September 7. Accessed December 23, 2014. http://www.thehindu.com/sci-tech/ health/india-rejects-patent-claims-on-two-hivaids-drugs/article15145.ece.

Rabinow, Paul. 1996. *Making PCR: A Story of Biotechnology.* Chicago: University of Chicago Press.

Rabinow, Paul, and Nikolas Rose. 2006. "Biopower Today." *BioSocieties* 1:195–217.

Radhakrishnan, Priti. 2007. "India and Second-line ART: Evaluating the Way Forward." Discussion paper. Chennai: Indian Network for People Living with HIV/AIDS. New Delhi: National HIV/AIDS Policy and Advocacy Centre. Accessed: March 1, 2016. http://archive.law.fsu.edu/gpc2007/materials/18%20FINAL_INP_March20.pdf.

Ranbaxy. 2015. "Ranbaxy Community Healthcare Society." Accessed January 30, 2015. http://www.ranbaxy.com/csr-ehs/ranbaxy-consumer-healthcare-science/.

Randeria, Shalini. 2007. "The State of Globalization: Legal Plurality, Overlapping Sovereignties, and Ambiguous Alliances between Civil Society and the Cunning State in India." *Theory, Culture and Society* 24 (1): 1–33.

Reddy, Prashant. 2013. "Victory has a Thousand Fathers: CPI(M) Stakes Claim to Section 3(d)." *SpicyIP*, [Web log], April 12. Accessed January 25, 2015. http://spicyip. com/2013/04/victory-has-thousand-fathers-cpim.html.

Reddy, Sita. 2006. "Making Heritage Legible: Who Owns Traditional Medical Knowledge?" *International Journal of Cultural Property* 13:161–188.

Reuters. 2007. "Gilead Pushes for Patent for HIV Drug in India." Accessed October 10, 2014. http://www.reuters.com/article/2007/05/11/us-gilead-aids-patent-idUSDEL2811220070511.

Rivers, W. H. R. 2004 [1924]. *Medicine, Magic, and Religion.* New York: Routledge.

Rose, Mark. 1993. *Authors and Owners: The Invention of Copyright.* Cambridge, MA: Harvard University Press.

Rose, Nikolas. 2006. *The Politics of Life Itself: Biomedicine, Power, and Subjectivity in the Twenty-First Century.* Princeton, NJ: Princeton University Press.

Sariola, Salla, Deapica Ravindran, Anand Kumar, and Roger Jeffery. 2015. "Big-pharmaceuticalization: Clinical Trials and Contract Research Organizations in India." *Social Science and Medicine* 131:239–246.

Satyanarayana, Kanikaram, and Sadhana Srivastava. 2010. "Patent Pooling for Promoting Access to Antiretroviral Drugs (ARVs): A Strategic Option for India." *The Open AIDS Journal* 4:41–53. doi: 10.2174/1874613601004020041.

Schlittler, Emil (assignor to Ciba Pharmaceutical Products). 1960. 18-O-Hetero Esters of Reserpine Acid Methyl Ester. U.S. Patent 2,964,527, filed November 14, 1957, and issued December 13, 1960.

Schlittler, Emil, and Johannes Mueller. 1956. Crystalline Reserpine, Salts, and Compositions Thereof. U.S. Patent 2,752,351, filed July 10, 1953, and issued June 26, 1956.

Sciolino, Elaine. 2008. "Time to Save the Croissants." *New York Times*, September 24.

Scott, James. 1985. *Weapons of the Weak: Everyday Forms of Peasant Resistance*. New Haven, CT: Yale University Press.

———. 1990. *Domination and the Arts of Resistance: Hidden Transcripts*. New Haven, CT: Yale University Press.

———. 1998. *Seeing Like a State: How Certain Schemes to Improve the Human Condition Have Failed*. New Haven, CT: Yale University Press.

Seema, Chawardol, and Jain Sapan. 2013. "Clinical Evaluation of Haridra Khanda and Anu Tail Nasya in the Management of Allergic Rhinitis." *International Journal of Ayurveda and Alternative Medicine* 1 (1): 43–49.

Selby, Martha Ann. 2005. "Sanskrit Gynecologies in Postmodernity: The Commoditization of Indian Medicine in Alternative Medical and New-Age Discourses on Women's Health." In *Asian Medicine and Globalization*, edited by Joseph Alter, 120–131. Philadelphia: University of Pennsylvania Press.

Sharma, Dinesh. 2000. "India Raises Standards for Traditional Drugs." *The Lancet* 356:231.

Sharma, Dinesh. 2005. "Indian Patents May Hamper Access to Antiretrovirals Globally." *Lancet Infectious Diseases* 5 (3): 136. Accessed October 20, 2014. doi: http://dx.doi.org/10.1016/S1473-3099(05)01296-X.

Sherman, Brad, and Lionel Bentley. 1999. *The Making of Modern Intellectual Property Law: The British Experience 1760–1911*. Cambridge, UK: Cambridge University Press.

Shiva, Vandana. 1997. *Biopiracy: The Plunder of Nature and Knowledge*. Boston: South End Press.

———. 2001. *Protect or Plunder? Understanding Intellectual Property Rights*. London: Zed Books.

———. 2005. "New Emperors, Old Clothes." *The Ecologist* 35 (6): 22–23

Silverman, Ed. 2014. "Why More Indian Generic Drugs Will Make Their Way to the U.S." *Wall Street Journal*, May 14. Accessed July 7, 2015. http://blogs.wsj.com/corporate-intelligence/2014/05/14/why-more-indian-generic-drugs-will-make-their-way-to-the-u-s/.

Singh, Khomba. 2007. "GSK Drops Claims on Two AIDS Medicines." *The Economic Times*, December 7. Accessed December 19, 2014. Available at: http://articles.economictimes.indiatimes.com/2007-12-07/news/28406347_1_patent-applications-patent-office-patent-act.

——. 2011. "Natco Seeks Pfizer Nod for Drug Clone." *The Economic Times*, January 6. Accessed October 25, 2016. http://articles.economictimes.indiatimes.com/2011-01-05/news/28426847_1_natco-pharma-pfizer-hiv-patients.

Singh, R. H. 1992. *Panca Karma Therapy: Ancient Classical Concepts, Traditional Practices, and Recent Advances*. Varanasi, India: Chowkhamba Sanskrit Series.

Sivaramakrishnan, K. 2005. "Introduction to 'Moral Economies, State Spaces, and Categorical Violence'." *American Anthropologist* 107 (3): 321–330.

Sivarajan, V. V., and Indira Balachandran. 1994. *Ayurvedic Drugs and Their Plant Sources*. New Delhi: Oxford & IBH Publishing Co.

Spector, Rosanne. 2005. "Me-too Drugs: Sometimes They're Just the Same Old, Same Old." *Stanford Medicine Magazine*, Summer 2005. Accessed February 28, 2017. http://sm.stanford.edu/archive/stanmed/2005summer/drugs-metoo.html

Srikanth, N., K. K. Chopra, and Jaya Prakash Narayan. 2001. "A Clinical Study of the Role of Nasyakarma and Ghritapana in the Management of Arddhavabhedaka vis-à-vis Migranous Headaches." *Aryavaidyan* 14 (3): 166–171.

Srinivas, Krishna Ravi. 2012. "Protecting Traditional Knowledge Holders' Interests and Preventing Misappropriation—Traditional Knowledge Commons and Biocultural Protocols: Necessary but Not Sufficient?" *International Journal of Cultural Property* 19 (3): 401–422.

Subramanian, Arvind. 2014. "The Thorn in India-US Business Ties." *Business Standard*, March 13.

Sunder Rajan, Kaushik. 2006. *Biocapital: The Constitution of Postgenomic Life*. Durham, NC: Duke University Press.

——. 2010. "The Experimental Machinery of Global Clinical Trials: Case Studies from India." In *Asian Biotech: Ethics and Communities of Fate*, edited by Aihwa Ong and Nancy Chen, 55–80. Durham, NC: Duke University Press.

——. 2012. "Pharmaceutical Crises and Questions of Value: Terrains and Logics of Global Therapeutic Politics." *South Atlantic Quarterly* 111(2): 321–346.

't Hoen, Ellen. 2005. "TRIPS, Pharmaceuticals, Patents, and Access to Essential Medicines: A Long Way from Seattle to Doha." In *Perspectives on Health and Human Rights*, edited by Sofia Gruskin, Michael A. Grodin, George J. Annas, and Stephen P. Marks, 203–222. New York: Routledge.

The Economic Times. 2009. "Patent on AIDS Drugs Could Hike Costs." March 14. Accessed October 15, 2014. http://articles.economictimes.indiatimes.com/2008-03-14/news/28419611_1_aids-drugs-quality-drugs-naco.

The Financial Express. 2009a. "Ranbaxy to Market Daiichi's Products in Mexico." October 5. Accessed October 29, 2014. http://www.lexisnexis.com.queens.ezproxy.cuny.edu:2048/lnacui2api/api/version1/getDocCui?lni=801X-5VX1-2NV6-T2YC&csi=270944,270077,11059,8411&hl=t&hv=t&hnsd=f&hns=t&hgn=t&oc=00240&perma=true.

——. 2009b. "Daiichi to Use Ranbaxy Network in Africa." December 22. Accessed October 29, 2014. http://www.lexisnexis.com.queens.ezproxy.cuny.edu:2048/lnacui2api/api/version1/getDocCui?lni=801X-5VX1-2NV6-T037&csi=270944,270077,11059,8411&hl=t&hv=t&hnsd=f&hns=t&hgn=t&oc=00240&perma=true.

The Hindu. 2005a. "India Wins Neem Patent Case." March 9. Accessed September 29, 2014. http://www.thehindu.com/2005/03/09/stories/2005030902381300.htm.

——. 2005b. "Many Left Amendments Accepted." March 19. Accessed January 12, 2006. http://www.thehindu.com/2005/03/19/stories/2005031906781100.htm.

——. 2016. "India, EU Aim to Break Free Trade Agreement Impasse." Accessed September 27, 2016. http://www.thehindu.com/business/Industry/india-eu-aim-to-break-free-trade-agreement-impasse/article8677993.ece.

The Statute of Anne. 2013[1710]. "The Statute of Anne." Yale Law School Library, The Avalon Project. Accessed July 8, 2013. http://avalon.law.yale.edu/18th_century/anne_1710.asp.

The Times of India. 2006. "US-based Mylan Buys Majority Stake in Matrix." August 29. Accessed October 29, 2014. http://timesofindia.indiatimes.com/business/india-business/US-based-Mylan-buys-majority-stake-in-Matrix/articleshow/1933730.cms.

The Toronto Star. 2008. "Daiichi Sankyo Buying into Indian Drug Maker." June 12. Accessed October 29, 2014. http://www.lexisnexis.com.queens.ezproxy.cuny.edu:2048/lnacui2api/api/version1/getDocCui?lni=4SRC-GF30-TWMB-514V&csi=270944,27 0077,11059,8411&hl=t&hv=t&hnsd=f&hns=t&hgn=t&oc=00240&perma=true.

Traweek, Sharon. 1988. *Beamtimes and Lifetimes: The World of High Energy Physicists.* Cambridge, MA: Harvard University Press.

Tu, Youyou. 2011. "The Discovery of Artemisinin (Qinghaosu) and Gifts from Chinese Medicine." *Nature Medicine* 17 (10): 1217–1220.

Ugalde, Antonio, and Nuria Homedes. 2006. "From Scientists to Merchants: The Transformation of the Pharmaceutical Industry and its Impact on Health." *Societies Without Borders* 1:21–40.

UNAIDS. 2015a. "The Gap Report." Accessed July 9, 2015. http://www.unaids.org/sites/default/files/media_asset/UNAIDS_Gap_report_en.pdf.

——. 2015b. "Information by Country." Accessed October 19, 2015. http://www.unaids.org/en/regionscountries.

Valecha, Neena, Sornchai Looareesuwan, Andreas Martensson, Salim Mohammed Abdulla, Srivicha Krudsood, Noppadon Tangpukdee, Sanjib Mohanty, Saroj K. Mishra, P. K. Tyagi, S. K. Sharma, Joerg Moehrle, Anirudh Gautam, Arjun Roy, Jyoti K. Paliwal, Monica Kothari, Nilanjan Saha, Aditya P. Dash, and Anders Björkman. 2010. "Arterolane, a New Synthetic Trioxolane for Treatment of Uncomplicated *Plasmodium falciparum* Malaria: A Phase II, Multicenter, Randomized, Dose-Finding Clinical Trial." *Clinical Infectious Diseases* 51 (6):684–691.

Veras, Juliana. 2014. "Making Tenofovir Accessible in the Brazilian Public Health System: Patent Conflicts and Generic Production." *Developing World Bioethics* 14 (2): 92–100.

Viiv Healthcare. 2013. "ViiV Healthcare Announces a Voluntary Licence Agreement with the Medicines Patent Pool to Increase Access to HIV Medicines for Children." Press release. Accessed October 16, 2014. http://www.viivhealthcare.com/media.

Vijayakumar, Sanjay, and Divya Rajagopal. 2013. "Natco's Compulsory Licence for Selling Generic Copies of Bayer's Cancer Drug Nexavar Upheld by Ipab." *The Economic Times*, March 4. Accessed January 26, 2015. http://articles.economictimes.indiatimes.com/2013-03-04/news/37437382_1_nexavar-compulsory-licence-leena-menghaney.

Vijayaraghavan, Bakthavathasalan and Poonam Raghuvanshi. 2008. "Impact of the Amended Indian Patent Act on the Indian Pharmaceutical Industry." *Journal of Generic Medicines* 5 (2): 111–119.

Whyte, Susan Reynolds, Sjaak Van der Geest, and Anita Hardon. 2002. *Social Lives of Medicines*. Cambridge: Cambridge University Press.

Wolf, Eric R. 1969. *Peasant Wars of the Twentieth Century*. New York: Harper and Row.

Wolfgram, Matthew. 2012. "The Entextualization of Ayurveda as Intellectual Property." *International Journal of Cultural Property* 19:313–343.

Woodmansee, Martha, and Peter Jaszi, eds. 1994. *The Construction of Authorship: Textual Appropriation in Law and Literature*. Durham, NC: Duke University Press.

World Health Organization (WHO). 2016. "Global AIDS Update 2016: UNAIDS Report." Accessed October 10, 2016. http://www.who.int/hiv/pub/arv/global-aids-update-2016-pub/en/.

World Intellectual Property Organization (WIPO). 2006. "Bioethics and Patent Law: The Case of the Oncomouse." *WIPO Magazine*, Issue 3/2006. Accessed March 2, 2015. http://www.wipo.int/wipo_magazine/en/2006/03/article_0006.html.

——. 2015. "WIPO Treaties: General Information." Accessed January 23, 2015. http://www.wipo.int/treaties/en/general/.

World Trade Organization (WTO). 1994. "Agreement Establishing the World Trade Organization. Annex 1C: Agreement on Trade-Related Aspects of Intellectual Property Rights." Accessed April 15, 2015. http://www.wto.org/english/docs_e/legal_e/legal_e.htm#TRIPs.

——. 2001. "Declaration on the TRIPS Agreement and Public Health." Accessed September 9, 2016. https://www.wto.org/english/thewto_e/minist_e/min01_e/mindecl_trips_e.htm.

Wujastyk, Dagmar, and Frederick M. Smith, eds. 2008. *Modern and Global Ayurveda: Pluralism and Paradigms*. Albany: SUNY Press.

Zimmermann, Francis. 1987. *The Jungle and the Aroma of Meats: An Ecological Theme in Hindu Medicine*. Berkeley: University of California Press.

——. 1992. "Gentle Purge: The Flower Power of Ayurveda." In *Paths to Asian Medical Knowledge*, edited by Charles Leslie and Allan Young, 209–224. Berkeley: University of California Press.

INDEX

abacavir, 38, 110–111, 112
Abbott Laboratories, 38, 48, 51
access to knowledge (A2K), 2, 148–149
access to medicine (drugs), 40, 50, 149
acquisition, 118–119, 121
active chemical ingredients, 7, 58, 69, 87, 118, 132
activists, 8, 10, 16, 17, 19, 35, 39, 47, 48, 50, 54, 59, 77, 89, 91, 101, 103, 108, 122, 142, 144, 149
Adelphane, 61
advocacy, 37, 49, 108, 149, 153n25
affordability, 51
Africa, 40, 53, 110
AIDS activists, 53, 54
AIDS/HIV, 6, 7, 15, 34, 36, 38, 50, 77, 90, 97, 105, 108, 112, 114, 115, 143
AIDS medication (drugs), 38, 51, 96, 111, 128, 129, 140, 144

AIDS treatment programs, 38, 50, 107
allopathy, 6, 67, 68
Angell, Marcia, 41, 45
antibiotics, 121
anticancer, 43, 45, 82
antifungal, 58
antihypertensive, 61, 82
antipsychotic, 8, 61, 82
antimalarial, 16, 102, 122, 126, 130, 138, 141, 143
anti-patent activists, 91
antiretrovirals (ARVs), 15, 19, 34, 35, 37, 38, 39, 50, 51, 92, 95, 104, 111, 113, 123, 126, 141, 142, 144, 149
anti-WTO protests, 83
artistic work, 76
Arya Vaidya Sala (company), 32
Aryavaidyani (journal), 73
atazanavir, 43, 144, 145

atorvastatin (Lipitor), 126
Aurobindo, 7, 34, 38, 105, 116
autonomous invention, 45
Ayush Tomorrow (journal), 73
Ayurveda, 4–6, 7, 8, 10, 11, 12, 56, 57,
58, 59, 62, 63–64, 65–75, 80, 81, 82,
83, 85, 87, 89, 136, 140, 142, 145,
146, 151n5, 157, 158; authentic, 66;
biomedicine and, 5, 7–8, 31, 66–67,
76–77, 78, 89, 136; creolization of,
75; defending, 57; exploitation of,
84; innovation in, 7, 22, 70, 76–77,
78; multinational pharmaceutical
companies and, 89; "new" treatments
in, 77; patent law and, 75, 78, 80, 88,
89; practitioners, 5, 7–8, 12, 17, 22, 24,
83, 89, 91, 120, 132, 142; principles of,
65; products (drugs) based on, 3, 4, 64,
79, 88; property claims in, 59; recipes,
71; research into, 67, 72, 73; search
engine, 87; threat to, 7, 59, 86, 89
Ayurveda colleges, 65, 67, 74, 80
Ayurveda hospitals, 67, 71
ayurvedic: activists, 58, 82; company,
82–83, 91; doctors (physicians), 55, 68,
88, 127; knowledge, 53, 79, 80, 89, 142;
practice, 58; principles, 71; professionals,
81; texts, 84; therapy, 57, 88
Ayyangar Committee, 32, 33

Bayer, 43
Bayh-Dole Act, 27–28
benefit-sharing, 4, 57, 62, 139, 145, 147,
157n11
Biagioli, Mario, 24
big pharma, 47, 48, 50, 92, 99, 103,
105, 114, 117, 119, 129, 131, 134,
141, 143
Bill and Melinda Gates Foundation, 107
Biocon, 131, 137, 138
biogenetic resources, 145
Biological Diversity Act (2002), 57, 62
biological material, 27–28
biomedical innovation, 77
biomedical methods, 75

biomedicine, 6, 66–67; chemically
isolated ingredients, 7; drug companies,
8, 82, 87, 88, 91, 98, 120; Indian
producers, 120; Western, 5, 6, 31
biopiracy, 3, 4, 7, 64, 124, 126, 141,
145, 151n5
biopolitics, 143
bioprospecting, 56, 60, 61, 62
bioprospectors, 58
biotechnology, 62
Bombay Stock Exchange, 137
Boyle, James, 8, 21–22, 48, 148
Brazil, 7, 34, 49, 96, 110, 112, 113, 117,
134, 144–145
Brazilian Interdisciplinary AIDS
Association (ABIA), 49
Bristol-Myers Squibb, 4, 30, 45, 53, 105,
107, 158n5
Brown, Michael, 24

Cancer Patients Aid Association, 47
Caraka Samhita, 63, 67–68, 72, 77
Central Council for Research in
Ayurvedic Sciences, 74
chemical entities, 43
Chennai Patent Controller, 44
China, 6, 9, 19, 34, 51, 96, 99, 110, 112,
118, 119, 144, 146, 161n22
Chinese medicine, 120, 126, 131, 132,
141, 146
Chinese scientist, 120
Ciba Pharmaceuticals, 53, 61, 82
Cipla, 31, 35, 38, 51, 95, 106, 117, 136
Clarinex (desloratadine), 40, 154n7
Claritin (loratadine), 40, 154n7
classical formulations, 86
classical texts, 73, 75
clinical trials, 45, 119, 130, 146
Clinton Foundation, 49, 50, 51, 103,
107, 114
Cochin, 60
*Colloquios dos simples e drogas e cousas
medicinaes da India* (da Orta), 60
commercialization, 62
commons, 21

communal, 70
Communist Party of India (Marxist)
[CPI(M)], 42, 155n8
competition, 38
compliance, 47
compositions, 75
compound, 43, 44
Congress Party, 42
constellations of power, 10, 12, 120,
141, 149
contemporary patent environment, 43
Contract Research and Manufacturing
Services (CRAMS), 119
Contract Research Organizations
(CROs), 119
Convention on Biological Diversity
(CBD), 4, 12, 56, 62, 89, 145, 147;
threats from TRIPS, 57
copyleft, 146
copyright, 1, 22–23, 25–26, 28, 76,
152n13; creativity and, 25, 26, 28;
Statue of Anne, 25
corporate citizenship, 52
corporate social responsibility, 92, 97,
98, 107, 122, 126
Creative Commons, 146
creative work, 76
cultural heritage, 60

Dabur, 32, 72, 73
Daiichi Sankyo, 118–119
Darwin, Charles, 60
data exclusivity, 148, 155n19
defensive measures, 89
Delhi Network of Positive People
(DNP+), 44
diabetes, 75
Diamond v. Chakrabarty, 26,
discovery, 41, 44
disease inflation, 102, 115, 145
Doctors without Borders (Médecins
Sans Frontières), 2, 37, 49, 96,
111, 112, 122; Access to Essential
Medicines, 2
Doha Declaration, 39–40, 96

dosas, 65–66, 71
Dr. Reddy, 116, 117
Drahos, Peter, 30
drug access, 39, 126
drug costs, 50, 85, 143
drug development, 43
drug prices, 43, 49, 50, 57, 89, 94, 95,
111, 113, 120, 136
drug testing, 45

Ecks, Stefan, 52, 71
effective, 42,
efficacy, 41, 43
emerging patent regime, 50, 57
epistemological problem, 88, 147
esomeprazole (Nexium), 42
essential medicines, 8, 15, 31, 37, 50, 51,
97, 108, 121, 142
esters, 41, 44
ethers, 41, 44
ethnobotany, 60
Europe, 53, 104
European Patent Office, 86
European Union, 47
evergreening, 40
existing chemical entities, 47
Ezhava caste (community), 60, 148

first-line drug, 38, 44
Food and Agriculture Organization, 12
free market, 14
free trade agreements, 10
free trade policy, 94

Gandhian ideology, 65
General Agreement on Tariffs and Trade
(GATT), 30
generic producers, 47, 117,
130, 146
generic production, 57
generic substitutes, 94
genetic modifications, 143
genetics, 45, 143
geographical indicators, 81, 87
GERD, 42

Gilead (Gilead Sciences), 15, 18, 95–96, 99, 102–105, 106, 110, 112, 114, 115, 123, 128, 133, 134, 136, 144–145; International Access Program, 103–104, 107, 111; representatives, 103, 109, 114, 131
Gilead model, 96, 104–105, 113, 114, 128, 133
Gilead voluntary licensing program, 19, 96, 104, 106, 113, 123, 128, 134
GlaxoSmithKline (GSK), 38, 46, 108, 110, 111, 130
Gleevec, 45, 95
Glivec, 45
global access programs, 52
global economy, 140
global health, 94
global hegemony, 48
global political economy, 98
globalization, 10, 12; amorphous forces of, 11
Gopalakrishnan, N. S., 57, 83–87
grandfathered drugs, 51
Greek humoralism, 65
Grove, Richard, 60
Grover, Anand, 36, 47
guru-sisya method, 65
Gusterson, Hugh, 17, 97

Hallowell, Irving, 24
health crisis, 106
Health Impact Fund (HIF), 110, 145, 146, 149
health problems, 49
healthiness, 114
high-income countries, 37, 52, 94, 118
Himalaya Drug Company, 75, 89
homeopathy, 6, 63, 65
Hortus Indicus Malabaricus (van Rheede), 59, 84, 147
Human Development Index, 95
Hyderabad, 17, 35, 105, 108, 114, 116, 119, 123, 124–125, 127, 133, 135

imatinib mesylate (Glivec, Gleevec), 45, 95
incremental changes, 46

India, 10, 98, 99, 110, 118, 144, 146; colonial period, 31–32; facing problems, 50; government of, 147; pre-colonial, 30–31; and the West, 56, 59, 89, 94, 120, 126, 142
India-EU Free Trade Agreement, 37, 47, 148, 155n19
India Patent Office, 13, 106
Indian, 2, 117, 131; bioresources, 57; courts, 36, 48, 113; government, 2, 41, 84; government program, 51; medical systems, 4; patent law, 31, 33, 142; pharmaceutical knowledge, 2, 58; pharmaceutical producers, 49, 113, 122, 131
Indian companies, 116, 121, 130, 133, 143; competition from, 38; representatives, 123–124, 127–128; "stealing," 2, 3; in the United States, 116–117
Indian Council of Scientific and Industrial Research (CSIR), 84
Indian generic producers (manufacturers, companies), 15, 96, 108, 119, 120
Indian Network for People Living with HIV/AIDS (INP+), 19, 37, 44, 49, 106, 111
Indian pharmaceutical companies (corporations), 6, 7, 8, 13, 14, 15, 16, 19, 33–34, 37, 57–58, 95, 104, 105, 115, 117, 120, 126
Indian schools of philosophy, 68
Indian Supreme Court, 13, 15, 140
Indonesia, 9, 10
information spillover, 52
Initiative for Medicines, Access and Knowledge (I-MAK), 37, 44, 48, 111
innovation, 48, 53, 77, 110, 131; balance, 48; narrow view of, 46
innovators, 47, 48, 129, 131, 133, 145, 148
intellectual property (IP), 3, 8, 99, 143; buying rights, 45; claims, 15, 29, 146; colonial laws, 32; enforcement, 47; environment, 76; history of, 19, 24; ideology of, 23; key forms, 22; laws, 9, 81, 148; myths, 8; new rules, 15; overextension, 8, 48; protections, 1, 8,

10, 48; secrecy and, 24; social contract behind, 25; struggles, 9, 10; TRIPS-related, 57, 102; WTO and, 6, 29, 120
intellectual property regime: new, 10, 11, 12, 15, 18; pricing under, 15; United States style, 3
intellectual property rights, 1, 83, 147; transferability of, 45
International AIDS Conference (Toronto 2006), 49
International Journal of Ayurveda and Alternative Medicine, 73, 74
international (multinational) pharmaceutical companies, 2, 3, 8, 13, 14, 15, 19, 37, 40, 48, 50, 117, 140, 143, 147
international treaties, 43
international Treaty on Plant Genetic Resources for Food and Agriculture, 147
invented illnesses, 102
inventions, 41, 71, 76–77; communal, 70; frivolous, 48; individual, 70

Japanese producer, 118, 119
Journal of Research in Ayurveda and Siddha, 73

Kerala, 17–18, 50, 55, 56, 60, 61, 67, 70, 72, 80, 84, 121, 123, 127, 135, 147, 157n11
Kerala AIDS Control Society, 50
Kline, Nathan, 61
knowledge exchange, 89
knowledge sharing, 89, 99, 142
knowledge transfer, 81
known substance, 41, 44

Langford, Jean, 66
Lawyers Collective, 19, 36–37
legal protection, 53
leftist allies, 43, 141
less developed, 56
leukemia, 45
LGBT discrimination, 36,
licenses, 7, 46, 95, 121, 128, 134, 144; compulsory, 40, 43, 96, 106, 112, 144,

145; compulsory and voluntary, 96, 106, 107, 111, 134; voluntary, 15, 39, 110, 135
Linnaeus, Carolus, 60
Lipitor (atorvastatin), 2, 126
local knowledge, 10, 58, 99
local production, 49
local variability, 23
lopinavir, 48, 51, 144
loratadine (Claritin), 40
loss of creativity, 9, 10
lovastatin (Mevacor), 42
lower caste, 60
Lowie, Robert, 23
low-income countries, 37, 39, 50, 51, 56, 94, 95, 104, 111, 122, 131, 137, 145

Malabar Coast, 60
Malaria Medicines Venture, 147
maraviroc, 46, 111, 159n26
marketable product, 45, 46
marketing, 47
Matrix, 49, 51, 119
Mayo Clinic College of Medicine, 60
medical anthropologists, 6, 66, 75, 98
medical knowledge, 1, 140, 142, 145; biomedical, 58; community, 9; digitizing, 81; indigenous, 4, 9, 15, 53, 145, 147, 151n5; local, 10, 145; non-Western systems, 2; restrictions on, 3, 9; traditional, 151n5; Western, 3, 4
medicines (drugs): affordable, 38; alternative, 6; biomedical, 11, 12; cheap labor, 15; chemical ingredients, 7; copies of, 2; existing, 41, 120; first line, 38; generic versions of, 1, 6, 129; low-cost, 6, 13, 94, 135; lower price, 38, 49, 52, 144; monopoly control of, 2; plant materials (derived), 7, 120; process of making, 2; product 2; second line, 38
Medico Friend Circle, 49
me-too drugs, 13, 35, 42
mental health, 50, 55, 61
mental illness, 55, 70
Merck, 38, 42, 92, 103, 117
metabolites, 41
metabolite switching, 40

Mevacor (lovastatin), 42
Mgbeoji, Ikechi, 4, 29, 62,
middle-income countries, 51, 95, 96,
    104, 111–112, 113, 141
Ministry of AYUSH, 63, 65
*Moore v. The Regents of the University
    of California*, 27, 45
multi-national corporations (companies,
    MNCs), 43, 89, 91, 99, 110, 117–118,
    121, 141, 144, 147

Nader, Laura, 17
Nagarjuna (journal), 73
Nagoya Protocol, 62, 145
Naraindas, Harish 75
Natco, 43
National Cancer Institute, 45
National Institute of Allergy and
    Infectious Diseases, 44,
national interests, 48
national property, 57
neem (case), 54, 58, 69
neglected diseases, 14, 109–110, 122,
    131, 137, 138, 142–143, 145
neoliberalism, 143
New Chemical Entities (NCEs), 69, 73,
    120, 130, 131, 132, 133, 135, 137, 138
New England Journal of Medicine, 41
New Molecular Entities (NMEs), 42
new patent environment, 8, 14, 15, 16,
    18, 39, 64, 92, 113, 116, 117, 133,
    136, 138, 149
new patent law, 1, 83, 90, 94, 122
new patent regime, 7, 8, 10, 13, 14, 15,
    16, 18, 19, 31, 34, 37, 39, 44, 50, 82,
    89, 90, 94, 109, 117, 122, 133, 135,
    136, 141, 143, 144, 145, 147
new product, 41
new property, 41
new reactant, 41
new use, 41
New York Times, 95
Nexavar (sorafenib), 43
Nexium (esomeprazole), 42
NGOs, 38, 49, 52, 54, 92, 120

Nobel Prize in medicine, 120
non-obviousness, 42
Novartis, 4, 13, 43–45, 46–47, 51–53, 61,
    64, 95, 111, 132, 133, 140, 155, 156
novelty, 42, 68, 69, 72, 75, 77, 78,
    162n22

Obeysekere, Gananath, 71
obfuscation, 99
Okasa, 49
omeprazole (Prilosec), 42
Open Source Drug Discovery program
    (OSDD), 63, 145, 146, 147
originator companies, 38
outsourcing, 119, 120
overriding of patents, 43
ownership rights, 6, 142

paclitaxel (Taxol), 45, 82
pancakarma therapy, 73
Paris Convention, 28–29, 43
Patent Cooperation Treaty (1970), 29
patent opposition database, 49
patents, 22, 23; advocates, 63;
    applications, 41, 86, 89; controversies,
    91, 122; expiration, 148; expired, 40,
    105; legal challenges to, 37; practices,
    48; problem with, 22; protections, 29,
    34, 39, 142, 149, 155n19; struggles,
    53, 144; transferable rights, 70
Patents Act (1970), 33–34, 38, 39
Patents Act (2005 Indian Patents
    Amendment Act), 3, 26, 30, 33, 38,
    39, 40, 57, 75, 85, 108, 111, 122,
    128, 135, 136, 137, 141; multinational
    pharmaceutical companies and, 41
pepper, black, 56
Pfizer, 2, 30, 46, 92, 99–102, 103, 105,
    108, 114, 115, 117, 120, 130, 133,
    140, 151n8; Global Health Fellows,
    102; Global Health Programs,
    100–101
Pfizer Foundation, 101
pharmaceutical companies, 92, 97,
    137, 138

pharmaceutical corporations (companies), 47, 58, 82, 117; Ayurveda and, 89; controversies over, 2, 8; global rules, 2; laws, 7, 80; new regime, 8, 14, 78; non-patent holding, 40; patents, 9; pre-WTO law, 2; special product exception, 2
pharmacology, 89
pharmacopoeia, 53, 54, 84
piracy, 9, 58
plant-based ingredients, 7
plant material, 58, 69
Pollock, Anne, 105
polymorphous engagement, 97
poor countries, 50, 95, 122, 140, 141
poor enforcement, 42
poverty, 50–51
pre-grant opposition cases, 49
President's Emergency Plan for AIDS Relief (PEPFAR), 50, 156n24
price reductions, 37
Prilosec (omeprazole), 42
prior knowledge, 12, 45, 58, 76, 83, 86
private interests, 48
privatization, 143
pro-corporate, 48
product and process, 33
profitability, 76, 86, 115, 126, 134
proprietary, 72, 89, 142, 148
proprietary patent, 75
proprietary protections, 75
protease inhibitor, 43
psychopharmaceutical drugs, 61
psychiatry, 61
public good, 48
public health crisis, 40, 96
public health effects, 50
public health priorities, 39
public image, 52
public research, 45

Quality Adjusted Life Years (QALY), 145
quality of life, 49

Ranbaxy, 7, 16, 33, 34, 116, 118–119, 120, 122, 123, 126, 130, 137, 138,
141, 142; Synriam, 16, 120, 122, 137, 138, 147, 161n6, 161n22
Randeria, Shalini, 12
Rauwolfia serpentina, 61
research and development (R&D), 23, 46, 47, 108, 119, 120, 121, 122, 130, 131, 132, 133, 135, 136, 137
reserpine, 53, 61, 82
resistance, 59, 63, 83, 85, 86, 88, 142, 152n24
reverse engineering, 33, 58, 63, 121
rhinoplasty, 53
rhizome, 11–13, 152n20
right to health, 47
right to knowledge, 148
rigorous patent standard, 48
Rio Earth Summit, 4
ritonavir, 48, 51, 144
Rivers, W. H. R., 53
Rose, Mark, 76
Rose, Nikolas, 143
royalty (obligation), 62, 107

SAHARA, 49
Sandoz, 45
Sanskrit, 55, 84
Schering-Plough, 40, 154n7
second-line drug, 38, 44, 51, 105
secrecy, 63–64,
section 2(1)j of the 1970 Patents Act, 50
section 3d of the 2005 Patents (Amendment) Act, 13, 15, 35, 39, 40–41, 111, 141, 143, 155n8; removing of, 47
self-sustaining partnership, 107
serpagandhi, 55, 61–62
Serpasil, 61–62
shankhapushpi, 55
Shiva, Vandana, 58
Siddha, 31, 63, 65
small companies, 45
social complexity, 141
social science research, 12, 100
sorafenib (Nexavar), 43
South Asia, 53, 156n6
sovereignty, 44

Srinivas, Krishna Ravi, 63
standard of care, 42
standard treatment, 42
standardized drugs, 70
standards, 44, 81, 89
statins, 2, 42, 131, 155n7
stealing, 2, 58, 59, 64
study-up, 17, 91
sub-Saharan Africa, 6, 38, 134, 144
subsidized prices, 95
Sun Pharmaceuticals, 7, 116, 117, 119
Sunder Rajan, Kaushik, 95, 114, 115,
    120–121, 137–138, 160n35
surplus health, 114, 121, 138, 161n13
surplus value, 138
Susruta Samhita, 67–68, 72, 77
sustainability, 128

Taxol (paclitaxel), 45, 82
technology transfer, 104, 144
tenofovir, 15, 39, 90, 95, 96, 104, 106,
    108–109, 110, 114, 127, 128, 134,
    144, 145
therapeutic access, 121, 137
therapeutic excess, 121, 137
therapeutic saturation, 145
Third World, 62
tiered pricing, 92, 94, 95, 107, 109, 112,
    156n31
Times of India, 43
Trade Related Aspects of Intellectual
    Property Agreement (TRIPS), 3, 7,
    10, 12, 13, 14, 19, 26, 29, 30, 34, 39,
    57, 81, 84, 87, 90, 96, 106, 117, 135,
    140, 144, 156; Ayurveda and, 54, 57,
    81, 147; before (pre-), 50, 57, 94; big
    pharma and, 143, 147; biomedical
    drug prices, 88, 159; CBD and, 12,
    57; compliant laws, 39, 48; Doha
    Declaration, 39–40, 96; flexibilities in,
    40; geographical indication in, 81, 87;
    Indian companies and, 92, 116–117,
    120, 135, 140; Indian government,
    43; India's Supreme Court and, 13;
    knowledge sharing, 89; low income

countries and, 39–40, 56; product
    patent, 34; propriety claims under,
    148; R&D, 122; requirements of
    (-compliant), 47, 48; uniform global
    system, 29; United States and, 30
trademark, 22, 62, 73, 75
traditional knowledge commons (TKC),
    62–63, 147
Traditional Knowledge Digital Library
    (TKDL), 4, 8, 9, 11, 16, 57, 79, 80,
    84, 85–87, 124, 152n15
transparency, 62
Trivandrum, 56
Trivandrum Ayurveda College, 71, 74
Tropical Botanical Garden and Research
    Institute, 55–56
true innovation, 26, 42, 46
Tu, Youyou, 120
Tufts University study, 46
turmeric (case), 54, 58–59, 69, 79, 84, 87

UCLA, 45
UNAIDS, 112
Unani, 6, 63, 65
UNESCO, 12
uniform global system, 29
United International Bureau for the
    Protection of Intellectual Property
    (BIRPI), 29
United Nations' Medicines Patent Pool,
    39, 46, 105, 111, 112, 113, 122, 134, 145
United Nations Special Rapporteur on
    the Right to Health, 37, 47
United States, 2, 6, 13, 53, 95, 121,
    137, 138; bilateral negotiations,
    47; companies, 2, 114, 115, 126;
    consumption of Indian drugs, 6;
    copyrights, 23; court decisions, 1; India
    and, 15, 18, 47, 61; interests, 47; IP law,
    23, 26, 30; Supreme Court, 15, 26–28
United States–India business ties, 47
university innovation, 45, 120, 131
University of Kerala, 60
University of Mississippi, 58–59
university research, 27, 42, 120, 131

US Food and Drug Administration
(FDA), 42
US Patent Act (1952), 26
US Patent and Trademark Office, 86
US taxpayers, 45

vaidyan, 65, 67
van Rheede, Hendrik Adriaan, 60
Viiv Healthcare, 108, 110–111, 112, 113

wait-and-see, 83
watch list, 47

World Health Organization (WHO), 46,
96, 105, 106, 108, 128, 142, 149
World Intellectual Property Organization
(WIPO), 28, 29, 34
World Trade Organization (WTO),
1, 2, 3, 6, 7, 10, 11, 14, 23, 26,
35, 47, 79, 120, 128, 140, 143;
policies, 88
W. R. Grace company, 58
wound-healing, 58

yoga, 1, 4, 9, 10, 63, 65, 67

CPSIA information can be obtained
at www.ICGtesting.com
Printed in the USA
BVHW031833080119
537339BV00001B/108/P